Ella S Armitage

The Childhood of the English Nation

The Beginnings of English History

Ella S Armitage

The Childhood of the English Nation
The Beginnings of English History

ISBN/EAN: 9783337366414

Printed in Europe, USA, Canada, Australia, Japan

Cover: Foto ©ninafisch / pixelio.de

More available books at **www.hansebooks.com**

THE CHILDHOOD

OF THE

ENGLISH NATION

OR THE

BEGINNINGS OF ENGLISH HISTORY

BY

ELLA S. ARMITAGE

SIXTH EDITION

LONDON

LONGMANS, GREEN, AND CO.

AND NEW YORK: 15 EAST 16th STREET

1894

All rights reserved

PREFACE.

THE aim of this little book is to awaken an interest in the study of English history in those who have never felt its charm. When first I began to write it, no short and simple History of England had appeared which made any attempt to give unlearned people an insight below the surface of the bare facts. Since then numerous works of the kind have appeared, and notably Mr. Green's 'Short History of the English People.' Yet, even after its publication, there appeared to me to be still room for a book of the kind I had attempted, a book which should act as interpreter to those who have no knowledge of history, and serve as an introduction to larger and better works. The early part of our history is so far removed from the thought of an average Englishman, that he cannot understand it without study; yet he is deceived by fancying that he understands it, and pronounces such words as monasticism, feudal system, English constitution, without knowing at all what lies behind them. Yet the interest of history lies in penetrating to the inner meaning of these things, in entering into the thought and feeling of past ages. To enable a modern reader of no great cultivation to do this, it seemed to me that some book was wanted which should be more diffuse in explanation than historians in general can find time to be; and in order to excite interest as well as to explain obscure phenomena, I have thought it best to pass briefly over the less interesting parts, and to tell in some detail the events of greatest importance. My great hope is to induce my readers to study those larger works which are in reality far more interesting than any small book can be. As Sir Francis Palgrave says, no small book can ever really teach great things. All I hope to do is to prepare my readers for books in which the secret of history is more fully unfolded. Of these works I have availed myself freely in the following pages; and as it was undesirable in so small a book to give references on every page, I have given at the end of the volume a table of the authorities for each chapter. If I should have any readers who are acquainted with such works as Professor Stubbs' 'Constitutional History,' or Mr. Freeman's 'Norman Conquest,' they will see at once what are my obligations to such writers; and as for those who are not, I wish I could inspire them with sufficient interest to read and find out from whom I have borrowed. It is a misfortune for my work that Mr. Freeman's fifth volume did not come into my hands until these sheets were passing through the press.

It may be thought by some that I have given too large a proportion of space to ecclesiastical affairs. My apology is, that no amount of space can be too great in proportion to the influence of the Church on mediæval history. The Church, in the early and middle ages, is not an institution which was working silently in the background while events were going on independently; she was the central figure in the drama—the power most active in moulding events. Being not only the medium through which we inherited the civilisation of the past, not only the great moral educator of the ages of which I am writing, but also a secular power of the highest social and political importance, her influence penetrated every side of life. It therefore seemed to me worth while to spend some time in trying to understand her, at the cost of some repetition. The struggle of Anselm with William II., of Becket with Henry II., must be studied as a prelude to the national revolt against the Papacy in John's reign.

I have not carried my work further than the end of the twelfth century, chiefly because by that time the reader will have made acquaintance with all those things in mediæval history which most require explanation, and from that time forward he can advance without further commentary; if he has understood what went before, he will understand what comes after, and is developed out of it. The twelfth century is also an important crisis in many respects. It saw the influence of the Church reach its zenith; it saw England united under a firm central government; it saw the rise of the forces which were ultimately to overthrow feudalism. With the thirteenth century a new period of history begins; the struggles of the nation against the despotism of John are wholly different from the struggles of the feudal baronage against the government of Henry II.

I have not followed the archaic spelling of Old-English names, simply because to call a man Eadwine or Ælfred is to put him farther off from us than if we call him Edwin or Alfred, and makes it more difficult to realise that he is not a foreigner, but is of our own flesh and blood. Many of these names have been handed down to our time by common use, and have been worn into their present form as naturally as other Old-English words. In other instances the Latinised forms have become more familiar to an English ear; and it is only in cases where there is no familiarity to lose that I have thought it worth while to use the archaic forms.

WATERHEAD, OLDHAM:
October 20, 1876.

CONTENTS.

CHAPTER I.

	PAGE
Civilisation and Organisation	1
The Family and Clan	3
The Kelts	4
The Roman Conquest of Britain	5

CHAPTER II.

The English Settlement in Britain	8
Political and Social Development of the Teutons	12

CHAPTER III.

Religion of the Teutons	18
Roman Mission to England	19
Scottish Mission	22
Character of Christianity at that period	26
Revolution it accomplished	29
Church and State	32

CHAPTER IV.

Royalty and Nobility among the Old-English	34
Tenure of Land	35
Commendation	37
The Witenagemot	39
The Shire and Hundred Moots	40
Northumbria, Mercia, and Wessex in the Eighth Century	41
Egbert	42
Invasion of the Danes	43

CHAPTER V.

	PAGE
Alfred	45
Battle of Ashdown	46
Danish Settlement in Northumbria and Mercia	49
Peace of Wedmore	51
Alfred's Reforms	52
His Translations	54
He repels the renewed Danish Invasions	57

CHAPTER VI.

Danish Settlements in England	61
The West-Saxon Kings recover England from the Danes	64
Battle of Brunanburh	65
Edgar	66
Dunstan	68
Religion and Art	69

CHAPTER VII.

Danish Conquest of England	72
Growth of the Royal Power	76
Feudalism	77
Feudal Jurisdictions	80
Hundreds and Frithguilds	80
Advantages of Feudalism	81
Slavery	84
Domestic Life	85
Compurgation and Ordeal	87

CHAPTER VIII.

Edward the Confessor	88
Godwin and his Family	89
Quarrel of Edward and Godwin	91
Harold's government	95
He subdues Wales	97
He becomes King	100
Invasion of Harold of Norway	103
Invasion of William	105
Battle of Hastings	107

CHAPTER IX.

William completes the Conquest of England	111
He lays waste Northumbria	113
Results of the Conquest	116

	PAGE
Feudalism	117
Royalty	119
The English Empire	119
Domesday Survey	122
Portrait of William	124

CHAPTER X.

The Mediæval Church	126
Gregory VII.'s Reforms	128
William I. and Lanfranc	130
William II. and Anselm	134
Henry I. and Anselm	139
Settlement of the Question of Investitures	142

CHAPTER XI.

The English People under William Rufus	143
Henry I.'s Charter	145
The Curia Regis	147
The Court of Exchequer	148
Stephen	149
Reforms of Henry II.	153
The Study of Roman Law	154
The Cistercian Order	156
Position of the Mediæval Church	158

CHAPTER XII.

History of Thomas Becket	161
Mediæval Theory of Church and State	164
Constitutions of Clarendon	168
Flight of Becket	173
His Return and Death	178

CHAPTER XIII.

Judicial Reforms of Henry II.	181
Revolt of the Baronage	183
The Assize of Arms	185
Character of Henry II.	187
Fusion of English and Normans	189
The English Language	189
English Literature	191
The English Empire	192
Wales	192
Cumberland	194
Scotland	195
Ireland	196
Henry II. in Ireland	199

CHAPTER XIV.

	PAGE
Pilgrimages to the Holy Land	201
Mohammedanism	202
The First Crusade	204
Results of the Crusades	207
Chivalry	210
The Home Life	213
Chivalric Literature	214

CHAPTER XV.

Reign of Richard I.	218
The Intellectual Revival of the Twelfth Century	219
Realism and Nominalism	220
The Arabian Schools	222
The Universities	222
The Church and Intellectual Development	224
St. Anselm	225
Abelard	226
Decline of the Church's Influence	228
Rise of the Towns	230
Merchant and Craft Guilds	233
The Jews	235
London in the Twelfth Century	237
Domestic Life	239
Art	240
Position of Women	241
Peasantry	241

LIST OF AUTHORITIES 245

INDEX 248

THE CHILDHOOD
OF
THE ENGLISH NATION.

CHAPTER I.

A NATION has a growth as truly as an individual, and a nation's history should be the story of that growth, and not a mere chronicle of disjointed facts. And just as the life of an individual receives its character to a large degree from the events of its earliest years, nay even from events which took place before its birth, so the key to the history of a nation must often be sought in its earliest days, and even in the time before it began to be a nation indeed. Inasmuch as this is the case in the history of the English nation, the study of the earlier periods of that history ought never to be thought uninteresting. They contain the germs of all that has since come to pass. The various changes and modifications which after history has brought about, can only be understood by knowing what the original elements were on which time and circumstance did their work.

The first great step in every nation's history is that by which it passes from barbarism to civilisation, from anarchy to organisation. That we may not use these words loosely, let us try to form some clear notions of what they mean.

The word civilisation is derived of course from the Latin word for a citizen, and thus the idea is suggested that life in cities is the life which, above all others, is the opposite of barbarism. People who live in cities dwell *Civilisation.*

in some kind of association. They have learnt to respect each other's rights, and to restrain their private desires in obedience to law. Through mixing with others, they have become more polite or *civil* in their manners. They have learnt, moreover, to build houses and to make roads, and to ply all kinds of useful crafts. They trade to other places, and get wealth, and when they have got wealth they do not need to spend their whole time in toiling for a livelihood, but they have leisure to turn their minds to learning and art.

And if by the word civilisation we thus mean to convey the idea of self-restraint, of mutual respect and friendly intercourse between man and man, of trade, wealth and leisure, of learning and art, by the word barbarism we mean to imply a state of life in which every man's hand is against his neighbour, where law is unknown, and where so little mastery over nature has been gained that the daily struggle for food leaves no leisure, and no strength for the search after better things. There are of course many stages both of barbarism and of civilisation, and we do not always use either word in its rigid sense.

And what do we mean by organisation? This word comes from a Greek one signifying an *instrument*; and a nation is said to be organised when it distributes its work among its different members in the same way in which the work of the body is distributed among its different *organs*. And a state of *anarchy* or no-rule is one in which no such arrangement is to be found.

Organisation.

If we examine the yolk of a fresh egg, we cannot see any traces of organisation in it; but if we could watch it day by day during the process of hatching, we should see the confused mass forming itself into different organs each with its different function, until at last the living bird is complete with all its parts. Very much like this is the process of organisation in a nation. At first there are no special organs for the work of governing; everyone does that which is right in his own eyes. Neither has any other kind of work its own organ; there is no division of labour. But gradually organisation begins. Leaders arise, and the governors become more and more separated from the governed. The labour of supplying the nation's wants is divided, and instead of each man turning his hand to all kinds of work, each learns to devote himself to some one kind only, and to look to others for the rest.

About the absolute commencement of human development history can tell us nothing. No records have come down to us of a time when there were not at least the rudiments of organisation present. But history invariably leads us back to the Family as the first known commencement of social organisation. The first bond that united human society was the tie of blood. When all other men were looked upon as natural enemies, kinsmen alone respected each other's rights. *The family.*

The Family, as we trace it in the primitive history of the Aryan nations, was governed by the Father. His wife, or wives and children, were wholly under his control, for there was no power to interfere with his authority.

Out of the Family was developed the Clan. The members of the clan were bound together by blood-relationship, and the chief of the clan succeeded to more or less of the patriarchal authority held by the father in the family. The clans of the Scottish Highlands have brought down almost to our own times some image of this primitive state of society. Among some nations, however, the authority of the chief was greatly limited by the self-governing power which the clan itself had developed. *The clan.*

Clanhood, in various phases of development, was the condition of all the northern nations of Europe, when we first become acquainted with them; not only of our Teutonic ancestors, but of the Kelts, who anciently possessed Britain. The Keltic and Teutonic nations were both daughters of that great Aryan race which had already given to the world the splendid civilisations of India, Persia, Greece, and Rome. The northern branches of the Aryan stock, the Keltic, Teutonic, and Slavonic nations, were far behind their four great sisters. While Rome was the empress of the world, and Greece was sovereign in the world of thought, the Kelts and Teutons had only reached that stage of civilisation when the cultivation of land takes the place of a wandering life. This transition probably took place when it was found convenient to spare the lives of captives taken in war, and use their services in tilling the land; so that Slavery at its first outset was a step forward *The Aryan race.*

in civilisation. Society then became divided into workers and fighters, the women and slaves being the workers, the free men the fighters.

The Kelts.
The Keltic race had preceded the Teutonic in Europe, and some centuries before Christ they held a great part of the Continent. The Keltic family is divid·d into two branches, the Erse or Goidelic (from which comes the word *Gaelic*), and the Kymric or Welsh. The Gaelic branch came first to this island, and some ethnologists suppose that it became mixed with a still older population, of non-Aryan race, whom it found in possession. The Kymric or Welsh people invaded Britain later, and drove the Gaels to the north and west. At the time of the Roman invasion the Welsh were the dominant race in Britain, and the inhabitants of Gaul, the ancestors of the French nation, belonged to the same branch of the Keltic family.

The Kelts, whose fate it has been to lose their nationality everywhere but in remote corners of Europe, such as Brittany, Wales, the Scotch Highlands, and Ireland, seem to have been a people of many brilliant qualities, quick and lively, and especially gifted with the powers of utterance. The two great Keltic tongues which still survive are said to be peculiarly rich in their vocabulary, and forcible in idiom. The remains of ancient Welsh poetry have a certain grandeur of epithet and imagery, though the absence of constructive power makes them often very unintelligible. The Erse branch of the race appears to possess greater richness of imagination. That the Kelts had reached a certain degree of intellectual development at the time of the conquest of Gaul by the Romans, is shown by the fact that an intellectual class had already separated itself from the ruling class. These were the Druids, about whom very much nonsense has been written; but if we may trust the simple statements of Cæsar, they were not only the priests of the national religion, but the depositaries of the law, and the judges in all disputes. It must be remembered that in early times, law grows up almost unconsciously in the form of custom, which is not written down like the rules of a legislator, but is preserved in the memory of the oldest and more thoughtful of the tribe, who through this intellectual power acquire a respect and an importance which gradually

The Druids.

confer upon them a distinct office. Besides their knowledge of law, the Druids were famed for many other kinds of knowledge and speculation, and they held schools which were eagerly attended by the quick-witted Keltic youth. Their wisdom was not committed to writing, but turned into verse, of which such an enormous body existed in memory that it took a Druid three years to learn it. Britain was the chief seat of Druidism, and to Britain the Druids of Gaul went for instruction. As there is no doubt that human sacrifices were part of the Druidic religion in Gaul, they doubtless prevailed in Britain also.

It was the destiny of the Keltic race to be overcome by Rome, and of her Teutonic sister to overcome Rome. The Romans had a hard fight to conquer Gaul ; nearly a million of brave Kelts are said to have perished by the sword of Julius Cæsar. The conquest of Britain became necessary in order to complete the conquest of Gaul, which drew help largely from her island sister. The conquest of Britain was begun by Cæsar in the year 55 B.C., and completed by the general Agricola about 78 A.D. The Britons resisted desperately ; but with their small population (probably scarcely equalling that of London now) their undisciplined hosts and clumsy weapons, and above all with their endless quarrels of clans and absence of national centre, they could not maintain the fight against the steady ranks of the well-trained, civilised armies of Rome. Agricola pushed his way up the Scottish lowlands, defeated the wild northern tribes in a great battle at the foot of their mountains, and shut them off from Roman Britain by a line of forts which he built from the Firth of Clyde to the Firth of Forth. *Conquest of Britain by the Romans.*

Then began the work of civilizing the Britons. Craftsmen from Rome brought into Britain all the useful arts of the great city. The Roman camps grew into cities, splendid with walls and towers, with baths, temples, theatres and court-houses, and houses with glass windows and painted walls. The sons of the British chiefs came to these cities, and learned to speak the Roman tongue, and wear the Roman dress, and do as the Romans did in many ways, both bad and good. Splendid roads were made from one town to another, roads which are still a won- *Roman civilisation in Britain.*

der to us who see their remains; for there was no hill so steep but the Roman would make a road straight up it, nor marsh so boggy but he would carry a causeway through it.

If we were now studying the history of France, it would be necessary here to enter into a careful examination of the nature of the government which Rome exercised over her subject nations, of the institutions which she founded in the provinces of the Gauls, of which Britain formed a part. It is not necessary here, because those institutions perished in the English conquest of Britain. Of the fabric of Roman civilisation in Britain, the only part which remained after the English had overrun the land, was the Roman roads. Some of these roads we still use as our great routes from town to town, though they have been so mended by successive generations that no visible trace of their Roman origin remains. The same is not the case with our institutions. We are not politically, any more than by race, the children of Rome. Our land dwelt once under the shadow of the Roman name, but our fathers never did. Rome has influenced us deeply, will ever influence us, by the potent seeds which she has cast into the field of modern civilisation, but this influence was not handed on to us by the Roman settlement in Britain. Our empire, which has grown to be a wider empire even than hers, sprang from a different root, was based on wholly different principles, and had a quite different benefit to bring to the world.

Roman institutions not permanent.

The Romans were governors and lawgivers greater than any nation that had gone before them, and there can be no doubt that the orderly government by which they replaced the anarchy of the Keltic clans, was a great blessing to the subject people. But the Roman dominion, great as had been the benefits which it conferred on mankind, was doomed to perish, because as the empire grew more despotic, more luxurious, and more corrupt, it became a curse instead of a blessing to those under its yoke. Slavery was a perpetual cancer at the heart of society. In Italy, agriculture, which in the early days of Rome had been thought a most honourable employment, was abandoned to slaves; the free population dwindled away through vice and idleness. Slave labour was unable to bring enough out of the earth to supply the enormous consumption

Decline of the Roman empire.

of the Empire; and in the provinces the free cultivators of the soil, as well as the free inhabitants of the city, were utterly crushed by the weight of taxation, and sank into a condition little better than slavery. The costs of the ceaseless wars of the Empire had to be wrung from populations which became daily more and more unable to pay. The whole fabric of government and of society began to fall to pieces of itself. Then came the great opportunity of the Teutonic nations, who hemmed in the northern frontier of the Empire. Received into the Empire first as soldiers and colonists, as the central authority crumbled away they took the part of conquerors. In 410 Rome was sacked by Alaric the Goth, and the same century saw the domain of the Empire in Gaul, Italy, and Spain divided amongst the Teutonic emigrants.

Britain shared in the fate of the Empire, but in an even sterner degree. The unconquered Kelts of North Britain, known to the Romans as the Picts or Caledonians, were ever a source of trouble to the Roman government. As the weakness of the Empire increased, the raids of these barbarians on the rich and civilised province became more frequent. In the fourth century we find them harrying Britain in alliance with the Scots, who then inhabited Ireland, and with the Saxons, who are spoken of as a nation of fierce pirates, terrible pests to the coasts of Gaul and Britain. It was in vain that the Romans built their magnificent wall from the Solway to the Tyne as a defence against the Caledonians; they were not able to defend their own defences. About the year 409 the Roman troops were withdrawn from Britain to share in the struggles of rebel generals which convulsed the dying Empire; and they never returned. Britain was left without defence, and the curtain falls upon its history; for we have no records of what took place between the withdrawal of the Roman troops and the settlement of the English in the island, except the most fragmentary traditions.

Fate of Britain.

DATES.

Julius Cæsar first lands in Britain	B.C. 55
Agricola completes the conquest of Britain	A.D. 78
Roman legions withdrawn from Britain about	A.D. 409

CHAPTER II.

The English settlement in Britain.

WHEN the curtain slowly rises again, we find the English in Britain. The oldest English historian, Bede, says that they came here in the year 449. There has been a great deal of dispute as to whether this date is the true one, and whether the English did not settle here a great deal sooner. The last thing that we know about Britain, before the period of darkness begins (when the Roman armies left the island in 409), is that the Saxons were constantly harrying the coasts. At first they probably came only as pirates. Absolute certainty as to the precise year in which they began to settle is not attainable; but our best scholars seem to be now agreed that there is no good reason to reject the account given by Gildas, and followed by Bede, that about the middle of the fifth century, the Britons, driven to despair by the inroads of the Picts, invited the Saxons to help them to drive off their enemies, offering them land in reward for their services. In this manner the first detachment of Saxons landed in Kent, led by the brothers Hengist and Horsa, and these were soon followed by a multitude of tribes of the same race. But after overcoming the Picts, the strangers quarrelled with their British allies, and began the conquest of the land for themselves. Probably because the first to harry the British coast had been Saxons, the Britons gave the name of Saxons to the whole race of the new comers. But they called themselves Angel-cyn, or English, the Angles being apparently the most numerous of the tribes who invaded Britain, and the others being so consciously akin to them that they willingly adopted their name.

The Teutons.

The Teutonic family is divided into three great branches: the High-Dutch, the Low-Dutch, and the Scandinavian; but the two latter have so many points of resemblance that they may almost be considered as one. The High-Dutch dwelt anciently in the high lands of South Germany; their language is now the ruling tongue of Germany, and is therefore called *the* German language. To the Low-Dutch, who dwelt mostly in the low countries near the mouths of the rivers flowing into the German Ocean, belong many of the North Germans, the Frisians, Hollanders, and our own English forefathers. These last were not all of one tribe. First there were the Angles, who dwelt, before they came to Britain, in those provinces in the south of Denmark, which are now called Holstein and Schleswig. A small district in Schleswig still keeps the name of Angeln. But the Angles, though the most numerous, were not the only tribe who shared in the conquest of Britain. From the mouth of the Rhine to the mouth of the Oder the whole coast was inhabited by Low-Dutch folk, Saxons, and Frisians, who all contributed to the hosts which set out to win the fair lands of Britain. The conquerors of Kent and the Isle of Wight belonged to the tribe of the Jutes, from Jutland. But it is important to remember that all these Low-Dutch tribes were so near akin that the Britons saw no difference between them, but reckoned them all under the common name of Saxons, a name which their descendants still bear in the speech of the Welshman and the Highlander. The conquerors, however, as we have seen already, called themselves English, and they called their British enemies Welsh, a name which in the old Teutonic languages simply means foreign.

It was in 449, then, that the conquest of Britain by the English began; and it went on for three hundred years at least. That is to say, during the whole of that time the English were fighting with the Kelts, more or less, and pushing on their own border ever further towards the West. But the main work of the conquest was done in the first hundred and fifty years. From 449 to the middle of the next century, swarm after swarm of the various Low-Dutch tribes came over to Britain, each host led by some man of royal or noble birth, and settling in Britain, they founded kingdoms there. By the end of the sixth century they had won for themselves a good deal more than half of that part of Britain which lies south of the Firth of Forth.

This conquest was no easy work. The Welshmen fought hard; the English only won the land bit by bit. The exterminating nature of the conquest, as related by Gildas and Bede, is confirmed by the evidence of later history and language, which shows a complete break between Roman and English institutions, and

Nature of English conquest.

between the Latin and Old-English languages. Christianity, which had come to Britain as it had come to the rest of the Empire, was blotted out along with Roman civilisation, or driven to take shelter in the West. Only a wholesale slaughter could have effected this entire breach between British and English history; and such a slaughter the chronicler relates: —' The priests were everywhere slain before the altars; the prelates and the people, without respect of persons, were destroyed with fire and sword; nor were there any to bury those who had been thus cruelly slaughtered. Some of the miserable remainder, being taken in the mountains, were butchered in heaps. Others, spent with hunger, came forth and yielded themselves to the enemy for the sake of food, being destined to live in perpetual servitude, if they were not killed upon the spot.'[1] Language confirms this last statement, by showing that a few Welsh words, relating to such things as slaves would have to do with, have crept into our English language. But there is no reason to think that in the early days of the English conquest of Britain any general mixture of Welsh and English blood took place. For the coming of the English to Britain was not merely a conquest, it was an immigration. The immigrant brings with him his wife and children. And the pride of race was so great in those days, as well as the mutual hatred between Christian and pagan, that it is unlikely that there were many marriages between the English and the Welsh in that part of the country which was conquered at first.

In the West of England the case is rather different. The greater part of Somerset, all Devon and Cornwall, Herefordshire, Shropshire, Cumberland and Westmoreland, were conquered by the English after they had been converted to Christianity. In these parts the Welsh were allowed to live under the protection of the law, though not ranked as equals with the English; and no doubt the folk of some of these countries have as much Welsh blood as English in their veins, though even there what once was Welsh is so overlaid with what now is English, that to-day it is scarcely to be seen at all. In Cornwall, however, this is not the case; it is really as Welsh as Wales itself, and spoke a Welsh tongue till about 150 years ago. So that if we take

Welsh element in the extreme west.

[1] Bede, *Ecc. Hist.* i. 15.

England as it is now, reckoning Wales as part of it, as well as those English shires which are of Welsh or of mixed blood, we cannot rightly deny that the old Kelts have given something to the making up of the English nation, though the laws, the institutions, and the character of that nation are mainly Teutonic.

The Jutes, Saxons, and Angles came to Britain at different times and under different leaders. Instead, therefore, of founding one great kingdom, they began a number of little kingdoms, some of which appear on the scene without any records of their first establishment. *Early kingdoms.* The most important of these kingdoms were :—(1) Kent, the first English settlement, founded by Hengist, the Jute ; (2) Sussex ; (3) Wessex, which covered at first Hampshire, Berks, Wilts, and Dorset, and in later times Somerset and Devon. Sussex and Wessex, as their names indicate, were *Saxon* kingdoms. (4) Mercia, the midland part of England between the Humber and the Thames. This kingdom seems to have grown up out of the amalgamation of several small Anglian and Saxon kingdoms or settlements. (5) Essex (the East Saxons), comprehending Middlesex and Hertfordshire as well as the present shire. (6) East Anglia, namely Norfolk and Suffolk. (7) The great Anglian kingdom of Northumbria, comprising all the country between the Humber and the Forth, except a Welsh kingdom, afterwards called Cumbria, which stretched from the river Clyde to the northern boundary of Wales. Besides this kingdom of Cumbria, Wales also was an independent Keltic kingdom, or rather a union of many little kingdoms, reaching to the Severn, at the time when Christianity came to England. Cornwall and Devon formed a third independent Welsh kingdom, called West Wales by the English chroniclers.

The period during which England was divided into these little kingdoms is often called the Saxon Heptarchy, a name which means the Seven Kingdoms. The number, however, was often more than seven, sometimes less ; and the name gives an idea of a more rigid state of things than could exist in such early times, when the very existence of states was as unsettled as their boundaries.

It now behoves us to inquire what sort of people the English were when they came to Britain, and what institutions they brought with them.

About the Angles and Saxons in their old land we know next to nothing; a few scattered references to them are all that we can find. But about those Teutons who dwelt nearer the borders of the Roman empire good accounts have been given us by Roman writers, and we have every reason to believe that what is said of their laws and customs is true of those of our own forefathers, only bearing in mind that these latter were more backward and barbarous. What we know of them after their settlement in Britain agrees generally with the accounts given of their German kinsfolk, and much of what is still wanting can be gathered from the Old-English laws and poems.

Teutonic institutions.

We naturally think of the Angles and Saxons as a very fierce and warlike people. So they were, when they had to fight for their lives against the Roman Empire in front, and against the pressure of other barbarian nations behind. But I believe that if they had one quality more distinguishing than another, it was their capacity for peace, for order and government, and that this, and not their warlike qualities, has been the real secret of their success in the world. They were then, as they are now, a law-abiding people.

I have already said that clanhood was the prevailing organisation of all the Northern nations at the time when the Teutons conquered the Roman Empire. They occupied their native seats in clans. The country was divided into small districts called marks, very like our parishes, and, like them, of varying size. These marks were each possessed in common by people of one kindred, whom we may look upon either as very large families or as very small clans. Such a thing as private property in land was, if not unknown, at least confined entirely to the homestead, the cottage with its garden and croft, which belonged to each household. The ploughland was divided every year into lots, one lot being given to each freeman to till for himself and his household. On the wastes and in the woods the flocks of the markmen fed in common. The mark grew all the corn and meat which the clan required; the women spun and wove the wool. The markmen had their regular meetings, in which they managed their common affairs.

The Mark.

But the organisation of clanhood appears to have made

great advances among the Teutons. These little clans, though so independent, were parts of a larger clan, or even of a nation. Besides the marks, there were larger divisions of the land, which appear to have been the same as what were called in England the hundred and the shire. These divisions had also their meetings for public business, especially for judicial matters. And no laws could be made, nor any great affairs settled, except at the great meetings of the nation, at which every man had a right to attend, unless he had forfeited his freedom. At these meetings, the nobles proposed certain measures; the common freemen, if they liked what was proposed, gave their assent by clashing their spears; if they liked it not, they groaned, and the proposal was rejected. So that at these various popular meetings, they helped in making and they helped in carrying out their own laws. They were in fact to some extent a free people. Another point in which the Teutons were remarkably free was that, instead of the chief having the patriarchal power which he held in the Keltic clans, the family appears to have formed a self-governing community, in which the noble was only an influential member. *The National Assembly.*

All men, however, were not equal among the old Teutons. There were three classes of men, more distinctly marked off than classes are now: nobles, freemen, and slaves (in Old-English, Eorlas, Ceorlas, and Theowas). *Aristocracy and Royalty.* In the most ancient societies, we always find that some families are considered to be of better blood than others; among the Teutons, the kings and princes were supposed to be descended from the god Woden. It is said by Bede that the Saxons had no kings in their old land, but only nobles, who had equal power among themselves. This may have been originally the case with all the Teutonic nations. In time of peace very likely these nobles were only the leading men in the mark, who were accustomed to preside at the meetings, and to take the lead in public business. But war is the great means through which aristocracy and royalty are developed. In time of war there must be a leader, and the leader must be obeyed. And the wars in which the Teutonic nations were involved with each other and with the tribes which pressed on them from behind, had already wrought this change in such of them as became known to the Romans. Their kings or nobles had gained a position of great authority, though they were not allowed to trample on the rights of the freemen.

Wherever clanhood prevails, there it will be found that vengeance for the blood of a kinsman is considered the duty of all the kindred. It is difficult for us, who have policemen, judges, and prisons, a complete public machinery for carrying out justice, to understand that in the beginning the only way to get justice done was to do it yourself. Public justice had its first beginning in family justice, in the duty of every member of a family to avenge the death of any member who had been slain, and in the responsibility of the family for the faults committed by any of its members. The duty of revenge was the most sacred and binding possible. In the ancient poem of Beowulf, which some scholars think was written before the English left their old land, and while they were still heathens in Schleswig, the singer says : 'Each of us must abide the end of worldly life ; let him that may, work doom before his death ; that will afterwards be best for the warrior, when he no longer lives.' By *working doom* he means executing justice, by avenging the death of his kinsman. But all the Teutonic nations had already found out that if everybody's death was to be avenged by slaying somebody else, there would be no end to it ; so they had made laws fixing a price on everyone's blood—so much for a noble, so much for a freeman—to be paid by the murderer to the kindred.[1] This price was called the *wergild*. If the kinsmen accepted it, they were to cease from *bearing the feud*, as it was called, that is, from keeping up the quarrel.[2]

Blood-revenge.

Almost any offence could thus be atoned for in money, or in what was used instead of money before money became common—a certain number of cattle or horses. The family, moreover, was responsible for its members; if a kinsman did wrong it was the duty of the kindred to bring him to justice. As all causes were tried and

Family responsibility.

---

[1] A part of it was paid, according to Tacitus, to the king or the State. This in the Old-English laws we find separated from the Wergild, and called the *man-bote* ; it was the fine due for the breach of peace.

[2] It was doubtless at first optional to the kindred whether they would accept the fine or have their revenge. See Palgrave's 'Proofs and Illustrations,' *Eng. Comm.*, p. cxii.

judgment given in those popular meetings already spoken of, it is plain that some sort of public justice did exist among our forefathers.

It was war which first brought in another bond of society than the tie of blood. Although in early times the clan system was carried out even in war, and the hosts of the Teutons were arranged according to clans, every man fighting among his own kindred, and under his own family chief; yet when war became a glory and an adventure, the chieftains and nobles who announced their intention of seeking their fortune in war, were followed by bands of volunteers, who were not of necessity their blood relations. They were young men of spirit, who followed the chief for the sake of glory and reward; they swore to fight under him, and he in his turn was to reward them with the spoils of war. Here we have a new beginning of order, faithfulness to a chosen lord, who is not of necessity a blood relation. It cannot be too carefully noted; for it was destined to be the great bond of society in Europe for more than a thousand years. When once the feeling of duty has been stretched beyond the narrow bounds of the actual family, a great step in civilisation has been taken. But this new relationship was modelled on that of the family. The companions of the chief were in the position of kinsmen to him, even when not really his kinsmen; they formed part of his household in time of peace, as they were his followers in war. To avenge the death of their lord was as urgent a duty as to avenge the death of a kinsman. In the poem of Beowulf, a warrior says: 'I had far liefer die in the fire where my lord's body is burnt, he who gave me gold, than bear back my shield to my own land, if I have not slain the foe, and defended the life of my lord.' No disgrace could be greater than to come alive out of a battle where the chieftain had been slain.

The chieftain and his followers.

The same old singer, when he wishes to praise his nation, calls them 'a people steady both toward friend and foe.' It was his idea of a man that he should both love well and hate well—be faithful in defence, and faithful in revenge. Treason and desertion were punished with death; so was theft, if the thief were taken in the act, for theft was a breach of faithfulness to the tribe. We are told that the unwarlike and slothful were put under a hurdle and drowned in a swamp.

Slavery existed in the forests of Germany, the slaves being either captives taken in war or those who had forfeited their liberty in punishment for their crimes or their folly. When the Teutons became a warlike nation they left the tilling of their fields to slaves, and agriculture came to be looked upon as an unworthy occupation for a freeman. This was no doubt one great cause why in all Teutonic countries the men of peaceful dispositions, who preferred tilling their fields to following some warlike chief, fell more and more into an inferior position, and were at last obliged to put themselves wholly under the protection and authority of some noble. But of this more hereafter. It is important to remember that in old Teutonic society, as we first become acquainted with it, almost the only workers were the women and slaves; the only honourable work for a free man was fighting or hunting.

Slavery.

Tacitus tells us that the Teutonic peoples paid a remarkable respect to women; they believed that something godlike, some spirit of foresight, dwelt in women, and they always listened to their counsels. But for all this the wife among the Teutons was bought from her parents or kindred, and was entirely in the power of her husband.

Women.

Among the Teutons there does not seem to have been any separate intellectual class, such as the Druids formed in the Keltic nations. We hear of priests, and even of priestesses, but they evidently did not form a very important class, still less did they engross the functions of judges. The singer or story-teller was an important person, and the great deeds of the heroes of old were sung to the harp at feasts. Some very interesting fragments of ancient English poems have come down to us which bear traces of having been composed at least in heathen times, if not before the English left their first abode. We may be sure that the race from whom came the poem of Beowulf, and from whom sprang afterwards Shakspeare and Milton, were not a people without imagination.[1]

Intellectual development and civilisation of the Teutons.

---

[1] The great superiority of the Old-English poem of Beowulf to those fragments of ancient Welsh poetry which have come down to us, has surely been overlooked by those who contend that English poetic genius is due to intermixture with Keltic blood.

In person the Angles and Saxons and other Low-Dutch peoples were tall, fair-haired, and blue-eyed. In battle they wore mail-coats made of iron rings, and helmets crested with carven boars' heads; they carried long ashen spears, and iron swords whose hilts were often richly worked in gold or silver, and sometimes graven with old stories written in the strange old letters of the North, which were called Runes. For the English had letters even then, though they were little used for writing, and were looked upon as charms; rude people always think the things which they only half understand have some magic in them. In the absence of paper or any substitute for it, letters cannot come into general use. But their having letters at all would of itself be enough to prove that they were not mere savages. They knew also how to make pottery, and, as the account of their armour shows, they were skilful workers in metals.

Such then, we may suppose, were the English at the time they came to Britain. We know little of their history until the time when they received Christianity, nearly a hundred and fifty years after their first conquest. At that time Roman civilisation was extinguished, and Christianity driven into a corner with the Welsh; and some seven or eight little Anglian and Saxon kingdoms were constantly fighting with each other, or with the Welsh, the Strathclydians, and the Picts.

About fifty years after the English settled in Britain, some tribes of Scots passed over from Ireland into Caledonia, and took up their abode in the western islands and highlands. From them *Scotland* has received the name which Ireland lost. This immigration of the Scots had afterwards an important influence on affairs in England, as the next chapter will show.

Settlement of the Scots in North Britain.

APPROXIMATE DATES OF THE ENGLISH SETTLEMENTS.

Hengist and Horsa bring the Jutes to Kent	A.D. 449
Ella conquers Sussex	477
Cerdic founds the kingdom of Wessex	495–519
East Anglian kingdom founded	before 519
Essex founded	527
Ida begins to reign in Northumbria	547
Mercia founded from Northumbria	584

See Haddan and Stubbs, *Councils and Ecclesiastical Documents.* Lappenberg. *Geschichte von England*, Band I.

CHAPTER III.

THE English, as has been said, were heathens when they came to this country. But they had a religion and a morality of their own; they believed in gods who would reward the brave and punish evil-doers in the next life. Only a few scattered hints about their religion have been handed down to us; but those few hints are enough to prove that the English and other Low-Dutch folk worshipped the same gods as the Scandinavians, that is the people of Denmark, Sweden, and Norway. In the language of the Norwegian colony of Iceland a number of ancient poems have been preserved, which tell us a good deal about this religion. These poems should be studied by all who wish to understand the deepest thoughts of our forefathers; here I can only give an outline of the religion of the North.

<small>Religion of the Teutons.</small>

The chief god of these nations was Odin, called in Old-English Woden, the father of gods and men; his name is still preserved in the fourth day of the week, *Wednesday* (O.-E. Wodnesdaeg), as well as in many names of places in England. All the English kings were said to be descended from Woden. Woden and Frigga his wife, and a multitude of other gods and goddesses dwelt in a heavenly hall called Valhalla, and there they received the souls of the brave who had fallen in battle, and feasted them with ale and boar's flesh. But evil men were sent for punishment to a dreary hall in the cold north, full of poisonous serpents. All who died of sickness or old age went to Niflheim, a land of ice and fogs. The gods would listen to the prayers of men; they would give victory and success and the power of song to those who asked it of them; but they were not all-powerful; the power of evil was destined to outwit them, and one day they themselves would perish in the great crash and burning of the world; though one ancient song tells vaguely of a new heaven and earth which should arise, more glorious, after this disaster. There were three great feasts in the year, at which solemn sacrifices were offered to the gods, and human victims were often slain upon the altars; slaves and captives taken in war were generally chosen. This fierce religion heightened the fierceness of the warfare between the English and the Welsh, who were already Christians. The Welsh regarded their conquerors with such bitter hatred that they never made any attempt to convert them to Christianity, and there is no saying how long the English might not have remained heathen, if Pope Gregory I., in the year 597, had not sent missionaries to bring them to the faith of Christ.

Gregory was Pope or Bishop of Rome from 590 to 604. In his time the popes of Rome had not yet risen to the position of universal bishops and supreme heads of the Church, though they were tending towards it. All men were agreed that there must be one and only one visible, united Church, but all had not yet made up their minds that the Bishop of Rome was to be the head of that Church. The Church of the Welsh, for example, and that of Ireland, owed no obedience to Rome. The Pope himself did not dare to call himself universal bishop; 'whosoever calls himself so is Antichrist,' said Gregory I. Still it was natural that Rome, which had been the ruling city of the one universal Empire, the queen of the West, should be the chief centre of the one universal Church, and that the Bishop of Rome should become the head of the Church, and all other bishops should bow to his authority. This was what did come to pass in time, but at the time of which I am now speaking it seemed very uncertain; for things had sadly changed with Rome. She had no emperor now; the emperor was at Constantinople; Italy was invaded by barbarians, Rome herself was scourged by plague and famine. The Bishop of Constantinople tried to set himself up as Universal Bishop and Head of the Church, and that the popes afterwards won the day in this struggle was largely due to the great influence which Pope Gregory I. gained by his wisdom and his powerful character. With so much work on his hands, with thousands of starving Romans clamouring for bread, with a barbarian king leading his armies up to the very walls of the city, with rebellious bishops denying his authority, and with important affairs in the churches of Gaul and Spain calling for his attention, Gregory yet found time to think about a handful of heathen tribes in Britain.

Position of the Roman Church.

There is a pretty story told that Gregory was first stirred up to the thought of converting England long before he became pope, by seeing some fair-haired English boys on sale as slaves in the market-place of Rome; they had been carried off by pirates. Touched by their beauty, he asked who they were and where they came from, and if they were Christians. Hearing that they were *Angles*, he declared that they had the faces of *angels*, and that the praises of God should be sung in that land. From that day he never forgot the thought; and when he was made Bishop of Rome (590) as soon as he had leisure to give his mind to it, he sent a monk named Augustine, with several others, to preach the word of God to the English nation. At that time the king of Kent, Ethelbert, had a Christian wife, Bertha, daughter of one of the kings of the Franks in Gaul. The monks, who were in such fear of the barbarous nation to which they were sent, that at one time they nearly gave up the journey altogether, were received by Ethelbert in a friendly manner. They landed in what was then the island of Thanet; after a few days the king came to the island and sent for them to appear before him. He would not receive them in a house for fear they should bewitch him, which the heathen thought could be done more easily in a building; so sitting in the open air, he awaited their coming. They came marching in procession, bearing a silver cross and a picture of the Saviour, and singing prayers for the salvation of the English. When Augustine had preached before the king, Ethelbert said in answer: 'Your words are very fair, but as they are new to us, and very uncertain, I cannot so far approve them as to forsake what I and the whole English nation have so long followed. But because you have come here as strangers from afar, and wish to make known to us those things which you consider to be true and good, we will not hurt you, but will supply you with whatever you need; nor do we forbid you to preach and to gain as many as you can to your religion.' And he allowed them to dwell in the royal city of Canterbury. Before long he himself believed and was baptized, and after him great numbers of his nation. But he did not compel any to become Christians, having learned (as Bede tells us) from his teachers in salvation that the service of Christ should be willing and not forced.

Pope Gregory's mission to England.

Thus Christianity came to Kent, and from Kent it spread to the other English kingdoms. The story of the conversion of Northumbria is interesting and important. King Edwin, of Northumbria, married Ethelburgh, daughter of Ethelbert, king of Kent. She of course, was a Christian, and brought with her as chaplain the Christian bishop Paulinus, whose mind (says Bede) was wholly bent on bringing the nation to the knowledge of the truth. He preached without much success for about a year. Then the king of the West-Saxons sent an assassin with a poisoned sword to murder King Edwin. The king was only saved by a faithful thane, who threw his own body between the murderer and the king, and was slain himself. The same night the king's first child was born. The king gave thanks to his gods for this blessing; but Paulinus told him that it was to his prayers to Christ that he owed the life of his infant daughter and his queen. The king was pleased with his words, and promised that if the Christian's God would give him victory in the war which he meant to begin forthwith against the king of the West-Saxons, he would himself become a Christian. He was victorious; but even then he would not hastily adopt the new faith, but would hear more about it, and consult with his wise men; and he often sat by himself alone thinking of these things. And having called a meeting of his Wise Men, he asked them what they thought of the new doctrine. The heathen chief-priest answered that he was very willing to try it, for though he had served his gods well for many years, he had never had a good turn from them. This was spoken like a heathen; but there was another man there who spoke as follows:

'O king, the life of man while on earth, compared to that which is unknown to us, seems to me like when a sparrow flies swiftly through the hall where thou art sitting at supper with thy thanes in the winter time, when the fire is kindled in the midst, and the hall is warm, but outside wild squalls of rain and sleet are driving past. The sparrow entering at one door flies quickly out at the other; while it is within, it is untouched by the wintry storm, but after a little space of calm it flies hastily away, and passing out of winter into winter again, is lost to thy sight. So the life of man is seen for a little while, but what follows it, or what went before, we know not at all. Therefore if this new teaching shall bring us anything more certain, it seems to deserve to be followed.'

This speech is deeply interesting, because it shows that at the time when our fathers are known to us chiefly as men of war, busied in laying the foundations of their dominion in blood and fire, there were yet thoughtful questioning spirits among them, and the practical character had its speculative side. We shall meet with this trait again in the English national character. When this meeting was over, the temples of the heathen gods were destroyed, and in due time the king, his nobles, and a large number of the common folk were baptized (627). As Kent had been the first kingdom converted, and Northumbria the most important, Canterbury and York, the chief towns of each, became the seats of archbishoprics, as they still are.

But in nearly every English kingdom to which Christianity came, after a time of success it had a time of trial. So it was in Northumbria. King Edwin was slain in battle by the heathen king Penda of Mercia, who allied himself with the Britons to attack the Christian kingdom. Penda harried Northumbria, Bishop Paulinus fled with the queen and the royal children to Kent, and Northumbria fell away from the faith of Christ. That faith was brought back again, not from Rome, but from Scotland, by a king named Oswald, who having been in exile for many years among the Scots, had learned Christianity from them. For the Scots had long been Christians, having received Christianity from their mother country, Ireland. A famous monk, named Columba, had founded a monastery on the island of Iona, on the western coast of Scotland. From that monastery many holy men wandered forth to different parts of Europe, seeking for some lonely place where they might lead what was then called the religious life, and they became missionaries who planted the faith of Christ in many places where it had been overthrown by the heathen. In the seventh century the learning and piety of the Scoto-Irish Church were famous throughout Europe.

A.D. 633.

Mission of the Scottish Church, 635.

It was to Iona that King Oswald of Northumbria sent for missionaries to teach his people. Aidan was the name of the monk who was sent to him—'a man of singular meekness and piety, says Bede, 'who taught no otherwise than he himself lived, neither sought nor loved anything of this world. Whatsoever gifts of money he received from the rich, he either gave them to the poor, or used them in ransoming such as had wrongfully been sold as slaves. All who were with him, whether they were shorn monks or laymen, were employed either in reading the Scriptures or in learning psalms.' King Oswald made the isle of Lindisfarne on the coast of Northumberland the seat of Aidan's bishopric. And Bede gives us a beautiful picture of the English king, who had learnt to speak Gaelic well during his long banishment, interpreting to his own people while Aidan preached in Gaelic. From that time many Scots came to England, and preached with great devotion to the people of King Oswald's kingdom; churches were built and monasteries founded, and Christianity took deeper root than before. It was from the Scotch missionaries that the English received the alphabet which was always used in Anglo-Saxon times. Therefore if the Southern English should ever remember Pope Gregory with thankfulness as their 'foster-father in Christ,' the Northern Englishman should look reverently on the ruins which mark the site of Columba's monastery of Iona, and should remember gratefully that the faith of Christ was brought to his fathers by Gaelic-speaking men, from those lonely cloisters by the Atlantic shore.

But it was not long before the two Churches, the Scottish and the Roman, came into collision in England. Though Pope Gregory did not claim to be Universal Bishop, it was believed that St. Peter had been the first Bishop of Rome, and that therefore his successor held the keys of the kingdom of heaven, which were supposed to be given in some special way to St. Peter and to no other; and there was a growing tendency to regard the Bishop of Rome as the natural head of the Christian world. The Scoto-Irish Church was the only rival to the Church of Rome. She asserted that she had received her Christianity from St. John, and maintained that he was at least as good as St. Peter. The Roman Church was very anxious to put down this rival, whose reputation and whose disciples had already secured her a wide influence. Iona was called the nursery of saints, the oracle of the West. The Scottish

Contest between the Romans and Scots.

monks had founded monasteries in many parts of Europe, and the Rule or order of monastic life which one of them named St. Columban had drawn up was a rival to the Rule of St. Benedict which the Roman Church had adopted. There were several differences between Scottish and Roman Christianity. The Scottish clergy were allowed to marry, and it seems that in general their religion was purer and simpler than the Roman. The Roman bishops, who were fighting for their own supremacy, were both more worldly and more practical than the Scottish monks. The Rule of St. Benedict was far superior to the Rule of St. Columban in the place which it gave to work. But what was then thought the great question between the Scots and the Romans was that they observed Easter at different times, and that they had different views of how priests should be shorn. We laugh at these differences now as idle forms; but when men believed that there must be one and but one outward and visible Church, no difference of form could be allowed, and therefore questions of forms, which are merely secondary, became primary. As Bede says, 'Many, when they heard these disputes about Easter, feared lest, having received the name of Christians, they might happen to have run in vain.' A great synod or meeting of the clergy was called at Whitby, where there was a famous monastery governed by the abbess Hilda.

A.D. 664.

King Oswy, of Northumbria, presided; Colman, the Scottish bishop of Lindisfarne, spoke for the Scots; and the English Wilfrith, afterwards Bishop of York, for the Romans. Wilfrith gained the day, for King Oswy declared that since the keys of heaven were given to St. Peter, he would obey him in everything, lest when he came to heaven's gate, it should not be opened to him.

So Rome prevailed in England, and it was well that she did prevail, for the time was not yet ripe for Christian independence.

Advantages of the Roman victory.

It was well for England to grow in the same school with the rest of Europe, and under the same teacher. It was good for her to be in close connection with the greatest and most civilized city in the world. When English priests looked upon Rome as their mother, and went to her for teaching, the arts and knowledge of Rome had a free channel into England. Workmen were sent for from Gaul to build stately churches of stone, with glass windows, and the bishops who travelled to and from Rome, brought back with them paintings and books. As there were no invasions of barbarians then in England, there was time for schools and monasteries to grow up, and for learning to thrive; and in the north of England especially, the monasteries soon had libraries and learned men such as were not to be found on the Continent. And England herself, instead of being an island cut off from the rest of Europe, became one of the sisterhood of European nations which, like herself, were then growing up.

In 669, the Pope sent, as Archbishop to Canterbury, a Greek named Theodore, who did a very important work in consolidating the English Church. He was the first Archbishop of Canterbury to whose authority the whole English Church submitted. *Archbishop Theodore.* He travelled over the whole of England, and established the Roman observance of Easter, and church singing, which had hitherto been known only in Kent; and being himself a learned man, he gathered round him a school of disciples who spread true learning throughout the country.

The English had the good fortune to have amongst them in the seventh century a Christian poet, Cædmon, who turned into English song the stories of the Old and New Testaments, 'besides many more about the divine *Cædmon.* mercies and judgments, by which he tried to turn all men away from the love of vice, and to stir up in them the love of and the effort after good deeds;' and thus, says Bede, ' by his songs the minds of men were kindled with scorn of the world, and with longing for the heavenly life.' In days when there were no printed Bibles, and written ones were very hard to get, it was a great thing to have Christian teaching put into English verse, which everyone could learn and remember, and which could pass from mouth to mouth. No other country in Europe had Christian poetry in the common tongue so early, and no doubt this greatly helped Christianity to take firm root in England.

Was England then thoroughly Christianised in the 6th and 7th centuries? One might almost as well ask, Is she thoroughly Christianised now? Pope Gregory said wisely to Augustine: 'It is impossible for rude *Heathen survivals.* minds to give up everything at once; for even he who struggles to climb to the highest place rises not by jumps, but slowly, step by step.' It was not possible to sweep away all heathen customs at once; and even to the present day some relics of Old-English heathendom survive not only in nooks and corners—such as the belief of country-folk in witchcraft, omens, and spirits—nor only in the fast-decaying ideas about the divinity of noble blood and the contemptibility of trade, but even in such an important instance as the subject position of women in the eye of English law. Besides, the Church herself had not gone through the long struggle with the heathen Empire without being deeply touched with heathenism.

The heathen notion that religion was a system of magic, whereby the powers of the unseen world were to be brought into compliance with human wills, had deeply infected the practice of the Church. The worship of the Virgin and the saints had arisen out of the thought that if the prayers of poor sinners on earth were not powerful enough to change the mind of God, the prayers of those holy beings who had passed into the heavens might do it. Rites and sacraments became magic spells which opened the door of heaven. The priest who had the charge of these holy spells was the wielder of the magic power, the gatekeeper of the heavenly kingdom. Thus the foundations were laid of an immense fabric of superstition, and of the overweening power which the priesthood gradually attained.

Religious magic.

Still more powerful was the infection of *asceticism*, which the Church had received from heathen philosophy. Superstition springs from the lower side of human nature, from the fatal tendency of sense-bound minds to petrify living ideas into dead forms. But asceticism appeals to the higher side of human nature, to its best aspirations. It is a voice which comes to men when they are attempting the hard task of self-conquest, and tells them that there is no victory possible unless all the natural desires and affections are utterly crushed and destroyed. Almost all great religions have had their ascetic phase, in which men have sought righteousness in the renunciation of every human affection and pleasure, and even in cruel self-tortures, that the body with its natural desires might be overcome. Eastern philosophers had taught that the soul of man came from God, but that the body and the outward world were the

Asceticism.

work of the Evil Spirit. The Church in her great councils had declared this to be a heresy, but not the less did it creep into her teaching. She could not get rid of the idea that the body was the source of all evil. Self-sacrifice was the greatest and most vital doctrine of Christianity; but self-sacrifice in its highest form is a subtle and a hard thing, too subtle for a rude age. Asceticism, or the sacrifice of the body, was an easier way, a way which all could understand. So the ascetic life soon became the model followed by the Christian Church. An eternal warfare between the body and the soul became the leading Christian idea. The body was to be despised and ill-treated in the hope that fasting and ill-usage would bring it more under the rule of the soul. All natural relationships were to be treated as belonging only to the body, and sharing in its degradation; the monk regarded the relationship of parent and child, of brother and sister, of husband and wife, as bonds springing only from the lower nature, to be despised and foregone by the soul that was truly seeking God. These ascetic ideas had become so powerful in the 6th century, that already it was esteemed more holy to be a monk than a common priest. And though there were still married priests—and it was not for five hundred years that the celibacy of the clergy was enforced—yet even then the best men in the Church thought it an unholy thing for a priest to have a wife. The monk and the nun were everywhere considered the highest types of holiness.

The Christianity, then, which Augustine brought to England was a Christianity deeply tinged with superstition and with asceticism. Perhaps on that very account it was well adapted to the time, and it may be shown that underneath these heathen accidents the genuine principles of Christianity maintained their vitality, and worked out an immense moral and social revolution, and that, so far from being hindered, it was greatly helped in this work by the ascetic forms which its institutions had put on.

In the first place, though Sacerdotalism always contains a large element of heathenism, the position of the priesthood as a separate caste was one which had been to some extent forced upon it by circumstances. The priesthood was the fighting army of the Church; and, during her long combat with the heathen world, the

Organisation of the Church.

Church had been obliged to organise her army more closely. She inherited the Roman power of organisation; and thus in her gradual progress through five centuries she stiffened more and more into a little kingdom within herself, with rank rising above rank, the priests owing obedience to their bishops, the bishops to their archbishops, the archbishops finally to the pope. Such a hard external form, such a rigid organisation, was needed in order that the Church might resist the pressure of the heathenism and barbarism which were surging around her.

Similarly, if we wish to understand the sway of asceticism, we must consider the circumstances of the time. The Empire in which Christianity had arisen was a very wicked society, more wicked than can be told. To a man who aspired to lead a holy life, the simplest and safest course was to flee from the world, and either lead a hermit's life, or join himself to those who felt as he did, and shut out the world behind the gates of a monastery. Again, when we consider the sensuality of the Roman world, and the animalism of barbarian races such as the Teutons, it is not strange that at a time when the wonderful construction of the body was quite unknown, it should have been looked upon only as a clog and a hindrance to the higher life. The sins of the body are those which have to be first overcome, and I do not doubt that it is owing to the discipline of asceticism that many of the grosser sins which were so rampant in the first ages of Christianity do not now dare to raise their heads openly. Moreover, asceticism, though to us it seems a coarse caricature of true Christian self-sacrifice, undoubtedly presented self-sacrifice in a form which the world was able to understand, perhaps better than a higher type. It taught men in plain language that the spiritual life was the only real life, the only life worth living. It was the standing miracle whereby the attention and the reverence of rude barbarian minds were drawn towards Christianity. Here were men who were content to forego all the joys of this life, to do the hardest work, to live on the coarsest fare, all for the sake of Christ and the kingdom of heaven. Wild barbarian kings bowed before the power of self-sacrifice in the person of half-starved hermits, who dared to rebuke them for their sins.

Value of asceticism.

Granting then that Sacredotalism and Asceticism were both made agents in the spread of Christianity, let us consider what the work was that Christianity actually accomplished. We are too much accustomed to look upon the introduction of Christianity as a mere change of opinions about God and the next life, instead of what it really was, a moral and social revolution of incalculable effect.

Christianity contained in its essential principles a most powerful solvent of clanhood and of the whole social system of our forefathers. To a people who recognised no tie between man and man except that of kindred, or that between the chieftain and the follower, it proclaimed the universal brotherhood of mankind. *Christianity a social revolution.* To people who looked upon noble birth as something divine, who bought their wives like slaves, and held other men in slavery, it proclaimed the equality of all human souls in the sight of God, without distinction of male or female, bond or free. To a people who exposed their children, and lived by war, it proclaimed the sacredness of human life. To a people who regarded all the members of a family as involved in the crime of one, it proclaimed individual responsibility. To a people who looked upon work as the portion of women and slaves, it proclaimed the dignity of free labour and initiated co-operation.

All these great seeds cast into the soil by Christianity could not bear fruit at once; some of them have not yielded their full harvest yet. But much was done even in those early days. The horrible custom of casting out young babes to die of cold and starvation was stopped. Christianity tried to check the absolute power of the father over his offspring. He was not allowed to sell his son into slavery after he was seven years old; nor to marry his daughter against her will after she was sixteen. The limited nature of these reforms shows the strength of the evil system against which Christianity was fighting. The position of women—though asceticism did much to lower it—was raised by Christianity through the sacred and binding nature which was impressed on the marriage contract. It was no longer a bargain which the man might dissolve at pleasure. The government of large convents opened a new field for the energies of women. And from the first Christianity undertook the protection of women, as of all the weak and oppressed.

Slavery was not at once put an end to, but a religion which declared the slave and his owner equals in God's sight entirely altered the position of the slave. An immense stimulus was given to the emancipation of slaves. The Church protected the slave, and would not allow his master to take from him any money which he might have earned. For all labourers the Church procured a day of rest on Sunday.

The avenger of a kinsman was ordered to do penance as a murderer. This was a great blow at the right of vengeance, which was one of the pillars of the clan system. The right of sanctuary which the Church claimed for her temples had also a great effect in sheltering criminals from private revenge.

While these reforms sprang out of the essential principles of Christianity, the monastic system, which was the model of Christianity in those days, has the glory of initiating a social reform whose consequences are felt to our own day. It was fortunate for England that monasticism was not brought to this country until it had been reformed and organised by the great St. Benedict. Monasticism in the Eastern Church, and in the Keltic Church likewise, meant simply retirement from the world into societies whose occupation was meditation and prayer. The genius of St. Benedict led him to organise his communities on a wholly different principle, more suited to the active spirit of the West. 'Idleness is the enemy of the soul,' was the cardinal doctrine of his rule, and therefore his monks were always to be busy, either in labouring with their hands or in studying holy books. From Easter to the beginning of October they were to work in the fields, in silence, from four o'clock in the morning till eight, and then to read from eight o'clock till ten. After the early dinner and the midday nap, which was allowed in all monasteries, they worked again in the fields till vespers. 'And if the poverty of the place,' says St. Benedict, ' or the needs of the crops or of the harvest keep them constantly employed, let them not complain, for they are truly monks if they live by the work of their hands. as did our fathers and the apostles; but let everything be done with moderation, for the sake of the weak.' It is impossible to overrate the importance of this consecration of labour. The great point in which our civilisation of to-day differs from the ancient civilisations which have preceded it, is that it is based on such an enormous development of industry as the world has never seen before, and that it recognises industry as the only honourable condition of national existence. Such an idea was indeed foreign to the thoughts of our barbarian forefathers. War was esteemed by them the only honourable occupation for a free man; as Tacitus says, ' they thought it shameful to earn by sweat what they might win by blood.' Now a nation which lives by war, lives by snatching from its neighbours the means of life. It lives by exhausting its neighbours, and even if it is always successful, in time it exhausts even that mode of subsistence. There is no true progress possible until war has been exchanged for the only lawful way of gaining a livelihood, honest toil. How immense then was the service rendered by the Church in trying to mitigate war,[1] and by the monks in vindicating the dignity of labour. Nor was it merely in theory that they did this. The Benedictine monasteries soon spread all over Europe, and while they softened the minds of the heathen by their preaching, they broke up the fallow earth by the labour of their hands, and made the wilderness blossom as the garden of God. They were the first examples of co-operative societies, working unselfishly for the common good; they were an example of order, discipline, diligence and economy, a constant practical lesson to the world.

The world, indeed, was slow to learn these admirable lessons from monasticism. It took centuries to quell the fighting spirit in our barbarian forefathers. But one result was gained; the position of the labourer was recognised as an honourable one. It was observed that society was divided into three classes—fighters, teachers, and workers, and that the two first live by the toil of the last.[2] Throughout mediæval literature, this dependence of society on the husbandman is acknowledged.

[1] To protect the husbandman in the field from the chances of war was the constant effort of the Church. The first instance that I know of is a decree of the Synod of Elne in Rousillon, 1024.
[2] See King Alfred's remarks in his Boethius, ch. xvii.

We must not omit to mention the services rendered by the monasteries to learning. They were the only havens in which thoughtful men could find peace and leisure for study. There was little creative activity of mind in those days, but in the monasteries ancient authors were copied, such knowledge as did exist was studied, and chronicles of contemporary history were begun. Efforts were made to establish schools in all monasteries and parish churches.

Monasticism and learning.

Before long, the attractions of monasticism became so great that kings and queens left their palaces to become the equals of their subjects in the cloisters, and so great was the influx of all classes that it seemed as if there would be none left to do England's work. This pressure of the world into the monastery naturally brought with it corruption and decline. The history of all the monastic orders is a history of rapid progress at first, and then of long decay. But as one order declined a new one arose, professing to return to a stricter observance of the true principles of monasticism, until at last the reign of asceticism was over, and monasteries lost their hold on the popular affections.

The Church was able to accomplish more rapidly what she did in the way of reform, by reason of the position which was given her from the first by the State. It was natural that the clergy, being the only educated class, the only men acquainted with the law and organisation of Rome, should become the councillors and ministers of the kings. The bishops and abbots took their seats with the nobles at the great meetings of the kingdoms. The laws of some of the early kingdoms, which now began to be written down, show the influence of the bishops. At the Shire-meetings, the bishop sat by the side of the ealdorman, and helped in carrying out the laws. The Keltic Church had bequeathed to the West the penitential system, which was maintained and developed under the Roman bishops. The penitential system was a complete moral education, by which the Church guided her children in all the acts of daily life, assigning penances for sins of which the Old-English laws took no cognizance. The State supported the authority of the Church, and enforced her sentences when necessary. But while this penitential system was valuable as a moral discipline, it led to

Church and State.

one great evil, the commutation of penance for money, the origin of the whole system of indulgences. It was early taught that almsgiving was an atonement for sin, and this doctrine was not without good effect when the penitent was bidden to spend his money on mending roads and building bridges, on helping widows and orphans, on setting slaves free, and providing the poor with fires, baths, and beds. But the principle of measuring offences in money, which had crept into the Penitentials from the laws of the barbarians, was made use of by the clergy to swell their own revenues, and became, as time went on, a fruitful source of corruption to the Church.

The unity of the English Church under the headship of Rome, accomplished by the struggles of Wilfrith and the labours of Theodore, prepared the way for the unity of the English nation, which had yet to be wrought out.

The conversion of England had most weighty results for Europe. In the first place, when the English had become Christians, they began to spread the kingdom of God among their neighbours. Germany, Friesland, Holland, all the countries from the Rhine to Denmark were still heathen. It was by English missionaries—Wilbrord, Winfrith, Willehad—that these countries were brought to the faith of Christ. All these English missionaries were devoted servants of Rome. Winfrith especially, who is more often called St. Boniface, and who was the great apostle of Germany, was the steadfast ally of the popes, and put down the Scoto-Irish 'heretics' wherever he found them. When he had built up the church of Germany, the Bishop of Rome had now two powerful churches wholly obedient to him, the English and the German; and these two acted like levers to lift him higher still. Further, St. Boniface, who was one of the most influential men of his age, had a great hand in raising the Carlovingian race to the throne of the Franks in Gaul and Germany. The Carlovingian kings and emperors were great allies of the popes. And when the great Frankish monarch Charlemagne, whose empire stretched from the Ebro to the Oder, wanted a helper and adviser in his plans for the improvement of his people, he sent to England for the learned Alcuin, who came and lived with him, though he often lamented that he had not as good a library in Gaul as

Conversion of Germany.

he had left behind him at York. It was through the influence of Charlemagne and Alcuin that learning, which was utterly dead in Gaul at that time, began to thrive again. Indeed, we may say generally that from that time Europe, which had been at a dead-lock since the break-up of the Roman empire, and the out-wandering of the Teutons, began to grow again. And though the conversion of England was not the only cause of this, for all great movements have many springs, it was one very important cause.

DATES.

St. Augustine arrives in Kent . . . . . . A.D.	597
Failure of his attempt to unite the British and English churches	603
Conversion of Northumbria and East Anglia . . .	627
King Edwin slain by Penda of Mercia . . .	633
Oswald king of Northumbria, and Aidan (Scottish) bishop of Lindisfarne	635
Conversion of Wessex	635
Conversion of Mercia	655
Synod of Whitby, and victory of the Roman party over the Scottish	664
Theodore Archbishop of Canterbury	668

CHAPTER IV.

I HAVE already spoken of the institutions which our forefathers had before they left the shores of Germany; of their *Old-English clans and popular meetings, and their chieftains institutions.* with their followers. We must now inquire how these old institutions throve on British soil. This inquiry ought not to be thought uninteresting, for we should not look upon the roots of our national constitution and our national character as dry and mouldy things, but should handle them with reverence and care; it is because our roots are so old and so deep that we have weathered so many storms.

First, let us look at Royalty. It was but a small thing among our forefathers in the old country. Bede says that *The king.* the old Saxons had no kings, but were governed by their ealdormen or nobles, and in time of war they chose one of these ealdormen to lead their armies. The hosts of Angles and Saxons who came to Britain were each led by some ealdorman. But he was always of the sacred race of the god Woden, and was respected on that account, as well as for the valour and skill which had made him the chosen leader; and he was surrounded by the band of warriors of whom I spoke, who thought it their greatest glory to fight and die for him. Had the conquest of Britain been a short war which came quickly to an end, the ealdormen might soon have lost their power, as they would have done in the old country in time of peace. But because the conquest was a long ceaseless war with the Welsh, the ealdormen who led the English armies did not lose their power, but gained more. 'Ealdorman' and 'king' had not a very different meaning in old times. 'Ealdorman' meant the *older man*, the head man; and 'king' in the ancient Aryan speech meant simply the father of the family.[1] But by degrees the word *king* began to mean much more, and the word *ealdorman* to mean less; so the most successful leaders of the English dropped the title of ealdormen and called themselves kings. Ealdormen then became the name of the nobles who governed the shires under the kings, and were chosen by the king and his council, or Wise Men's Meeting.

The power of the kings, then, was growing. So was the power of the nobles. In old days the nobleman had perhaps been little more than the head of the leading family in the mark, respected for his high descent; when he came to Britain he was a successful chieftain, who was not likely to give up his power if he could help it. If he did not call himself a king, it was only because he found it better to be the servant of some more powerful king, and to govern the shire as his ealdorman. And those young men of noble family who had come over with their chieftains, and had at first been called his *gesiths* or companions (afterwards the name of *thanes* or warriors[2] became more common), when they settled down in lands of their own formed a new class of nobles, with more independent power than any nobles had possessed in the old country.

The nobles.

The great change in fact which the English settlement in Britain made in the old English customs was the change from a system dependent on personal relations, the relations of

---

[1] See Stubbs, *Const. Hist.* i. p. 140, note 1; Morris, *English Accidence*, p. 85.

[2] Stubbs, *Const. Hist.* i. p. 155, note 2; Schmid, *Gesetze der Angelsachsen*, p. 664.

man to man, to a system in which everything depended on a man's relation to the land. Private property in land, as I have said before, was unknown in the old country, or at least it was only the homestead itself which the freeman looked upon as absolutely his own. The noble received a larger share of ploughland than the common freeman in the yearly division, but it was not his private estate. But as soon as we know anything of the English settled in Britain we find the nobles holding land as their own *allod* or possession (whence the term *allodial tenure*).

There are but scanty allusions to guide us as to how the land was held by the common people when first the English came to Britain. We should naturally expect that they would settle in marks after the old pattern, and would bring with them all their old institutions. But except some scanty mentions in laws and charters, the only proof we have that they did so is that we find traces of the ancient mark system in England hundreds of years after. Those common fields and common rights in pasture, possessed by certain villages up to a very recent date, point to the day when our old English village communities owned the land in common. These village communities were no doubt in many cases real kindreds, united by the tie of blood and a common ancestral name;[1] in other cases there may have been no real relationship, but the association of villagers was copied from that of the mark. The importance of the family bond continued long after the English conquest; the laws make the kindred responsible for their members, and they share in the wergild paid for the murder of their kinsman. But whether the markmen ever in England had wholly independent possession we cannot be certain; and it would seem more likely that they were always more or less under the sway of some lord (the lord of the manor of later times). We can see very plainly that in the warlike character of the English colonisation, and the state of constant warfare with each other and with the Welsh in which they continued for so many centuries, there were causes sufficient to increase the influence of royalty and aristocracy at the expense of the older independence of the free members of the mark.

The people.

[1] Such as the Harlings, Wælsings, Scylfings, &c., who have given their name to Harlington, Wolsingham, Shilvington. See Taylor, *Words and Places*, p. 128. See note, p. 247.

The unoccupied land which had not yet been distributed among the nobles or the village communities was called the *folkland*, and was regarded as the property of the nation; the king could not dispose of it without the consent of the national assembly. But to obtain grants of *bookland* out of the folkland was the constant ambition of the king's thanes and favourites, and of the Church. Bookland was the name given to private estates secured to the owners by *book* or charter.

Folkland and Bookland.

It must often have happened that the most convenient way in which a king could grant estates to his thanes was by giving them the lands of some village mark. And when there were a number of small kingdoms in England often fighting against each other, it was easy for a victorious king to make grants of the conquered markland to his thanes. This would be one of the causes through which the old mark-system gave way.

The mark-system giving way.

Another cause was this. All who held land owed fighting service to the nation; not because they were land-holders, but because they were freemen, and fighting was the first duty of a freeman. All freemen were obliged to turn out and fight at the summons of the ealdorman of the shire, just as they were obliged to keep in repair all roads, strongholds, and bridges on their lands. But the expense of military service was very great, as the freeman had not only to find his own armour but his own food during the campaign. Consequently the nobles who had got the largest share of landed property and stock were the men who were best able to undertake this expense. Hence the freemen of the mark were willing to become the vassals of some rich neighbour if he would provide them with arms. In the language of those times, they bowed to him and became his men. They kept at first all their old rights in the common land; it was only by degrees that the lord encroached upon them. The townships, with their right of making their own by-laws and choosing their own officers, handed on many of the ancient rights of the mark.

The townships.

The relation of the peasants to their lord, in fact, was the same as that of the king's thanes to the king. It was called *commendation*, and was in truth only a carrying out of that personal obligation of the follower to the chieftain which I have spoken of so often as existing in the

Commendation.

forests of Germany, and which is the key to social and political history for a thousand years. It implied, on the side of the lord, guardianship; on the side of the man, service; and in England always some fixed service. The very name of *lord* (in its old form *hlaford*) means a bread-giver. The young men of noble birth who devoted themselves to some powerful chieftain looked to him to provide them with food, clothing, and arms, while they in return fought for him. The peasants who had commended themselves to a lord were armed at his expense in return for certain fixed services.

This is the oath which was sworn by anyone who became the man of a lord:—

'By the Lord, before whom this halidom[1] is sacred, I will be faithful and true to N., and will love all that he loves, and shun all that he shuns, according to God's right and the world's law, and never with will or purpose, word or work, do anything that shall be to his hurt, on the condition that he keep me according as I deserve, and do all that we agreed to when I bowed to him, and chose his will.'

Oaths like this were continually being taken then and for ages to come, by ceorls or common freemen to thanes or country gentry, by thanes to greater thanes, by greater thanes to kings, by under-kings of Scotland or Wales to more powerful English kings. In later times they were called oaths of *homage* (from the Latin *homo*, a man), because he who swore homage promised to be the *man* of his lord or king, whoever it was he swore to.

Commendation, the feudal relation between lord and man, had at first nothing to do with the holding of land. It was a purely personal relation. But in time homage and the tenure of land became inseparable things. And it was out of the double relation which grew up between the lord and his man and the land that the state of things which we call feudalism was developed.

Origin of Feudalism.

I am glad to use the word feudalism at so early a stage of our history, because it is important to remember that, although that word is now generally used to express a system of land-holding on condition of

[1] The *halidom* is the holy thing (saints' relic, host, or book of the Gospels) upon which the oath was sworn. This oath is probably of the time of Edward the Elder or Athelstan. Schmid, *Gesetze der Angelsachsen.*

military service, the personal relation of lord and man was really the first element out of which later feudalism grew; and the germs of feudalism existed wherever clanhood was found. Where the family was the type of social organisation, the only way in which that organisation expanded was by forming communities on the model of the family. The village community was such an imitation when its members were not actually blood-relations; the lord and his followers were another imitation of the family. This explanation of the origin of feudalism, which I take from Sir Henry Maine, appears to me to give the best key to the history of social development. He has shown how clanhood tended everywhere to a kind of feudalism, even in countries uninfluenced by Roman institutions. The history of England from the fifth to the thirteenth century is the history of her transition from clanhood to feudalism, and from feudalism to central government. It has been the singular good fortune of England to make these transitions more quickly and easily than any other European nation. But wherever the conquering Teutonic races settled they brought with them the binding personal relation between lord and man, which was the germ of feudalism. The new relationship of both to the land—and in Continental countries the rigidity given to these relationships by ideas derived from Roman law—were the other elements of feudalism; and from these things grew that mighty system which prevailed in Europe for so many centuries, which it took so many storms to break, and whose relics are only finally perishing now.

But neither the power of the king nor the power of the nobles grew up unchecked in England. The king could do very little without the consent of his *Witenagemot*, The Witena- or Wise Men's Meeting. This was the old Teutonic gemot. assembly, where every freeman had a right to be present and help in settling the affairs of the nation. But as the kingdoms grew larger, and the clans were scattered over a large extent of country, it is easy to see that it would become difficult and irksome for all the people to attend these national meetings, and by degrees they would only be attended by the king's thanes, the great ealdormen, the bishops and abbots, and such people of importance as happened to be in the neighbourhood where the meeting was held. Thus the democratic assembly became more and more an aristocratic one. This assembly had great powers. It chose the king; for in old times our kingship was elective, though each tribe had its own royal family, supposed to be descended from Woden, out of which the king was always chosen. But it was not thought then that the king's eldest son had a sacred right to succeed; the worthiest of the royal family was always the one chosen, for it was absolutely needful to have a king who was fit to be a leader. As the Witan made the king, they also could depose him if he deserved it. Without their consent the king could not make laws or treaties, nor impose taxes, nor give grants of the public land to his thanes. For it was never supposed then that the king was the owner of the public land, nor was he ever called king of the land, but always king of the people, king of the West Saxons, of the East Angles, of the Kentish men, and so forth.

Nor did the growing power of the nobles utterly destroy the old freedom of the people. Though they were *The Shire-moot.* seldom to be seen in the Wise Men's Meetings of the kingdoms, they were still present at the folk-meetings of the shires, which were held twice a year in the open air. These shire-moots, as they were called, were to some extent representative meetings, for they were attended by the reeve, or head man, and four of the best men from every township (or mark). And at these shire-moots the people were still called upon to declare what the law was in difficult cases, because the old law of England never was all written down, nor is it yet. And when the king and his wise men had made new laws, the sheriff brought them down to the shire-moot that the people might give their pledge to *The Hundred-moot.* keep them. There were also the lesser courts of the hundred, which were holden once a month, where all civil and criminal causes were tried before passing to the higher court of the shire. At these hundred-moots also the townships were represented in the same manner as at the shire-moots. The free townships, carrying on the ancient rights of the mark, still held their own meetings, made their own by-laws, and sent their reeves and four best men to represent them at the shire- and hundred-moots. And though the noble, or 'eorlish man,' was rated so much higher than the ceorl, or peasant, that the fine for killing an earl was six times as much as for a ceorl, yet it was possible for the ceorl to rise by industry and thrift to the higher ranks; if he could gain five hides of land, he won the rank of thane; so did the merchant who had thrice crossed the sea on his own account. Even the slaves, who on account of the endless wars became a very large class, might buy their freedom; so that one class was not hopelessly marked off from another.

It must be remembered that this is a rough sketch of the development which took place during a period of five hundred years, from the English conquest to the time when England was welded into one kingdom in the tenth century; therefore the changes which it describes were very gradual. I must now go back to tell how England became one kingdom.

While there were still seven or eight small kingdoms in the country, there was often some one king who obtained greater power than his fellows, and who was called the Bretwalda, a title conveying some amount of superiority, though what amount it is difficult to say. Several of the Bretwaldas were kings of Northumbria, and at one time it seemed as if Northumbria would be sovereign of the rest of Britain. But soon Mercia became very great, and all England south of the Humber became subject to her. Then the power of Northumbria revived again under a king named Eadbert, who conquered the Cumbrian Welsh, and gained such glory that Pepin, king of the Franks, sought his friendship. But after him divisions sprang up in Northumbria, and it became weaker than the other kingdoms. Then Mercia again became very powerful under a king named Offa, who beat the Welsh and took from them the country that now is Shropshire, and built a dyke of turf from the mouth of the Wye to the mouth of the Dee, to be a landmark between the English and Welsh; it is still called Offa's Dyke, nor has the boundary between England and Wales very greatly changed since then. Offa had friendly relations with Charlemagne, the great king of the Franks, who was afterwards Emperor. Mercia was then and for some time after the

A.D. 716. Ethelbald, king of Mercia.

A.D. 756. Eadbert, king of Northumbria.

A.D. 755-794. Offa, king of Mercia.

most powerful kingdom in Britain; but this did not last, for in the year 800 Egbert became king of Wessex, and in his time the chief power passed over to Wessex, and stayed there.

Egbert, king of the West Saxons, is often called the first king of all England. He was not that, but he was the first English king who became the head of all the others. Kent, Surrey, Sussex, and Essex he made parts of his own kingdom, their old lines of kings having come to an end. The kings of the East Angles, of the Mercians, of the Northumbrians, and of the Welsh, were subject to him in that way already spoken of, which became so common in those times, that is, they acknowledged him as their over-lord, and promised to do nothing against his interest; but he had no authority over their people, so it cannot be said that he was king of the Northumbrians or of the Welsh, though he was over-lord of the Welsh and Northumbrian kings. But the Strathclyde Welsh, and the Scots and Picts, who had sometimes been subject to the Northumbrian kings, were not in any way subject to Egbert.

<small>A.D. 800.
Egbert, king of the West Saxons.</small>

We know very little of Egbert, but we are told that he spent thirteen years in banishment before he became king, at the court of Charlemagne, the great king of the Franks. who ruled all Gaul and Germany. It is very likely that at his court Egbert's ideas of kingly government were enlarged, and that he came back to England with a distinct purpose to be a more powerful ruler than any English king had been before him. In his time forces began to work which in the end brought all England under the rule of one king, so that the king of the West Saxons became at last the king of all England. Why did Wessex obtain this power, rather than any of the other kingdoms? I have said that in Egbert's time Kent, Surrey, and Sussex were joined to Wessex, so that it included all the south of England. Now the south of England was no doubt the most fertile and the richest part; it lay nearest to the Continent, where the tide of civilisation was flowing fullest. And the people of Wessex settled their Welsh question before Northumbria or Mercia were able to do so; Egbert ravaged Cornwall from east to west, and just before his death he won a great victory over the Cornishmen (835), after which they never shook off the English rule.[1] But the chief reason that Wessex became the cradle of the monarchy of England was that Egbert was followed by a long line of brave and wise kings, a race of heroes, and they alone were able to make head against the sea of troubles in which the other English kingdoms were overwhelmed and sank.

We have now come to that crisis in the history of England when she had to fight for her very life with those fierce pirates of the north, who in our old histories are called the Danes. These Danes, who came not only from Denmark but from Norway also, were a nation of pirates, as fierce and barbarous as the English themselves had been when they came to Britain. They were a people of the same stock as the English, speaking almost the same language. But whereas our forefathers had been Christians for about two hundred years, and had become on the whole a sober respectable people, tilling the land and practising all the arts of civilised life, as civilised life was then, these Danes were heathen, with all the barbarity and brutality of heathen. When they landed they slew all the people they could find, they plundered everything they could lay hold of, and seemed to take a wanton delight in burning whatever they could not carry away. Wherever they went the churches were burnt, the monasteries were sacked, the peaceful monks, who had given their time to labour and study and prayer were driven out or slain, the precious pictures and books which had been brought from Rome or copied in England with so much trouble, were wantonly destroyed, and the work of centuries was undone. When the Danes had got as much booty as they could carry, they went back to their ships and sailed off in triumph, laughing at the English who could not pursue them, for Englishmen were not then masters of the seas, and the Danes were far the better sailors. Sometimes they seized horses for themselves when they landed, and scoured the country, plundering place after place for a whole summer, then returning with their stolen goods to spend the winter in Denmark. Another common feat of

Invasion of the Danes.

---

[1] Cornwall appears to have continued for some time to be a separate principality, but subject ecclesiastically and civilly to the church and king of Wessex. In 875 the *Annales Cambriæ* record the death of Dungarth, apparently the last king of Cornwall. Haddan and Stubbs, *Councils and Ecc. Documents*, i. pp. 673, 675.

theirs was to sail up some river, robbing, slaying and burning on either bank as they went, and then, if the people of the country had gathered together to fight them on their way back, they dragged their light ships overland to the next river or firth, and then sailed off scot free, for they were as cunning as they were fierce.

It was thirteen years before Egbert began to reign, in the year 787, that the first ships of the Danes or Northmen came to England. The crews landed on the coast of Dorset, and slew the reeve of Dorchester with all his men, who had come down to see who these strangers might be. After that they came often in the days of Egbert, and oftener still in the days of Ethelwulf his son. When they had harried England in this way for some seventy or eighty years, plundering in summer and generally returning home for the winter, they began to aim at a more complete conquest of the country. In 866 a formidable army came to England, and gradually overran Northumbria, Mercia, and East Anglia. The two kings of the Northumbrians were slain, and the Northumbrians and Mercians made peace ignominiously with the heathen; the help which Ethelred and Alfred, the sons of Ethelwulf, gave to the Mercians in besieging the Danes in Nottingham seems to have been all in vain. The Danes defeated and slew King Edmund of East Anglia, who was afterwards revered as a saint and martyr by the English, and had the great abbey of St. Edmundsbury built to his honour.

Danes invade Northumbria, East Anglia, and Mercia.

Up to the time of this Danish invasion there were still kings of Northumbria, East Anglia, and Mercia, though we are now in the reigns of the grandsons of Egbert.

Wessex was now the last English kingdom which held up its head against the Danes, and it seemed a question whether Wessex would be able to hold up long. For wherever the Danes went they spread panic; the English had become so cowed by their long ravages that they had lost heart. Yet the struggle between Englishmen and Danes was one between Christianity and heathenism, between civilisation and barbarism; and the fate of England hung upon the fate of Wessex. Happily for England, the hour of need brought with it the man who was able to save his country. This man was **King Alfred**. We must pause awhile to study a life in which the life of the English people was gathered and bound up.

DATES.

Wessex pushes her frontier to the Severn	A.D. 577
Edwin of Northumbria conquers Lancashire	(probably) 616
Mercia extends over the centre of Britain	626
Kenwalk of Wessex conquers Somerset, driving the Welsh to the Parret	658
Ina, king of Wessex	688
Offa, king of Mercia, conquers Shropshire, and fixes the Welsh frontier at Offa's Dyke	777
First coming of the Danes	787
Egbert king of the West Saxons	800
Ethelwulf	836
Ethelbald	857
Ethelbert	860
Ethelred	866
Alfred	871

CHAPTER V.

ALFRED was the youngest son of Ethelwulf, king of Wessex. His father is said to have loved him above his other children, and because he loved him so much he sent him to Rome when he was only four years old to be blessed by the Pope. Two years afterwards, when Ethelwulf himself went to Rome, he took the little Alfred with him; and though Alfred was then only six years old, yet as he stayed in Rome a year, no doubt he remembered for the rest of his life the great sights he had seen in Rome, and by such sights his education was begun. His mother was a good and wise woman, of Mercian race. There is a pretty story told that she encouraged her children in the love of the national English poetry by promising a beautifully painted book to the one who should first learn the poems it contained, and that the little Alfred went to his tutor and earned the prize by learning the poems. Much doubt has been thrown on this story, because it is said to have happened when he was twelve years old, and we know that his mother had been dead a long time then. The mistake in the age is no reason for entirely rejecting the story, and we may well believe that Alfred's mother encouraged him in the love of old English songs. But though

Alfred learned to read and to write at some period of his life, he used to lament in his manhood that he could not get teachers when he was young and had the leisure and the desire to learn.

But Alfred learned riding, hunting, fighting, and the other accomplishments which were thought proper to an Etheling or prince, and became very skilful in them all. He lived from his youth up among wars and rumours of wars; when he was eleven years old the Danes sacked Winchester, the royal city of Wessex, and when he was sixteen they ravaged Kent. His father, Ethelwulf, and his brothers who reigned before him, had a constant struggle to defend their kingdom against these pirates. Before it was Alfred's lot to fight with the Danes he had to win the conquest of himself. It is said that in his youth, in the agony of his struggle with temptation, he cried to God : ' Give me any suffering, any pain which a man may bear without his life's work being hindered, rather than that I should give way to sin.' And he deemed it an answer to his prayer that from that time to the end of his life he was constantly afflicted with a painful disease, in one form or another, which never left him for more than a short season.

In the year 871 the great Danish army which had overrun the north, middle, and east of England, invaded Wessex.

The Danes invade Wessex. Alfred's brother, Ethelred, was then king of Wessex. Ethelred was a brave man, and he and his brother Alfred were firm in the defence of their country. The Danes took up their quarters at Reading, which lies on the south bank of the Thames, between that river and the Kennett, which flows into it not much farther down. Part of the Danish forces went out to plunder the country, while the other part set to work to build a dyke from the Thames to the Kennett, so as to make a stronghold for themselves between the dyke and the two rivers. They were attacked in this stronghold by Ethelred and his brother Alfred, but they rushed out with such resistless fury that the English were forced to flee. Four days after a more successful *Battle of Ashdown.* battle was fought at Ashdown, in the Vale of the White Horse, in Berkshire, of which we have a long account. There runs an old Roman road from Reading into Wiltshire, along the top of the chalk downs, called the Ridge Way. Along this road the heathen army no doubt had come. They were in great force, for they had with them two kings and many earls, and they were well posted on the top of a hill. They divided their host into two parts, one commanded by the kings, the other by the earls, and each half formed itself into a *shield-wall*, as the manner of fighting was then in the north, that is, the men stood so close in their ranks that their shields touched, and made a firm wall all round them. When the English saw this they also drew up their army in two bodies, one of which was commanded by Alfred, the other by Ethelred. Ethelred was to fight with the kings, Alfred with the earls. The Danes had the higher ground, so that they could throw their missiles down on the English. The English were eager to attack them, but King Ethelred was hearing mass in his tent, and he vowed he would not come out till the priest had ended the mass, nor leave divine service for human. Alfred at last could no longer wait for Ethelred's division, but forming his men into a shield-wall, he charged up hill. There was on the hill a short squat thornbush, round which was the hardest shock of the battle. Fiercely and long did both sides fight, the Danes (as the old chronicler says) for their evil ends, but the English for their lives, their loved ones, and their fatherland. Ethelred with his division came up and fought against the Danish kings; one king and five earls were slain, but not till the greater part of their host was killed did the heathen take to flight. The English pursued them all that day, and even through the night, till they reached their stronghold at Reading; the bodies of the slaughtered Danes were scattered far and wide over the downs. There is still in that valley, on the slope of the White Horse Hill, the rude figure of a white horse, carven in the turf by cutting away the sods down to the chalk soil; it seems very likely that it was cut in memory of this battle; for the white horse was the ensign of one of the old English tribes, and still forms part of the arms of Kent.

This was Alfred's first victory, but it was of little use as long as the Danish army held fast at Reading, like an arrow sticking into the heart of England. And now we read of battle after battle, in which sometimes the Danes were victurious and sometimes the English. A fresh army of Danes came from over sea, and joined their countrymen at Reading. King Ethelred's strength gave way under so many troubles; he died the same year, and Alfred, his brother, was chosen king of the West Saxons.

Alfred was only twenty-two years old when he began to reign, and the fate of England was hanging upon him alone.

<small>A.D. 871. Alfred, king of the West Saxons.</small> He had not been king a month before he had to fight the Danes again, at Wilton, with very unequal forces; for a long time the English had the upper hand, till they were deceived by a pretended flight on the part of the Danes; then, when the English had broken their ranks in pursuit, the Danes turned round and overwhelmed them. In that one year, 871, nine battles were fought south of the Thames between the English and the Danes, besides skirmishes without number. On the whole, the English seem to have had the best of it in this campaign, since they made peace with the Danes at the end of the year on condition that they should leave Wessex.

The enemy then drew off their forces from Reading, and wintered next year at London, which was then a city of

<small>Danish conquest of Mercia.</small> Mercia. The Mercians escaped their ravages for a while by paying them money, but in 874 they began a regular conquest of the Mercian kingdom. They drove out King Burrhed, who was the husband of King Alfred's sister; he fled to Rome and died there. According to a plan which they had already followed in the conquest of Northumbria, they set up an under-king in Mercia, who was to hold the kingdom of and for them. The next year a large part of the Danish forces under the leader Halfdan went into Northumbria, and harried not only that country but also the kingdom of the Cumbrian Welsh, now called Strathclyde, because Anglian conquest had reduced it to the valley of the Clyde. They rased to the ground Alclwyd, the chief city of Strathclyde, which stood where

<small>A.D. 875.</small> Dumbarton now stands. It was in those days that Eardwulf, the bishop, and Ealdred, the abbot of Lindisfarne took up the body of St. Cuthbert from the island where it lay, and wandered about with it for nine years, fleeing from place to place before the face of the

barbarians. Halfdan divided the lands of Northumbria amongst his men, and from that time they ploughed and tilled them. It was probably Yorkshire which was thus divided in lots, as we still find in Yorkshire a much greater number of Danish names of places than in Northumberland or Lothian, and we know that the under-king whom the Danes had previously set up was still reigning between the Forth and the Tyne. *Danish settlement in Northumbria, 876.*

Meanwhile, though the great army was gone, Alfred had still to fight with other bands of vikings. But this time he met them at sea. He went out himself with a fleet, and fought against seven ships, one of which he took, and put the rest to flight. The next year (876) the other half of the great Danish army, which had been spending a year at Cambridge, left Cambridge secretly, took ship, and appeared suddenly at Wareham, in Dorset. It is not said whether there was a battle. Probably Alfred was not in condition to fight then. But he made peace with them, and they swore on the holy bracelet, the most solemn oath in their country, which they had never sworn by in any treaty before, that they would leave Wessex forthwith. But for all that, the false heathen, as soon as they could get horses, stole away by night to Exeter; and though King Alfred rode after them with all his forces, yet he was unable to reach them before they got within the town, which had still good Roman walls. But their fleet was wrecked in trying to get round from Wareham to Exeter, and being besieged by the king, they gave hostages and swore oaths again. This time they kept faith better. They went away into Mercia, and divided the Mercian lands among themselves, as Halfdan had done those of Northumbria. As Lincolnshire and Leicestershire are thick with Danish names, no doubt it was there they settled themselves, giving the other shires of Mercia to Ceolwulf their under-king. *Second invasion of Wessex.*

This was only a short respite. The time of Alfred's greatest trial was now to come. Whether new swarms of Danes came over and joined their comrades is not stated; but in January 878, the restless heathen again broke faith, and their army 'stole away to Chippenham and overran the land of the West Saxons, and sat down there; and many of the folk they drove over sea, *Third invasion; Alfred forced to flee.*

and most they overcame and forced to obey them, except King Alfred; and he, with a little band, fared hardly in the woods and in the moor-fastnesses.'

All must have seemed lost then when the last English king was driven from his throne and from his royal city, and was wandering in the cold winter with only a few followers among the woods which cover the hills of Somersetshire, or the marshes of the lower ground, with nothing to eat except what they could get by making a foray upon the Danes, or on those who had submitted to the Danes. But the king's mind was still unconquered, and there were still some brave men left to rally round him. An attack made by twenty-three pirate ships on the coast of Devonshire was bravely resisted by some Devonshire men. The Danish leader was slain, and the magic banner of the Danes, called the Raven, was taken. Alfred, during his wanderings in Somersetshire, observed a little island formed by the junction of two rivers, but higher than such islands generally are, and surrounded by swampy country which was often overflowed by the tide. He saw that a little labour would render this place impregnable. Here, then, when the long winter was past, he built a stronghold. Here he raised again the down-trodden banner of Wessex. The nobles and people of Somersetshire began to flock to him, and from time to time he made sallies against the Danes from the island-fortress of Athelney. Seven weeks after Easter he felt strong enough to leave Athelney and move forward into Wiltshire, intending to attack the chief camp of the Danes at Chippenham. The people of Somerset, Wilts, and Hants now flocked around the standard of their king, and, as the old chronicler says, 'they were fain to see him.' In two days he came up with the whole Danish army at Edington, and fought the great battle which saved England. But we have no details given us of this battle as we have of the battle of Ashdown. We are only told that the armies were each formed into a massive shield-wall; that they fought fiercely, stubbornly, and long; and that when at last the Danes gave way, the English chased them up to their stronghold. There King Alfred besieged them fourteen days, till they were overcome with hunger and cold, and offered him peace on such terms as they had never

Fortifies Athelney.

Battle of Edington.

given to any king before—namely, they gave him as many hostages as he wished but he gave them none, and they swore to leave his kingdom with all speed. But the great point was that they gave up heathenism, and desired to be baptized. They were as much vanquished by the moral superiority of the religion and civilisation of Alfred's kingdom as by the force of his arms.

The Danes fulfilled all that they had promised. Three weeks later their king Guthrum was baptized, Alfred himself standing godfather to him. Guthrum spent twelve days with the king, who 'greatly honoured him and his companions with gifts.' At Wedmore a solemn league was made between Alfred and the wise men of Wessex on the one hand, and Guthrum and his Danes on the other, the text of which is still in being. This treaty settled the boundary between the English and the Danes: 'up the Thames to the Lea, up the Lea to its source, then right to Bedford, then up the Ouse to Watling Street.' This arrangement left more than half England in the hands of the Danes; yet Alfred was a gainer by it, since nearly half Mercia, which had never belonged to Wessex before, fell to his share. It was agreed that each king was to rate his subjects equally, whether English or Danish. This put the English in Guthrum's dominions on an equality with their conquerors, and arrangements were made for carrying on trade between the two peoples.

Treaty of Wedmore, 878.

This peace of Wedmore ends the first period of the Danish wars. Alfred's dangerous guests left his kingdom and settled down in other parts of England. In 880 they divided the lands of East Anglia among themselves. In the course of years they became absorbed in the mass of the English people. Those whose love of wandering and plunder was too strong to allow them to settle down and become Christians joined themselves to a great body of Danes which came over sea in 879, and wintered at Fulham, on the Thames. But whether they were awed by Alfred's name, or whether they thought they would have better luck elsewhere, they seem to have done no mischief in England, and in the spring they sailed away to Flanders, where they did much evil during the next two or three years. The eyes of the English chroniclers were so fixed on the Danish vikings that for the next seven years they tell us more of what the army did in the Frankish empire than of what was going on in England. For the next fifteen years Alfred seems to have had comparatively little fighting, though the peace was not unbroken; for the Danes still gave him trouble at times, either by sea or land. And it must have been during these years that Alfred took those measures for building up his shattered country which have earned him the gratitude of his countrymen as much as his victory over the Danes.

His first care was to provide for the defence of his country. He had no standing army to rely upon, and it would *Alfred's reforms. The* not have been possible in those days to keep a standing army. But there was a sort of militia *army.* called the *Fyrd*. Every freeman was bound to serve in the fyrd, and to turn out at the summons of the ealdorman or governor of the shire; but he was only bound to serve a certain time, and when the time was up he went home. It is easy to see what a hindrance this must have been in fighting such an enemy as the Danes. Alfred improved this by dividing the fyrd into two parts, which were to relieve each other in turn. He also arranged to have always a troop under arms in each important town as a garrison. He caused forts to be built in various parts of the country, as strongholds against invasion; and one of the cities which he repaired was London, which had been broken down by the Danes. London had not then the importance which it afterwards gained; but it was one of the greatest cities of England.

Alfred's next great care was to bring about good government and order in his kingdom. The invasions of the *The administration.* Danes had upset everything; when there is war in a country, the bonds of society become dissolved, and everyone does what is right in his own eyes. It needed a strong hand to put things straight. We find that in Alfred's time the power of the king increased very greatly. It was above all things necessary in those days, when disorder was so mighty, that there should be a strong hand to rule. Alfred tried to have the laws carried out with strictness. He was most anxious that the poor should have their rights as well as the rich. If he found that any judges had acted unjustly, he sent for them, and rebuked them most severely, sometimes dismissing them from their office.

As there was some difficulty in knowing what the laws were, Alfred had a fresh code of laws drawn up. This code contains scarcely anything really new; it is almost all taken from the laws of the West Saxons. Alfred himself tells us that he carefully looked over the laws of his predecessors, and kept all those which he approved of, rejecting some which he did not approve of; all with the advice and consent of his wise men's meeting. He adds that though he had some intention of putting in ideas of his own in place of what he had cut out, he did not do so, because he did not know how those who came after him would like them. The age, indeed, was one which was little used to innovations in law; for the more undeveloped a people are, the more they are bound hand and foot by custom; and Alfred, though full of theories, had the practical English instinct which told him that theories must not be forced upon a people who are not ripe for them. At the beginning of his code he puts in the Ten Commandments and some others of the laws of Moses; but this is only by way of a little sermon, telling his subjects what all laws should aim at. He finishes it with Christ's rule: 'Whatsoever ye would that men should do unto you, do ye even so unto them,' and adds, 'By this one commandment a man shall know whether he does right, nor will he need any other law-book.'

The law.

But what Alfred had most at heart was the instruction of his people. He saw that the people were perishing for lack of knowledge. How could good order be kept when the judges could not read the laws, and the priests could not translate their mass-books? In those days very few children were taught to read, except those who were intended to be priests. Nobody cared about reading; what people cared about was hunting or fighting. And why should they have cared, when there were no English books to read? all the few books there were were written in Latin. Two hundred years before King Alfred there had been a good many books written in English; part of the Bible had been translated into English. This had been done in the North, for Northumbria was the place where learning had first flourished in England. But, unfortunately, the North was just the part which had suffered most in the wars with

Education.

the Danes; the monasteries, which were almost the only places where books were kept and people could read and write quietly, had been burnt, and the books with them. English literature had quite died away. There were plenty of English songs, which the people used to sing, but they were not written down, they were carried in the memory only.

Think, then, what a great idea this was of King Alfred's: 'That all the free-born youth of English race should be put to learning, while they can do nothing else, until they can read written English well.' This idea Alfred tried to have carried out. He set the example himself in his own household; he not only had his children properly taught, but also all the children of the nobles who attended his court. He did more than this; he saw there was not much use in making folks learn to read as long as there were no English books which they could read. So amidst all that pressure of business which there was upon him, the reform of the army and navy, the remodelling of the laws, and all the other ceaseless work which the business of government brought upon his shoulders, he set to work to learn Latin, and to translate books from Latin into English for the good of his people. Books were written in Latin at that time, because Latin was the language of Rome, and all learning had come from Rome. In every country the learned men were but a handful, and they were always churchmen, that is, priests or monks. Latin was a natural language to them, because it was the language of the Bible and of the mass; for the Bible had been translated into Latin out of the Hebrew and Greek, and this translation, called the *Vulgate*, was what churchmen always used. England was the first of the great modern nations of Europe to have a literature in the language of the common people.

Alfred's translations.

Alfred chose the books which he thought would be most useful to his people, and wrote them in English; not always sticking closely to his Latin author, but improving him sometimes by adding facts which he knew himself, or putting in thoughts of his own. He translated Bede's 'Church History of the English Nation,' because he wished his people to know their own history. Another book, called the 'History of the World,' by Orosius, he translated because it began with a description of the world as it was then known, so that it would serve as a manual of geography as well as history. He has inserted in it two accounts of voyages to the Baltic and the White Sea, which had been given to him by two sea captains whom he knew. He translated another book specially for his clergy, a sort of priests' guide, called the 'Pastorale,' or Shepherd's Book, which he thought would help them to guide their flocks.

But the book from which we learn the most of Alfred's own mind is his translation of the 'Consolations of Philosophy.' This book was written in prison by a Roman philosopher named Boethius, who does not seem to have been a Christian, though he lived in Christian times, since the book contains nothing more than the best wisdom of the ancient poets and philosophers, those wise men in Greece and in Rome who had taught how far nobler the soul of man was than the body, and how beast-like it was to live only for bodily pleasure, and not for the nobler blessedness of the soul, which is goodness; and how uncertain life is, how quickly riches and fame and pleasure pass away, and how goodness alone abides, and is the only thing worth living for. Alfred felt these words ring in his heart; he wished that they should ring in his people's hearts also. Alfred was a Christian, and to him goodness meant God and the love of God ; therefore he has added to Boethius out of his own full heart passage after passage in which he speaks of God as 'the beginning and end of every good, and the highest bliss.' He calls on men to cease from seeking rest and happiness in anything else but God. He has shrewd sayings on many subjects. Of noble birth he says : 'A man will be little the better for having a good father if he himself is but naught.' He acknowledges that many things in this life are dark, that 'we have little ready knowledge free from doubt.' But not the less 'we should with all our powers inquire after God, from the dignity of that understanding which He hath given us.' He says he is sometimes burthened with the great question which has puzzled all earnest thinkers, the question of the existence of evil. I will quote this passage in full, because it is Alfred's own, and it shows us a great deal of his mind :—

'How would it now look to thee, if there were any very

powerful king, and he had no freemen in all his kingdom, but only slaves ? Then said I, I should think it very wrong and unreasonable, if only slaves should wait upon him. Then quoth he : It would be more unnatural if God in all His kingdom had no free creatures under His rule. Therefore He made two rational creatures free, angels and men. He gave them the great gift of freedom ; hence they could do evil as well as good, whichever they would. He gave them this very fixed gift, and a very fixed law with that gift. The freedom is that man may do what he will ; and the law is that he will render to every man according to his works.'

This passage is interesting because it shows that the mind of this practical English king was far from being exclusively practical, but was busied with speculations on the deepest questions of life; the combination of practical activity with thoughtful speculation is a great feature of English national genius. It shows us also that Alfred had some very advanced ideas about freedom; he saw that the end of God's government was not to force men to do right, but to teach them to choose it because it is best in itself.

Alfred was obliged to send to other countries for learned men to teach himself and his people, and help him in his His learned men. translations. Through the Danish wars, times had greatly changed since a hundred years before, when England had given teachers to France and Germany; now Alfred had to send to France and Germany, and even to Wales, to get teachers for England. One of these was Asser, a Welsh priest from St. David's, who wrote Alfred's life. He found, however, some learned Englishmen in Mercia; and a story is told that when he was wandering in Somerset he was struck with the natural quickness of a swineherd whom he met, and whom he afterwards had educated, and raised to the bishopric of Winchester.

Alfred was not so busy that he could not find time to think of the welfare of other countries as well as his own. He kept up regular intercourse with Rome, always sending money to the church there. He had correspondence with the patriarch of Jerusalem, and his interest extended even to India, for he sent alms to the Christian churches there. It is a touching thing that so long ago, before the English had set foot in that great country, which they were afterwards to win with so much bloodshed and so much wrong, an English king should have thought about India, and cared to do all the little that was in his power to further Christ's kingdom there. Alfred found money for these foreign gifts in the same way that he found time for all his various undertakings; he carefully divided both time and money, and spent them according to a fixed plan. And though he was the poor man's friend, and a most liberal giver, yet even in his charity he followed the maxim of St. Gregory, 'Do not give much to him who needs little, nor little to him who needs much.'

This was Alfred's work during the fifteen years of peace— to provide for the safety, the good government, and the enlightenment of his people. And all this was done by a man who, instead of being strong and robust, was in almost constant bodily pain. The disease—we do not know what it was, but some painful disease—which had afflicted him during his youth, never left him all his life, and he was always liable to severe attacks of it, which incapacitated him for the time for any business. Add to this that he had to struggle always against the slothfulness and incapacity of many of those who ought to have helped him. But through disease and pain and all other obstacles the light of his strong soul burnt only the clearer.

And now the result of his labours began to be seen. Wessex, as the only state in England where there was order and enlightenment, began to earn the respect of her neighbours. The Welsh came of their own accord and chose Alfred for their over-lord; and they were afterwards his faithful allies. The Danes of Northumbria also entered into relations with him, and probably if his life had been prolonged he would in time have obtained supremacy over the whole of England. But this was reserved to his grandsons. *His ascendency in Britain.*

In the meanwhile the marauding armies of the Danes had been harrying the coasts of France, Flanders, and Germany for several years. They plundered those countries until a general famine came on, so that there was really nothing more to get; and then they turned their greedy eyes again towards England, which during the years of peace had had time to recover her former prosperity. *Renewed Danish invasions, 893.*

In the year 893, a large army of Danes came to the mouth of the river Lymne in Kent, in 250 ships. They towed their ships up the river into the heart of the dense forest with which half of Kent was then covered, till they came to an unfinished fort which was still in process of building, and was only defended by a few workmen. They easily stormed this fort, and then encamped at Appledore; and as they had brought horses with them, they went forth in bands and plundered the surrounding country. In the meanwhile another army of Danes, commanded by a famous and valiant leader named Hasting, had landed on the shores of the Thames, and made a stronghold at Milton in North Kent. Defended as both armies were by the almost impenetrable forest, Alfred did not feel strong enough to attack them; but gathering his forces, he encamped between them to prevent their joining, and to give them battle if they should venture into the open country. Their bands when they sallied forth to plunder were chased by the king's bands. At last the Danes at Appledore left their quarters, and attempted to cross the Thames. But the king's forces, under his son Edward, were down upon them directly, gave them a bloody defeat at Farnham in Surrey, and retook all the booty which they were trying to carry away. Edward pursued them across the Thames, but before Alfred was able to come up and utterly crush them news came that the English Danes, those who had settled in Northumbria and East Anglia, had broken faith, and had gathered a fleet and were besieging Exeter, at the very opposite end of the kingdom. Alfred had to turn about with all his force, except a strong body of troops which he left to carry on the struggle in the east. These were joined by the townsmen of London, and they advanced to Bamfleet in Essex, where Hasting and his army had now joined the remainder of the great army which came from Appledore, and had been defeated at Farnham. There they had built a fortress and had stored their plunder and their wives and children. The English stormed the fort while Hasting was out on a raid, and took everything that was in it; the wife and sons of Hasting they sent to King Alfred, the ships they destroyed or brought to London. Only a short time ago the faithless Hasting had sworn fidelity to Alfred, who had stood godfather to his son. But Alfred, with a chivalric spirit rare in those times, restored to the Dane his wife and children in all safety.

Alfred was now in Exeter, where as soon as he arrived the Danes raised the siege and took to their ships. When Hasting had drawn his men together after their defeat at Bamfleet, he went up the Thames; his troops were joined by a great number from East Anglia and Northumbria, and they went up the Thames to the Severn, and then up the Severn. Then Ethelred the ealdorman of Mercia, who had married King Alfred's daughter Ethelfled, and had already done good service against the Danes, gathered an army from every quarter whence he could summon one, even from parts of England which did not belong to Alfred, and from the Welsh. They overtook the Danes at Buttington on the Severn, and beset them on either side of the fort where they entrenched themselves. When they had besieged them many weeks, the enemy began to suffer from hunger, and after having eaten all their horses, they made a desperate sally. The English, however, were victorious, and made a great slaughter of them, and they fled away to Essex. But they soon gathered an army again, and marched at one stretch day and night across the country to Chester, following no doubt the Watling Street, the ancient Roman road which led from London to Chester. The English rode after them, but could not reach them before they got within the stronghold, for Chester had Roman walls; so they burnt the corn round about, and seized the cattle. Then when the Danes could stay no longer at Chester for want of food, they went into North Wales, and after plundering there, they went back again to Essex by a more roundabout way than they had come, still pursued by the English forces.

Meanwhile Alfred and his fleet had driven away the Danes from Exeter; but as they were going homewards they landed near Chichester, where the townsmen bravely fought them, slew many hundreds of them, and took their ships. The next year the army of Danes in Essex built a work on the river Lea, twenty miles above London. The Londoners attacked them, but were put to flight with slaughter. 'Then after this,' says the chronicler, ' during harvest, the king encamped near to the town, while the folk reaped their corn, so that the Danish men might not take their crop from them. Then on a certain day the king rode up the river, and noted where the river might be dammed up, so that they might be unable to bring out their ships. And they then did so; they wrought two works on tw' sides of the river.' But when the Danes saw the trap which was being laid for them, they left their ships and went across the country to Bridgenorth, on the Severn, where they wintered. The Londoners took their ships, destroyed those they could not bring away, and brought the rest to London.

The next summer (897), the Danish army broke up; they scattered themselves in the Danish parts of England, where some got ships and went to France. 'Thanks be to God,' says the old chronicler, drawing his breath, 'the army had not utterly broken down the English nation.' It had been a hard time, not only on account of the Danes, but also because of much sickness and death amongst men and cattle. But Alfred's kingdom was now so organised and so firm that the invaders were met at every point, and Hasting was outwitted in all his manœuvres. Instead of the Danes always seeking to give battle, as they had done in their first invasions, they skulked in forests or in fastnesses, only coming out to plunder, and they were chased by the English army from sea to sea.

Alfred's last triumphs were at sea. As for about a year the disbanded Danes who had got ships gave trouble by harrying the sea coasts, Alfred caused new ships to be made, which were both swifter and steadier and higher than the enemy's, after a model of his own, not copied from the Frisian or the Danish. Nine of these ships fought with six Danish ships off the Isle of Wight in 897, and though they did not succeed in taking them all, they were so damaged that the sea afterwards cast them ashore in Sussex. The crews being brought before the king at Winchester, he ordered them to be hung, a severe but needful justice. That same summer no less than twenty Danish ships with their crews perished wholly upon the south coast. After this come four years in which we read of no fighting at all, so we may hope that King Alfred had rest for a while before his death. He died in 901, when he was only fifty-three. His wife, Ealhswith, whom he seems to have much loved and valued, survived him only one year.

Alfred's name is such a great one in English history, that

many things have been put down to him which are not really his doing. He did not invent trial by jury, nor divide England into shires and hundreds; these things are older in their germ than Alfred's time, though later in their present form. Nor did he found the University of Oxford. But he saved England from the Danes; founded the English monarchy; organised an army and navy; and created an English literature. It was reserved to his children and grandchildren to conquer the rest of England from the Danes, and to turn the kingdom of the West Saxons into the kingdom of England. But Alfred made Wessex the cradle of the English Empire, because he secured in Wessex a firm seat for the English laws, polity, and language; and he made Wessex so much better organised and more enlightened than its neighbours in the island, that its future supremacy was inevitable. Through all the conquests and changes which England has since undergone, the laws, the institutions, and the language of this country have remained English; English influence has eventually conquered the conquerors and the foreigners, and turned them into Englishmen. To this permanence and supremacy of the English element in our history Alfred contributed most powerfully, because he wrought for it a stable footing in England, and put it in a position to begin that work of conquest which was carried out by his successors.

DATES.

Alfred King of the West Saxons	A.D. 871–901
Battle of Edington and Peace of Wedmore	. 878

CHAPTER VI.

THE last chapter has given an outline of the settlements of the Northmen in England. All the country between Watling Street (the old Roman road from London across the island to Wroxeter and Chester) and the Firth of Forth was under their hand. Yorkshire, Lincolnshire, and Leicestershire were thickly colonised by

Danish settlements in England.

them, not to speak of their settlements in East Anglia and elsewhere. Besides these Danish colonies, the Norwegians had taken hold of the western coasts, and settled in Cheshire, Lancashire, Cumberland, and Dumfries. We can trace these Northmen, Danes and Norwegians, by the names they have given to places. Such endings as *by*, a town; *thorpe*, a village; *beck, tarn, dale, fell*, and many others, mark the places where the Northmen settled. And these places are so numerous, especially in the shires above-mentioned, that it is plain the country must have been very thickly peopled by the Northmen, and therefore there must be a great deal of Danish blood in the people of those parts, for we know that the Danes brought their wives and children with them. Perhaps we should not be wrong in saying that the folk of North England are half Scandinavian by race.

England to the north of Watling Street was now called Denalagu, that is Dane-law, because it was ruled by the Danes. As far as we can tell, there were three Danish kingdoms there, besides a sort of independent confederation of five great Danish cities in Mercia; Guthrum's kingdom in East Anglia; a more purely Danish kingdom in Yorkshire, to which Lancashire and Cumberland, and perhaps Strathclyde, were subject; while north of the Tyne, in the old Anglian kingdom of Bernicia, an English king reigned under the Danes. In East Anglia the Danish conquest was of a milder kind than in Yorkshire; the English and Danes were on equal terms. But in Northumbria the Dane was the superior, and the *wergild* of the Danish landed gentleman was reckoned at twice as much as that of the thane or English noble.

Results. Had this settlement of the Danes in England any great and important results for England? It is often said that the English at the time of the Danish invasion had become a tame, feeble, priest-ridden folk, that the Danes brough fresh life and vigour into the nation, and that we get from the Danes that love of freedom of which we have boasted so long.

Now I think the account given of the resistance which Wessex under Alfred made to the Danes does not show the English as a feeble people at all. In fact, the English and the Danes were very near akin in blood, and they had much the same national character. There is a description of the old Saxon pirates, by a Latin poet of the fifth century, which might have been written of the Danes in the ninth; it tells of their fierceness, their unconquerable boldness, their delight in danger, and their equality amongst themselves. The Northmen's religion, the religion of Odin, was the same as that of the English had been; and with them, as with the heathen English, revenge was a duty, and infanticide a right. They had no free institutions which the English had not; they had their Things, meetings or parliaments of the freemen, and many places in the British isles called Thingwall, Dingwall, or Tynwald, tell that the parliaments of the Northmen were once held there. But these free assemblies, as has been said before, were common to all Teutonic nations. The Danes had certainly not learned so much self-government as the English, they had not those institutions, which I shall speak of later on, which made the people themselves the guardians of the public peace. In fact the Danish invasion was more of an aristocratic and less of a popular migration than the English conquest had been. These Danes were men who had been landholders living almost independently on their own land in Denmark or Norway, who fled from their native country because the kings were trying to bring them into settled obedience. They were therefore no doubt a very independent set of people, and it is certain that in the parts of England where they settled there were fewer serfs and more free small landholders two hundred years later, than in the other parts of England. But we must set against this that for hundreds of years the north of England was the most turbulent and disorderly part, the quarter where troubles were constantly brewing. There is so much delusion in the word freedom that it is well for us to bear in mind that submission to a king who had such an ideal of freedom before him as King Alfred had, was a far higher state than any amount of such independence as seemed good in the eyes of heathen Danish chieftains.

Nevertheless, there was in the Scandinavian as well as in the English character an inborn respect for law. 'With law shall our land be built up and settled, but with lawlessness wasted and spoiled,' said one of their wise men in Iceland. By reason of this good quality, they soon fell under English influences, and the most ardent worshippers of Odin became Christians. And English priests planted Christianity in Norway.

In the great struggle between Alfred and the Danes the English nation was born. That is to say, the great work of the making of the English nation was begun; but it was not finished for many hundred years, not till after the Norman conquest. Even the little English England south of Watling Street, Alfred's kingdom, was not wholly one in law and government; and it had yet to win and absorb the great Danish England to the north of Watling Street. This was the work of the successors of Alfred.

English nationality founded.

Edward the son of Alfred, generally called Edward the Elder (901), began the winning of middle England from the Danes, and followed it up steadily all his life. In this work he was greatly helped by his brave sister Ethelfled, called the Lady of Mercia because she had married Ethelfred, ealdorman of Mercia, and after his death became herself a sort of queen in Mercia. The brother and sister both spent their lives in fighting, and we see them gradually pushing their frontier northwards beyond the Watling Street, and building strongholds at every important point, till a chain of forts ran across the island from east to west, a firm barrier against the advances of the Danes. There were no fresh invasions of Danes in the tenth century, so that Edward and his successors had only to fight with those already settled in the island. Gradually, shire after shire that had once owed obedience to the Danes submitted to King Edward, till East Anglia and all the country south of the Humber were reclaimed. The lady Ethelfled herself overcame the Danish union of the Five Cities (Lincoln, Leicester, Nottingham, Stamford, and Derby), and she was just awaiting the surrender of York when death took her, and as the old chronicler says, 'she fared forth' to rest from her labours. After her death, Edward kept Mercia in his own hand. He still pushed forward his arms, till the Danish kings of Northumbria, acknowledging his greater might, chose him for their over-lord; so did the king of the Scots, and the king of the Strathclyde Welsh.

Edward the Elder.

Athelstan, the son of Edward (925), drove out the Danish

kings from Northumbria, and thus earned the title of the first king of all England. And now the power and influence of the English kings began to be felt abroad as well as at home, and we find the sisters of Athelstan marrying the greatest kings and princes of the Continent. One married the German emperor, another the Carlovingian king of France, another the great duke Hugh, the ancestor of the future kings of France. And we see for the first time an English king interfering in foreign affairs when, in 936, Athelstan caused his sister's son Louis, who had been banished from France, to be restored to his throne by the help of the duke of Normandy. *Athelstan.*

The wild Danes of Northumbria were restless under Athelstan's yoke; and in 937, uniting with the Scots and Cumbrians, and helped by a large fleet from the Northmen settled in Ireland, they rebelled against the English king. And then was fought the famous battle of Brunanburh, where the Danes and Kelts were crushed by Athelstan and his brother Edmund, where five kings and seven earls were slain, and Constantine, king of Scots, and Anlaf, king of the Danes, were put to flight. I call it famous because songs were made about it, which were sung by harpers at feasts; and one of these songs has been preserved for us by the *Anglo-Saxon Chronicle*, as that old record is generally called, which is our most truthful guide for many centuries of English history. Here are a few lines of this song rendered into modern English, but keeping the curious kind of verse, without rime, in which English poetry was then written:— *Battle of Brunanburh.*

Then forth fared
The northern foemen
The spears' bloody sparing,
Over sparkling ocean,
O'er deep waves driving,
Dublin seeking,
And Ireland once more.
Aching in heart;
Likewise the brothers
Both together,
King and Etheling,
Came to their kinsmen
To West Saxon land
In war well-famed.
They left behind

On the battle-field bloody,
The swart raven sharing
The sallow corpses
With horny beak;
And the bravely feathered
White-tailed erne
The carrion eating,
The greedy goshawk,
And that grey beast
The wolf of the wood.
Never was witnessed
Erst in this island
Sorrier slaughter,
Folk so fearfully
Fallen before the

Sharp sword's edge ;	O'er broad-brimmed ocean
So the books say,	Britain seeking,
Old tale tellers ;	Wise war-smiths
Since the time when	The Welsh overcame,
Angles and Saxons	Greedy for glory
Came from East hither,	They gained this land.

But the Danes were not so pressed down by the defeat of Brunanburh that they could not spring up again when Athelstan died, and his brother Edmund became king (940). They again chose themselves a Danish king, and the revolt was so widespread that it was joined by the Mercian Danes, and sanctioned by Wulfstan, archbishop of York, and for some time Edmund was obliged to yield to them the country north of Watling Street. But Edmund, like Athelstan and Edward, was a hero strenuous in arms. In 943 he overcame the Danes and brought the Denalagu again under his sway. More than that, he conquered Cumberland from the Norwegians, and gave it to Malcolm, king of Scots, to hold under him, on condition 'that he should be his fellow-worker by sea and by land.' The king of Scots was found a rather dangerous neighbour to the new kingdom of England, and Edmund thought it well to keep on good terms with him. Edmund could now style himself 'king of the English, and governor and ruler of all the nations dwelling round about.'

Edmund.

Yet still his successor Edred (946), though he received the submission of the Scots and Strathclydians, had to begin his reign by a fierce struggle with the Yorkshire Danes. Having overthrown the last Danish king of Northumbria, Edred gave the country to be governed by an earl of his own choice (954). In the reign of his nephew Edgar, it was divided into two earldoms—one to the north, the other to the south of the river Tyne (966). In later times the southern earldom lost the name of Northumbria, which was kept by the earldom north of the Tyne; and that is the reason why we now find the shire of Northumberland so far from the Humber.

Edred.

It was in the reign of Edgar, the son of Edmund (959), that the glory of the new English kingdom reached its height. The work of conquest was completed; the Danish pretenders were all expelled from English ground; the Welsh, Scots, and Strathclydians bowed

Edgar.

before their overlord, so that Edgar could proudly say, 'God has reduced under my power all that this island within it holds.' A powerful fleet was stationed to guard the shores; peace was maintained, and with peace commerce and wealth were increased.

But still, England, though welded into one kingdom, was not yet fused into one nation. The old divisions of Wessex, Mercia, and Denalagu were still governed by their own laws. And the extreme northern portion of Northumbria, that part which had been governed first by English under-kings, then by English earls, and which was less Danish than Yorkshire, was so far from one with the rest of England that Edgar found it convenient to grant part of it (namely, Lothian) to Kenneth, king of Scots, to be held under himself. *Cession of Lothian.*

The kingdom of the Scots has now begun to emerge out of darkness. It was founded by the Scots, who came over from Ireland about the same time that the English settled in Britain. In the ninth century it absorbed the old kingdom of the Picts, and thus covered all the northern part of the island, the firths of Clyde and Forth being the boundary between the Scots and English. But towards the end of Edred's reign, the Scots, being themselves pressed by the settlements of the Scandinavians in the extreme north, began to advance southwards. They crossed the Forth; and the royal city of Edinburgh, which our king Edwin of Northumbria had founded, fell into their power (954). It is a sign that Edgar had not much direct power over the more northern part of this kingdom that he was willing to yield such a province as Lothian to the Scots. *Scotland.*

When Lothian was joined to the Scotch kingdom, its English inhabitants were undisturbed, and were still governed by their own laws, which in the end became the laws of all Scotland. And though we now call the dwellers between the Tweed and the Forth the Scotch, we ought not to forget that they are as English as ourselves in blood, and that the true Scotland is beyond the Clyde. An old proverb says that whoso crosses the Clyde, going southwards, goes out of Scotland into Largs.

Whether Edgar was a man altogether worthy of so much

glory as brightened his reign we do not know. Many stories are told of him which are not at all to his credit. But they do not rest on the best authority, and his good government does. He had the wisdom to choose the best men for his councillors and ministers. The leading man in his government was Dunstan, archbishop of Canterbury; and to Dunstan's influence were probably due most of the wise measures which were taken in Edgar's reign for the establishment of peace and order.

Edgar's government.

Dunstan.

The name of Dunstan is most commonly associated with the religious revival which took place under his inspiration. Like all religious revivals in those ages, the form which it took was a return to a stricter asceticism. Owing to the wars with the Danes, monastic life in England had fallen into great decay. The monasteries often had laymen for abbots, and had become places to which people retired with their families to spend a life of jollity and idleness; and the lay abbots handed them on to their children as inheritances. Nor were the English priests in general inclined to the monkish views about marriage which were held by the leading churchmen of that day. Dunstan endeavoured to reform the Church by turning out the married clergy from the cathedral bodies, replacing them by monks, and by establishing a strict observance of the rule of St. Benedict in all monasteries. To the men of that day there was no way of keeping the Church pure except by drawing a hard line between it and the world. To preserve the purity and moral power of the Church, strictness of rule was above all things needed. Therefore, the man who worked for monastic reform, and for the spread of monasteries, was a true civiliser; for such a man was also working for learning, for science, for art, for mechanics, which in those days had no other seats but in the monasteries.

Monastic revival.

Under the guidance of Dunstan, Edgar is said to have founded more than forty Benedictine monasteries. Ethelwold, bishop of Winchester, who appears to have been even more active in the cause than Dunstan, and who was called the Father of Monks, drove out the married clergy from the minsters of his diocese. These reforms naturally roused great anger among the laxer monks and the married clergy, and the consequence is that by one party Dunstan's character has been blackened with many stains, while by the other side he has been praised as a saint. In particular, he and his predecessor Odo, archbishop of Canterbury, have been very much condemned for their conduct to King Edwig, Edgar's brother, who reigned before him, and to his wife Elfgifu. I do not attempt to unravel the truth out of this perplexed story.

It cannot be said that Ethelwold's warfare against the marriage of the clergy was wholly successful; for at the time of the Norman conquest the English clergy were still in the habit of marrying, and most of the cathedral churches were served by secular canons instead of by monks. *Secular,* which means belonging to this world, was the name now given to priests; while the monks, who had retired from the world, and lived according to a rule, took to themselves the title of *regular* clergy. And, as might be expected, there never ceased to be jealousy and strife between the seculars and the regulars.

Dunstan himself was no narrow ascetic, but an artist, a painter and musician, and a cunning worker in metals. We still have his portrait, painted by himself in an old missal. It is often said that the study of the Greek and Latin poets was discouraged by churchmen; but it was Dunstan's opinion that though the Scriptures were the great objects of Christian study, yet the writings of the poets and other ancient authors were not to be neglected, because they tended to polish the minds and improve the style of those who read them. Dunstan's enemies made it a charge against him that he was too fond of the old English songs and tales. We know how fond Alfred was of these, and how he caused his children to learn them. It is worth noting that these two great Englishmen thought so much of their own tongue and their native poetry. Poetry and art had their work in that age as in every other. Whatever man has seen, felt, or imagined, he strives to make again in some form, solely for the delight of it, and that others may know it too. The very lowest savages draw figures of themselves and animals upon the rocks. That is the first rude working of the art-instinct; but the true power and charm of all art lies not in its giving us a mere imitation of the things we see and hear, but in its raising in our minds the same feelings

Dunstan and Art.

which the objects themselves would give. The poet and singer in Old-English (as in Greek) was called the maker, because by singing of the things which thrilled and stirred men most deeply he made those feelings in their minds. These ideal feelings raised them out of the vulgar rut of their common life. It is true that the gleeman or minstrel at the Anglo-Saxon feasts sang chiefly of wars and battles, the things which his hearers liked best, and never failed to put in a hint for a good reward at the end of the song; but every now and then he touched a deeper chord; he spoke of duty and faithfulness, or across his music flitted the dark question, Whence come we? whither do we go? which, even in heathen times, continually rose to the earnest minds of our forefathers.

When Christianity came, this power of song was made use of to spread the Gospel. We are told how Aldhelm, one of the most learned churchmen of the seventh century, finding that the people were apt to rush away from mass without waiting for the sermon, used to post himself on a bridge, and begin to sing sweetly to his lute the old tales which the people loved; then when they thronged about him, he changed his song and sang the Gospel stories, and such things as he thought it good for them to hear and remember. I have told of Cædmon's hymns, and how useful they were. Painting the Church had already pressed into her service, and brought it with her to England as her handmaid. The walls of Benedict Biscop's Church at Wearmouth (where the same good Benedict had collected a library, which Bede afterwards used) were adorned with 'the lovely image of Christ and his saints,' or with pictures from Old and New Testament history placed side by side to illustrate each other. By these pictures the unlearned folk who could not read were taught the truths which were most useful.

Poetry, painting, and the Church.

The danger in those days was lest the Church should keep painting and poetry entirely to herself; and therefore one is glad to hear that Dunstan was so fond of the Old-English songs. In those days everyone, even the poorest, could play and sing a little; and at night, when all the company were met in some great hall, after the feast, the harp was passed round, and each man in turn had to give a song. We may be sure that men would not be content to sing only hymns at such times; therefore it is pleasing to know that even the monks in their cloisters were humming the 'Battle of Brunanburh,' and one of them could not help putting it into his chronicle. These national songs are of the very greatest importance to us. They were the only form in which history lived then among the common folk, and therefore they teach us what the people thought about events of which we have only scanty notes elsewhere.

It is pleasant after so much fighting with the Danes to think of Dunstan and his civilising work, to listen to his harp, or to watch him working at his anvil, where his cunning fingers wrought the twisted gold, and where between whiles he had fights with the devil. For conflict was still the great thought of this age, and of all the middle ages. The old heathen songs told of wrestlings with dragons and giants. That time has gone by; but the Christian songs sing of another warfare, not less deadly, not less absorbing, between the Flesh and the Spirit—the Soul and Christ on one side, the Flesh and the Devil on the other; and the man who wins in it is the man whose soul, in the words of an ancient Anglo-Saxon song, 'is filled with brand-hot love.' I have said enough about this conflict before;[1] I only note it now in passing, to remind you that all the deepest moral life of the middle ages is set to that tune, 'Who shall deliver me from this body of death?'

DATES.

Edward the Elder	A.D. 901
Conquest of Central England from the Danes	
Athelstan	925
Conquest of Northern England from the Danes	
Battle of Brunanburh	937
Edmund	940
Conquers Cumberland and gives it as a fief to Malcolm King of Scots	
Edred	946
Division of Northumbria into two earldoms	
The Scots get possession of Edinburgh	954
Edwig	955
Edgar	958
Administration and reforms of Dunstan	

[1] See Chap. III. p. 26.

CHAPTER VII.

AND now we must look the Danes in the face again. It may seem at first sight a strange thing that the glorious wars of Alfred, Edward, Athelstan, and Edmund, and the triumphant peace of Edgar's reign, when all the island owned his sway, should be followed by the conquest of England by the Danes.

Edgar was succeeded by his son Edward, who reigned only four years, and was murdered to make way for his half-brother, Ethelred the Unready, so called because he had no *rede* or counsel. When the time for action came, he never had any plans to act upon, and was driven like a ship before the wind. He was the weakest man that ever sat upon the English throne; and in those days it was a much more serious matter to have a bad king than it would be now. For almost everything depended on the king then; and with an incapable king the nation was like an army without a leader.

Ethelred the Unready.

The reign of Ethelred is a weary tale of mismanagement, treachery, weakness, and ruin. Often we hear of brave resistance in some parts of the country, as at Maldon, where Brithnoth, the heroic ealdorman of Essex, fell in a battle about which a noble song was made; or in East Anglia, where Ulfcytel, the ealdorman, a Dane by race, was one of the best defenders of England; or at London (a city whose growing importance begins now for the first time to be clearly seen), where the brave citizens themselves drove back the Danes four times from their walls. But we hear far more often of treason and cowardice. In 991 Ethelred tried the wretched plan of bribing the Danes to go away, by paying them the tribute so well known as the *Danegeld*. Of course this only made them more greedy; and now for twenty-two years England lay an almost helpless prey to their merciless harryings.

The Danegeld.

It is not my purpose to tell in detail the history of that dreary time. A few passages from the *Anglo-Saxon Chronicle* will give an idea of what it was like:—'This year the army landed at Watchet, and wrought much evil by burning and manslaying. And after that they went up the Tamar till they came to Liddyford, and burnt and slew everything that they met with; and they burnt Ordulf's minster at Tavistock, and took unspeakable spoil with them to their ships (997).' 'And forces were often gathered against them, but as soon as they should have joined battle, then was there ever, through some cause, flight begun; and in the end they ever had the victory' (998). 'Then became the dread of the army so great that no man could think nor discover how they could be driven out of the land, or this land held against them; for they had sadly marked every shire in Wessex by burning and harrying' (1006). 'And oft they fought against the city of London; but praise be to God that it yet stands sound, and there they ever fared ill' (1009). 'And when they went to their ships, then ought the fyrd to have gone out against them again until they should land; but then the fyrd went home; and when they were eastward, then was the fyrd kept westward; and when they were southward, then was our fyrd northward. Then all the Witan were bidden to the king, that they might *rede* (counsel) how this land should be guarded. But though they *red* something, it did not stand even one month. And next, there was no head man that would gather the fyrd, but each fled as he best might; and next, no shire would even help another' (1010). 'All these woes befell us through *unrede* (lack of counsel), that they were not offered tribute in time, or fought against; but when they had done most evil, then peace and truce were made within them. And, nevertheless, for all the truce and tribute, they fared everywhere in bands, and harried, and robbed and slew our wretched folk' (1011).

The end of it all was the complete conquest of England in 1013 by Sweyn, king of Denmark. King Ethelred fled into Normandy, and 'all the people held Sweyn for full king.' But Sweyn died the next year; Ethelred came back to England; and now there was a struggle for the kingdom between Ethelred and Cnut, the son of Sweyn. After Ethelred's death, in 1016, his doughty son, Edmund Ironsides, kept up the struggle like a hero, fighting no less than six battles in seven months. Had he lived longer, the fate of England might have been different; but in the same year, 1016, he died, some say by a traitor's hand. 'Then Cnut obtained the whole realm of the English

Conquest of England by the Danes.

kin.' Not by main force alone however; the form of election by the Witenagemot of all England was gone through as regularly as in the case of any English king.

To understand the bearings of this Danish conquest of England, we must give a glance both forward and backward into English history. There is one great event now looming in the distance before us, the conquest of England by the Normans, that remarkable people, whose Scandinavian fathers, led by the Norwegian Rolf, had wrested from the Carlovingian king in 912 that goodly slice of country in the north of France, which received from them the name of Normandy. The Danish conquest is a link in the chain of events leading up to the future subjection of England by the Normans. But this chain begins with the great Danish settlement in England in the ninth century. The Danish folk were not yet melted into the English nation; the *Denalagu* was ever ready to throw off the yoke of the English king; and in the Denalagu any Danish invader could always find a foothold. When we remember that England was half Danish, we can understand why the old chronicler just quoted complained that 'one shire would not help another.' Even the English parts of England were imperfectly united, and had as yet no strong common feeling of patriotism. Besides this, there was yet another cause which may have powerfully contributed to the victory of Sweyn and Cnut.

Causes of Danish conquest.

Disunion of England.

It was the general belief of Christians at that time that the world would end in the year 1000. It is easy to understand how this belief would damp the national ardour, and make people careless of what happened, cowardly and panic-stricken. It is equally easy to understand how, when the fated year 1000 was past, and the world did not end, a reaction took place, and as often happens when the strain of a great fear has been taken away, the bonds of society were loosened, and the world was worse than it had been before. We are told that there never was such a time of faithlessness, vice, and contempt of right. A sermon preached about 1014 notes these evil signs of the times, that the rights of poor men and thralls were trampled on, that no man cared more for his kin than for strangers, that priests did not live by the church's rule, nor laymen by

End of the world expected.

the laws, and above all that treason to lords was become a common sin; the gravity of this last sin must be measured by the fact already spoken of, that faithfulness between lord and man was the chief bond of society in those days. One pirate, says the preacher, will often put ten Englishmen to flight.

Now look at another link in the chain. In 1002 King Ethelred married Emma, sister of Richard, Duke of Normandy. From that time a connection between Normandy and England began. When Ethelred and Emma were driven from England, it was to the court of the Norman duke that they fled, and there their sons were brought up; so that when in after years one of them (Edward the Confessor) came to be king of England, he was more than half a Norman, and he put Normans into important offices in England. Already the province of Normandy was becoming too small for the Normans. They kept the restless energy of their Scandinavian fathers, though they had been polished by the civilisation of France. Just about this time (1016) they began their conquests in Italy and Sicily, the beginning of that career of conquest which made them famous throughout Europe. Ready as they were for any adventure which promised glory and reward, it was natural that they should turn their eyes towards England if there seemed a chance of conquest there. In the same way, after Cnut's time, the kings of Norway and Denmark fix greedy eyes upon England. We shall find that the great reason why England fell a prey to the Norman conqueror was because she was raked by a double fire, from Norway on the north, and from Normandy on the south.

Connection with Normandy begun.

Yet the wars and toils of Alfred and his successors were not in vain, though in the end England was handed over first to a Danish, then to a Norman conqueror. For under Alfred's rule an England was born which should in the end conquer her conquerors, both Dane and Norman. And even in Alfred's time, the English, being the more civilised and Christian people, had made the Danes feel that they were so; the Danes by taking baptism had shown that they confessed the higher power of Christianity and civilisation. When Cnut conquered England, he also accepted Christianity, and made himself a soldier of civilisation.

Permanence of English nationality.

Cnut was a good specimen of a Northman of that age; brave, crafty, not shrinking from a cruel deed if it served his purpose, but able to see the advantages of civilisation, and to choose the cause of order. Denmark was but a barbarous kingdom, in spite of great advances which the North had made in some of the arts of life; but Denmark and Norway were heathen or only half Christian, and Christian, civilised, refined Wessex was much more to Cnut's taste. He made his home there, and only left England on such expeditions as were necessary to keep up his sway in Denmark, and to conquer Norway (1028).

Cnut; union of England, Denmark, and Norway.

England, Denmark, and Norway were now united under one crown, to the great benefit of the whole North, where English priests were foremost in spreading Christianity. Cnut seemed every year to become more of an Englishman, and under him England enjoyed eighteen years' peace, order, and prosperity. The under-kings of Scotland and Strathclyde did homage to him, though a further cession of Lothian was made to the King of Scots by a defeated earl of Northumberland. The most important posts in the state were trusted to Englishmen; the English parts of the country were still governed by their old laws; and England, safe from foreign invasion and from inward revolt, was better off than she had been for years. Cnut protected the Church, founded monasteries, and enforced the payment of tithes and of Peter's pence, a subscription to the English school at Rome.

Prosperity of England.

The chief results of the Danish conquest were an increase in the power of the king, and a fresh impulse given to that tendency towards feudalism which has been already spoken of. Cnut, when he sent home to Denmark the fleet which had helped him to conquer England, kept with him the crews of forty ships, and formed them into a sort of body-guard to himself, called the king's house-carls, which became a little standing army. No English king before him had ever had any standing body of soldiers, and this force at his back must have helped him greatly to keep his power over the great nobles, who, in Ethelred's time, had been very independent. But the Danish conquest altered that matter in another way, for most of the old nobility had perished in the wars, and their places had been filled by men appointed by King Cnut. Writs

Results of Danish conquest.

Growth of the royal power.

now begin to be issued by the king to the bishops, thanes, and reeves of the shires, without the consent of the Witenagemot. These writs are mostly grants of land, and we now see that the old ideas about Folkland are giving way, and that the king, instead of the nation, is beginning to be looked upon as the owner of the public land.

On the other hand, the division of the kingdom by Cnut into four great earldoms, Wessex, Mercia, East Anglia, and Northumbria, opened the way for the rise of great feudal families in whose hands a weak king would be almost powerless. This was not contemplated by Cnut, who regarded the four great earls[1] as his officers; bound to obey his writs, and removable at his pleasure. But in the next reign the possible evil of the division was fully realised. It seems also, as far as we can speak with certainty on a very obscure subject, that since the Danish conquest the jurisdiction of the nobles in their own lands was prevailing more and more, and that in this direction also the tendency towards feudalism was growing. *The four great Earldoms.*

It is now time that we should take a closer look at feudalism, and see what it was really like. We shall better understand what it was in England if we look at it first in France. In France, in the eleventh century, feudalism was fully grown, and its evils were at their height. All the land of the country (at any rate in the north of France) was held by feudal tenures; that is, it was not held as absolute property, but as a loan or *fief*, on certain conditions, generally on condition of military service. Every lesser noble was the man or *vassal* of some greater noble, and the greater nobles in turn were the vassals of the king; but the authority of the king was a mere shadow, the great nobles were in reality quite independent. The land was covered with castles; in every castle dwelt a noble, a seigneur as he was called in France, whose power over all around him was absolute. The people who dwelt in the village which clustered round his castle were his serfs, bound to till the land for his benefit; the burghers of the neighbouring town had to pay him tolls, and very often he made his castle a robber's nest, from which he pounced on all *Feudalism.*

---

[1] The old title of Ealdorman is now dropped, and the Danish word Earl is used instead.

travellers and merchants, and plundered them. The seigneur's life was utterly idle; he had no amusements but hunting and fighting. He was always quarrelling with the neighbouring seigneurs; indeed, causes of quarrel could not fail to arise, because of the thousand ins and outs of the feudal relations, one seigneur being often the lord of another seigneur for a fief which he had granted him, and at the same time vassal of the same seigneur for a fief which he held of him. The variety was also immense in the conditions on which fiefs were held. There were courts to judge these quarrels, courts of peers they were called, meetings of the barons. But these courts were of very little use, because there was no State, no central authority higher than the nobles, and able to enforce its decrees. The only remedy for private grievances was that the seigneur took the law into his own hands, and sallied forth to attack his enemy.

The wretched country people were exposed to all the storms of these private wars, as well as to all the exactions of their seigneur. They were bound to the soil, and could not change their lord. If he was a bad lord, they were wholly in his power; his bailiff could squeeze out of them the uttermost farthing. There was no State to protect them; the king had no authority within the domains of the count or baron. The seigneur made laws, and was supreme judge. The Church was the only helper of the poor, but even in the Church their merciless lord could pursue them; the escaped serf who had taken orders could be claimed by his lord even in the ranks of the clergy. No wonder the people said the castles were built by the inspiration of the devil; no wonder feudalism has left behind it such a hated name.

The worst features of feudalism were unknown in England. The great reason of this was the entire difference *Feudalism in England.* between the English conquest of Britain and the Frank conquest of Gaul. The English conquest was an immigration as well as a conquest; the English were not a handful of conquerors scattered over an immense territory. The original Roman-Celtic inhabitants formed the mass of the nation in Gaul, and many of them kept their wealth and high position. The English were themselves the nation in England; for the Welsh (except in the western shires) were slain or driven out. The mass of the people being English, the old free customs, the meetings of the people, their laws and rights, lived on, instead of dying out as they did in Gaul. For in Gaul too the Franks at first had their popular assemblies, the meetings of the county and of the hundred, but these meetings died of neglect, because people could not take the trouble to go to them, and because Charlemagne, who wished to be a great Roman emperor, appointed judges instead. Then there were no castles in England; the noble did not build himself a nest whence he might tyrannise over the people, but lived in a great hall, where he kept open house at night; and in early times the villagers round about him were more or less his kinsmen. He had jurisdiction in some cases over his vassals, but he did not give laws to them; the law of England was above him. He was a magistrate and not a tyrant. The ceorl had his rights as well as the noble. Above all, in England there was a king; there was a central authority to keep the nobles in order.

It is not needful to point out again that if the kingly power had not grown steadily from the ninth century onwards, the power of the nobles would have grown much more independent than it was, and England might have been split up into a number of feudal states like France. The growth of feudalism in England consisted mainly in the increase of the power of the great landlords. Allodial land, that is, land which was wholly a man's own, was becoming less and less common, for those who had commended themselves and their lands to the protection of some thane or earl had lost the direct right of property; they now held their lands on condition of certain fixed services to these thanes or earls. *Commendation on the increase.*

I have already spoken[1] of the way in which the ancient marks or parishes tended to become absorbed in the estates of the nobles. The freemen of the mark, either because they were not strong enough to hold their own, or because the expense of freeman's service in war was greater than they could bear, or perhaps because they were too poor to furnish their lands with stock, *commended* themselves and their lands to some neighbouring thane, who henceforth looked upon their lands as his own, granted to them at his pleasure, and their ancient rights in commons and forests as grants

---

[1] See Chap. IV. p. 37.

proceeding from his favour. This was how the *mark* passed into the *manor*.[1]

Feudal jurisdiction. The most important consequence of this change was the rise of *manorial jurisdictions*, that is, the right of the lord to try the causes of his dependents in his own court. This right arose naturally out of the lord's right to take away from his vassal the land he had bestowed, or was supposed to have bestowed on him, and out of his obligation to answer for those who were in pledge to him.[2] For since the time of Athelstan it had been made law that every man should be in pledge, that is, that he should find some one to answer for him, in case he were accused of any crime.

Popular courts not discontinued. The mark meeting, in which the local affairs of the mark had been settled, now became the court of the manor. This, of course, put a great power into the hands of the nobles. The hundred courts also fell largely into their hands. But the old popular forms were still observed in these courts, and were the safeguards of ancient liberties. And the folk-moot of the shire had still a jurisdiction superior to that of the manorial courts, and prevented the whole administration of justice from falling into the hands of the nobles. At these shire-moots, as has been already remarked, the voice of the people was constantly appealed to to declare what the law was, or to give evidence about rights in land.

The Hundreds and Frithguilds. Another thing which tended to keep up an independent spirit among the people, was that they were themselves called upon to help in carrying out the law. From the time of Edgar, if not before, the inhabitants of every hundred formed a sort of association which was bound to pursue thieves and recover stolen property. I will not enter into the perplexed question of the origin of the name hundred, which now belongs to the divisions of the shires. But it would appear that these associations for protection against theft were at first voluntary. In the reign of Athelstan we find in the city of London frith-guilds, or peace-clubs, (which were also called tithings) consisting of ten men each, both nobles and ceorls, who not only sub-

---

[1] The word Manor was at first used only of the lord's house. It properly belongs to Norman times only; but the thing existed before, and the word is the most convenient one to use.

[2] The civil jurisdiction arose thus; the criminal jurisdiction was conferred by royal grant sometimes, but generally reserved by the Crown.—See Stubbs, *Cons. Hist.*, i. 187.

scribed to a common purse to make good losses by theft, but also undertook to pursue the thief, and recover the stolen property. This idea of association once grasped, it was extended on all sides, and the law took hold of it. In Edgar's reign (959-975) we find the hundreds apparently divided into tithings, and the tithing-men are bound to ride after a thief, and do justice upon him. And it would seem (though this is a much-disputed question) that in the reign of Cnut this responsibility of the tithings for the maintenance of peace was extended so far, that the members of a tithing were bound to hold one another to right in case any one of them were accused; an institution which appears in a more developed form after the Norman conquest under the name of frank-pledge.

Beside the tithings, the frith-guilds upheld by law, there were many other kinds of guilds, some of them very like the friendly societies or benefit clubs of the present day.

On the Continent also these associations were formed by the people to protect themselves when the law was too weak to protect them. But on the Continent they were put down with a high hand by kings and bishops; they were not trusted. In England, on the contrary, the kings trusted them, and made use of them as a means of keeping order. The reason no doubt was that England being a smaller country, and king and people being of the same race, they knew one another, and there was sympathy between them.

Thus, while society was taking more and more a feudal shape, the old forms of popular participation in the carrying out of the law kept up the life of the people, and prevented them from becoming entirely the passive serfs of the nobles. Feudalism in England never had all things its own way. But feudalism was a needful step in the development of England as of other European countries. *Vitality of popular institutions.*

In the first place, society was not yet ripe for organisation on a large scale. It could only form into clusters of small organisations. When a great wind has blown over a sandy shore, the sand collects in tiny heaps round every little pebble on the shore. By degrees the larger heaps join together, and form sand-hills. So after the storm-wind of Teutonic inva- *Feudalism a necessary stage of development.*

sion had passed over the Roman Empire, out of the ruins and confusion rose the feudal baronies and duchies, a thousand small centres, and it was long before out of these swarms of sovereignties any one solid State was formed. One reason why England became a State sooner than any other European country was that England was an island, and it is much easier to get organisation on the limited scale of a small island than on such an immense scale as a country like France, for instance, would need.

Secondly, the change from the mark system to the manorial system must not be looked upon as an evil, as regards the tilth of the land. It is certain that the tilth of the lands held in common was very bad. There were endless rules about fallows and crops which prevented any progress of agriculture, because no art can make progress unless it has free scope. It has been proved by experience that land which a man holds and tills as his own will feed many more people than land which he holds in common with others. The lord who had succeeded in making the mark his own property could reclaim the wastes without being hampered by the rules which bound those who held their land in common, and therefore could not do as they would with it. Moreover, though the mark was held in common, and held by the people, and though it helped to develop many valuable qualities, such as mutual helpfulness and honesty, there were many bad points about it. It was every man's interest to prevent his neighbour from working his land in the way that he thought best, because next year the same land might be his by lot, and might be spoiled for him. Besides this, though this old system of public property in land answered very well up to a certain stage of civilisation, it did not answer well when population and wants began to increase, and the old tribal bond was broken up. It was a good thing in its day, but private property in land was also a needful stage in the development of society.

Advantages of manorial system.

Thirdly, the feudal relationship called forth many fine qualities. It was not a bad thing that society should be built up on the faithfulness of man to man. These relations called for truth and honour in an age when, the old family bond being relaxed, truth and honour

Feudal virtues.

would otherwise have had but little soil to grow upon. How this idea of personal faithfulness has blended with Christian influences, and given us our modern notions of what is honourable in a gentleman, we shall have occasion to trace hereafter.

But the very fact that personal relations were the only bond of society in that day, shows that people lived in a state of general distrust. For they could only trust those whom they knew. We should never for- *State of society.* get that now-a-days, besides the policeman who stands at the corner of the street, we have another policeman, unseen but very powerful, who helps to keep order in the most effectual way. That policeman is public opinion. Because public opinion does not allow people to do just what is right in their own eyes, we are able in many things to trust people whom we do not know at all. But in the eleventh century, public opinion was young and ungrown. It was therefore needful that every man should have his guarantors, who could give an account of him. The head of every house was in pledge for his wife and children, the lord was in pledge for his dependents. No one, in fact, had a right to live unless he could find some one to answer for him. The man who could find no one to vouch for him might be slain as a thief. Even a man of rank could not freely leave his land; he would be hunted from shire to shire, and the law would punish those who sheltered him. No sales could take place without full witnesses, and the charge for witnessing sales was a fruitful source of income to those who had the privilege of it. It is easy to see what a clog this must have been to trade. And in truth, trade was confined to the great towns, which were growing in wealth and importance.

Since every man of lower rank was dependent on the knowledge which his neighbours had of him, it follows that it was no easy thing for a poor man to change his place of abode. In fact, the greater part of the freemen were sinking into the condition *Freedom and Serfdom.* of serfs, bound to the soil, they could neither leave their land nor change their master at will. But we must not allow ourselves to be deceived by the word *freeman*. What we call freedom, freedom to move from place to place, to think and speak as we like, to engage in what trade we like, was unknown in early times. It could not exist where every man was watching his neighbour suspiciously. In the Danish parts of England there was still a class of freemen who, though not holding by military service, could change their lord, or could even sell their land. This class did not exist in other parts of England (except in Kent); there was no class (except in the towns) between the thane who held by military service and the villeins [1] who were bound to the soil. But although the population of South England were falling into a state of serfdom, we have no reason to think that they were very badly off, because in almost all cases the services which they owed were fixed, either as to kind or as to time; and though they had to work hard for their lord, yet on the other hand the duties of the lord towards them were fixed, as for instance, to provide them with live stock and seed on their farms, and with tools and house furniture; and all these relations were watched over by ancient custom. And if there were more so-called freemen in the North than in the South, we must remember that society was less organised in the North, and that there was much more violence and robbery there.

The only class which had no rights was that of the thralls. The master had power of life and death over his thrall; but *Slavery.* the Church was active in trying to lighten his burthens, and punished any master who killed his slave unjustly. He could earn money in his leisure time, and (before the Norman conquest) could buy his freedom. The Church encouraged the setting free of slaves. But slaves were increasing, for not only were all captives and many classes of criminals made slaves of, but fathers could sell their children as slaves (up to the age of seven years), and were too often tempted to do so in needy times. The name of the saintly Wulfstan, Bishop of Worcester in the reigns of Edward the Confessor and William the Conqueror, should ever be remembered for his steady and successful efforts to put down the slave trade which then made Bristol infamous.

We have some materials from which we can form a

---

[1] Villein is a name used only in Norman times. It meant simply a farm-labourer. In Anglo-Saxon times this class was divided into many with many names and different rights.

rough picture of the life and manners of the Anglo-Saxons. We must imagine the country almost covered with forests or moorland. In the forests, here and there, were clearings, where stood the villages of our forefathers with their tilled land lying round them. At one end of the village was a large hall, where the thane or noble lived. Around the village lay the common fields, where each villager had his own portion of land. The common field was divided into three strips, of which one in turn lay fallow as pasture every year, and there the flocks of the villagers fed in common, guarded by the village herdsman. In the forest which lay round the clearing, the villagers kept large herds of swine; there also they cut their firewood, or they dug turf from the bogs, no man saying them nay, for their lord had not yet altogether deprived them of their ancient rights. There also they were free to hunt the deer and the wild fowl, for no game laws were passed before the time of Cnut, and the forests were so large and so full of beasts of prey as well as of game, that it was a public benefit to hunt. Bee-keeping was much followed, for there were such vast heaths in England that bees were easily fed, and honey was quite an important article of food, cane sugar being then unknown in England. Stray cattle were looked after by the village pounder, and there were very strict orders about them. The villagers were bound to work for the lord for a certain fixed portion of their time, and their little holdings, generally furnished by the lord with stock and tools, were looked upon as payment for these services. Each of these small communities supplied its own wants; grew its own corn and malt, baked, brewed, spun the wool of its own sheep, made shoes and clothes of home-grown leather; and the bakers, tailors, shoemakers, and smiths were paid for their work by allotments of land. *Village life.*

The hall in which the Old-English noble lived was a large wooden building, consisting of one great room, which served both as a dining-room, sitting-room, and sleeping-room. Rushes were laid on the floor of the hall, instead of carpets, but when a great guest was expected, the floor was sometimes strewn with flowers, and the walls were hung with shields. A great fire was kindled in the middle of the room, and as chimneys were not yet intro- *Domestic life of upper classes.*

duced, a hole was made in the roof for the smoke to escape by. Dinner was at noon, and supper in the evening; when the dinner-hour came, tressle-tables were brought into the hall. A cloth was laid on the dinner-table, but knives were only used to carve with; forks there were none, and the company ate with their fingers, for which reason water was always handed round to wash the hands with before and after meat. After dinner or supper the tables were cleared away, and the rest of the evening was spent in drinking, while the gleeman sang songs or recited tales. The Old-English were deep drinkers, according to all accounts. The song of the gleeman to his harp was the only refined enjoyment to which even the noble could aspire in those days.

Along the sides of the hall were sleeping berths, sometimes furnished with curtains; to these the guests retired when night came on. The attendants had bedding spread for them on the floor, or on the long benches which formed almost the only furniture of the hall; for chairs were rare, and used only for persons of distinction. The ladies of the household alone had separate sleeping-chambers built apart from the hall, and called *bowers*, the same word which we still use for a little house in a garden; the bowers, the hall, and the chapel or other outbuildings were all surrounded with a wall, whose gates were shut and guarded at night; and the whole enclosure was called a *tun*, the word from which our word *town* is derived.

Although we are now describing a state of society in which clanhood was merging into feudalism, we must not imagine that the old family bond was a thing which quickly gave way. Throughout Old-English times, the kinsmen of a murdered man had the right to take the law into their own hands, and to avenge themselves on the murderer, if he refused them the pecuniary compensation fixed by law. The Church, which had valiantly struggled against the evils which this right of revenge gave rise to, had succeeded in curtailing it within certain limits; and the law of Edmund, whereby the kinsmen of a murderer were allowed to renounce him, and were then released from bearing the feud, shows an advance in the direction of individual responsibility.

The family bond.

The way in which criminal cases were tried in those days shows how dependent every man was on his fellows, and how necessary it was that he should have some one to answer for him. Now-a-days, if Tom Dodd stole a hen, witnesses would be called to prove that Dodd was seen skulking about the hen-roost on a certain evening; that later on, he was met with a suspicious-looking bundle under his arm; and so forth. This is what is called evidence. The Old-English did not go about things in this way. They wisely did not trust their eyes and ears; the devil played such tricks in those days![1] Therefore if Dodda was accused of stealing a hen, in the first place he had to swear in court that the charge was false; then five or six of his neighbours (the number varied according to circumstances) were called in, not to prove that Dodda had not committed the theft, but to swear that they believed he had sworn 'a clean and true oath.' The value of the oath varied according to the rank of the swearer; a thane's oath was worth that of six ceorls. It has sometimes been thought that we have here the germ of trial by jury, but we can see what a wholly different thing it was, since this jury had not to try the evidence, but simply to support the oath of their comrade. If the neighbours were doubtful about Dodda, and would not swear for him, he had then to go to the ordeal. First he must fast three days; then he went to church, where mass was sung, and he took the communion, the priest first solemnly adjuring him by all holy things not to partake if he were in any way guilty. Then the ordeal was got ready; the accused had either to plunge his hand in boiling water, or to carry a lump of red-hot iron for a distance of nine feet. His hand was forthwith bound up, and not opened for three days. If at the end of that time it had festered, he was pronounced guilty; if not, he was innocent.

Compurgation.

Ordeal.

The object of the ordeal was to appeal to the judgment of God, but it took effect by working on the mind of the accused. After the fasting, the solemn service, and the adjuration, while the boiling water was hissing, he was a bold man who could brazen it out to the end, when he knew that God and the saints were looking on, able and willing to confound his cause. If he trembled or turned pale, the case went against him.

[1] If a thief was taken in the act, he might be slain at once by his captors.—Palgrave, *Engl. Commonwealth*, p. 210.

As has been said before,[1] the Church of that day took an active part in punishing crime. She imposed penances, which the State gave her power to enforce. In fact, while the State only undertook to make good the losses caused by crime (by its system of fines for every offence), the Church undertook to root out sin, and was supported in this work by the secular power.

DATES.

Edward II. (the Martyr)	A.D. 975
Ethelred II. (the Unready)	978
Danegeld first paid	991
Ethelred marries Emma, daughter of Richard duke of Normandy	1002
Ethelred driven out by Sweyn	1013
Edmund Ironsides	1016
Cnut King of Denmark and England	1016
Cnut conquers Norway	1028

CHAPTER VIII.

THE STORY OF THE NORMAN CONQUEST.

WE need not stop over the short reigns of Harold and Harthacnut, the sons of Cnut. At the death of Harthacnut, *Edward the Confessor.* in 1042, the old line of native kings was restored in the person of Edward, son of Ethelred, known as Edward the Confessor. His reign brings us to the direct story of the Norman conquest. And here our history must again become personal, and we shall only have a glimpse now and then of the English people; while we are chiefly taken up with kings, earls, and bishops.

First we have the white-handed, waxen-faced King Edward, with his snowy hair and beard, who was said to have the gift of healing, and whom his people reverenced as a saint. He was a good man, no doubt, of pure life and kindly disposition (except in occasional fits of rage), very reverent to holy things, and wishful to govern his people well. But he had no ability or energy. If other people would take the trouble of governing for him, he was only too glad to give his whole time to singing and dreaming in church, to church business, and to the amusement of hunt-

[1] See p. 32.

ing, which he greatly loved. The last of the old kingly race of Wessex, he was very little of an Englishman. Half Norman by his mother, he was wholly Norman by education and tastes. He preferred the sprightly Norman-French to the grand Old-English tongue, and the English manners and customs seemed to him barbarous compared to the refinement of Normandy. Especially was he shocked by the lax discipline of the English Church, and he brought Norman monks to England to set an example of strictness. He surrounded himself with Norman favourites, who had his most intimate friendship, and managed the affairs of his palace. Many of these Normans received lands and high offices in England. Ulf was made bishop of Dorchester; Robert of Jumièges archbishop of Canterbury. Richard Scrob, who received an estate in Herefordshire, built a castle there after the fashion of the barons in Normandy. Such a castle England had never seen before. Her nobles were not used to shut themselves up, as if in an enemy's country, in strongholds from which, while safe themselves, they could oppress the poor people round about; and this castle-building was looked upon with great horror by the English. *Edward's Norman tendencies.*

But as yet the Normans had not got everything to themselves. The fourfold division of England made by Cnut still stood, and the four great earls were the chief ministers of power. Whether the doughty earl Siward, earl of Northumbria from the Humber to the Tweed, was often seen at Edward's court we know not. Northumbria was a turbulent region, not very obedient to the English king; yet we shall find Siward marching at his sovereign's bidding more than once. Leofric, the earl of Mercia, who was very wise both in church matters and in worldly business, was thought to be 'a great blessing to all this nation;' but his sons and his grandsons, as we shall afterwards see, wrought England much sorrow. But the figures of chief interest at the court of Edward are those of Godwin, earl of Wessex, and his sons; Swegen, who held a new earldom in the western shires; Harold, earl of East Anglia; and Tostig. *The four great earls.*

The origin of Godwin is doubtful; but he married the sister of Earl Ulf, one of the companions of Cnut; his sons therefore were half Danish by blood. *Earl Godwin.* It is difficult to give a sure verdict on the character of

Godwin and his sons, because the Norman writers, and those who followed them, have heaped most bitter blame on all the house of Godwin; while the modern English writers, regarding them as the heroes of the national party, have equally overladen them with praise. When we look at the old chronicles which were written at the time, we find the figures of Godwin and Harold somewhat dim. We can only guess at what they were from what they did. But what they did does not seem to justify either the extravagant blame of the one side, nor the overdone praise of the other. There is, however, a marked difference between Godwin and his son Harold. Godwin, the clever and eloquent earl, hangs under suspicion of a dark crime, the murder of the innocent Etheling Alfred, the brother of Edward, who was entrapped and slain in the days of Harold, son of Cnut. Godwin, it is true, has long ago purged himself of this crime by oath before the assembly of his peers, in ancient English fashion; and the king, who has never accused him of it, has received him at his court—nay, he has taken his daughter Edith to wife. Yet still the suspicion is revived from time to time, and one of the old chroniclers quotes it against him from an old rime of the day. But Harold, he tells us in another rime, is the noble earl, who at all times loyally served his lord in word and deed.

Harold.

As to Swegen, it is plain he was a violent young man, who did not shrink from the darkest deeds; but he repented him of his sins, and died on his way back from a pilgrimage to Jerusalem—a very common mode of expiating sin in those days. Swegen does not greatly concern us; but the history of England turns on the history of Godwin and Harold. Whether of their own free will, or because their interest and their patriotism ran together, they were the champions of England against the 'outlandish men' with whom the king had filled his court.

Swegen.

Great was the anger of Englishmen when the highest office in the English Church, the archbishopric of Canterbury, was given by the king to the Norman Robert of Jumièges (1051), while Elfric, whom the monks of Canterbury had chosen, and Earl Godwin had recommended to the king, was rejected. But this Robert, who had already been seven years bishop of

Jealousy between English and Norman party.

London, had got possession of the king's ear, and for some time back had been stirring up the king's mind against Godwin, by whispering the old story of his brother Alfred's murder. The jealousy between the English and the Norman party was increasing. A slight event threw the whole country into a blaze.

Eustace, count of Boulogne, a French nobleman, had married a sister of King Edward. In the autumn of 1051 he crossed the Channel, and paid a visit to his royal brother-in-law. What his business was we are not told; but it was successful, and Eustace appears to have been so puffed up with pride that on his homeward journey he deemed he had a right, like the king, his brother-in-law,[1] to demand free quarters from the citizens of Dover. As he and his men drew near to Dover, they put on their byrnies and rode into the town like men who are monarchs of all they survey. But when one of his men tried to take up his quarters at the house of a certain townsman, the townsman, who deemed that every Englishman's house was his castle, slew the insolent Frenchman. A skirmish took place; many were slain on both sides, but the Frenchmen were driven off, and hastened back to the king at Gloucester, to complain of the treatment they had received. The king was very wroth, and ordered Earl Godwin, in whose earldom Dover lay, to chastise the rude townsmen. But the earl, because he was loth to hurt his own people, who had only defended their rights, refused to go. 'It is monstrous,' said he to the king, 'that you should judge unheard those whom it is your duty to care for.' Then the king sent for his nephew Ralph, the Norman earl of Hereford, and for Leofric, earl of Mercia, and Siward, earl of Northumbria, with their forces, and held a Witenagemot to judge Godwin; while the earl and his stalwart sons gathered together the men of their earldoms, intending also to go to the meeting.

Affair of Count Eustace.

Edward quarrels with Godwin.

But when Godwin heard that the influence of the Frenchmen was likely to prevail, he and his men trimmed themselves

---

[1] *Feorm*, or the right of demanding board and lodging free wherever they went, was one of the privileges of the old English kings, at least on all lands which had been originally Folkland; booklands were exempted from these obligations.—Allen, p. 144.

for battle, and marched towards Gloucester, 'though it was loathly to them to stand up against their royal lord.' Then some of the Witan thought that it would be a great evil for them to come to blows, seeing that the noblest of England were arranged on either side, and that by killing each other they would only leave the land more open to the Frenchmen. So they made peace between the king and Godwin, and fixed another meeting, to be at London, a few weeks later.

Meanwhile the king sent for all the fighting men, both north and south of the Thames, and when the meeting came together at London, Godwin dared not appear before it, though he had brought with him a great force out of Wessex. But the king's party found means to entice to their side the thanes who were under Godwin and Harold, and Godwin's force dwindled away. He asked for a safe-conduct to come to the meeting, but the king would not grant it him. Godwin was at dinner in his house at Southwark when the news was brought to him that the safe-conduct was refused. He pushed the table from him, sprang on his horse, and rode all that night to Bosham, where he shoved out his ships and sailed for Flanders. On the morrow the meeting declared him an outlaw, and all his sons. His daughter, the queen Edith, shared in the family disgrace. The king took all her goods from her, and sent her to a convent. Harold escaped to Ireland. The bishop of Worcester was sent after him with a force to take him, but 'they could not, or they would not.'

Godwin outlawed.

This sudden fall of Godwin has a good deal that is strange about it, seeing that only such a short while before he had been at the head of a powerful army, with the sympathy of at least all the South of England. Even the men of that day do not seem to have been able to account for it. 'It would have seemed wonderful to every man who was in England,' say the chroniclers, 'if any man had said before that it should end thus; for he had been erewhile so greatly exalted as if he wielded the king and all England; and his sons were earls and the king's darlings, and his daughter wedded to the king.'

Thus the Norman party triumphed; and while they were

at the height of their triumph, a visitor of ill omen came to England; no other than William, the young Duke of Normandy. This William had already shown himself a prince of great shrewdness and valour.

<small>Visit of William the Norman.</small>

The proud barons of Normandy had despised him because he was not born in lawful wedlock, and was the son of a tanner's daughter, and they had rebelled against him; but he had made them feel his strong arm, and was now undisputed lord in his own dominions, and the most powerful vassal of the French king. He was already beginning to be famous in Europe for his valour, his wisdom, and his success. As he was the great nephew of the Norman Emma, wife of Ethelred and afterwards of Cnut, and mother of Edward the Confessor, he could claim kindred with Edward; and he came to visit Edward at the time of all others when the king was most inclined to welcome and honour his Norman kinsmen. Very likely it was at this time, if ever, that Edward made some kind of promise that when he died William should have the English crown. This promise was afterwards made one of the grounds of William's invasion of England; but it is not spoken of by the English chroniclers, neither had any English king either the right or the power to promise his crown to whom he would.

As the king refused to listen to any messages which were sent by Godwin in his banishment, praying for peace, the summer of the next year (1052) saw Godwin in the English channel with a fleet, harrying the Isle of Wight and the south coast.

<small>Return of Godwin.</small>

Harold also came with nine ships from Ireland, and was heard of on the coast of Somerset, man-slaying and cattle-lifting. This does not look very patriotic in Godwin and Harold, but in those days men who had been ousted from their own were not very scrupulous as to what means they used to get their own again. And we must remember that one reason why armies always plundered in those days was that as people lived then from hand to mouth, it was almost impossible to buy up large stores of provisions beforehand as we should do if preparing for war.

King Edward's fleet, which had lain in wait for Godwin many weeks, dispersed at last, because the seamen's serving-time was up. Godwin met with no opposition, and at Portland he joined his forces with those of Harold. As the men of the south coast swore to live or die with Godwin, he now ceased plundering, or at least confined it to seizing provisions. 'Except this,' says the chronicler, 'they did not much harm after they came together; but they drew to them all the landfolk by the sea's rim, and eke up on land; and they fared towards Sandwich, and ever gathered to them all the boatcarls whom they met, and came to Sandwich with an overflowing army. Then when Edward King heard that, he sent after more help, but they came very late. And Godwin fared ever towards London with his ships, till he came to Southwark, and there he abode some while till the flood came up. And erst he treated with the townsmen, that they almost all would what he would. When he had mustered his host, then came the flood, and they weighed their anchors, and held through the bridge by the south bank, and the landforce came up and trimmed them on the strand; and then the ships went about towards the north shore, as though they would hem in the king's ships. The king had also much landforce on his side besides the ship-men; but it was loathly to almost all of them that they should fight against men of their own race, for there was little that was worth much on either side, except of English men; and eke they would not that this land should be left more empty to outlandish men, through their killing one another themselves.'[1]

'Then the earls sent to the king, and asked of him that they might be worthy of everything that had unrightfully been taken from them. And the king withstood some while, until the folk that were with the earl were greatly stirred against the king, so that the earl himself with difficulty stilled the folk.'[2]

'And they made peace on both sides. And Godwin landed, and Harold his son, and as many of their fleet as seemed good unto them. And there was a Wise Men's Meeting, and they gave Godwin his earldom clean, as full and as free as he had it at first, and to his sons all that they had before, and to his wife and his daughter as full and as free as they had before. And they fastened full friendship between them, and promised good law to all the folk. And they outlawed all the Frenchmen who before had set up unlaw, and doomed

---

[1] Anglo-Saxon Chronicle, Abingdon version.
[2] Anglo-Saxon Chronicle, Peterborough version.

wrong judgment, and counselled ill counsel in this land; except so many as they agreed upon, that the king liked to have with him, who were true to him and to all his folk.'[1]

'When Archbishop Robert and the Frenchmen heard that,[2] they took horse and fled, some west to Pentecost's castle, some north to Robert's castle. And Robert Archbishop, and Ulf Bishop [of Dorchester] went out at East gate, and their companions, and slew and wounded many young men; and he went to Eadulfsness and threw himself into a crazy ship, and fared over sea, and left his pall and Christendom on land, as God would have it, seeing he got this dignity before as God would not have it.'[3]

This story comes from that old 'Anglo-Saxon Chronicle,' which we are sometimes told is 'a dry, bare, monkish, record.' But how full of life and patriotism it is! The English monk writes, not like a monk, but like an Englishman, rejoicing in the revolution which rid the land of 'outlandish men,' and once more put Englishmen at the forefront of the kingdom.

Godwin did not long survive his triumph; he died the next year (1053). Since many stories were told in later times about his death, I may as well say that those trustworthy chroniclers who wrote at the time when the things happened, simply tell us that while sitting at the king's table one day, he suddenly fell senseless, no doubt from a fit of paralysis or apoplexy, and remained speechless till the fourth day, when he died. The people wept for him as for their father and guardian, we are told. *Godwin's death.*

His son Harold was appointed to the vacant earldom of the West Saxons. Two years later (1055) when Siward the doughty earl died, Tostig, the third son of Godwin, and King Edward's special favourite, was made Earl of Northumbria. Not very long after the two youngest sons of Godwin were provided for; Gyrth was made Earl of East Anglia, and Leofwin of Kent, Essex, and Hertfordshire—in fact, of South-Eastern England generally. *Harold, earl of the West Saxons.*

The House of Godwin was now at its highest point of

---

[1] Anglo-Saxon Chronicle, Abingdon version.
[2] Namely, that peace was made between the King and Godwin; they did not wait for the great meeting, but fled the evening before.
[3] Anglo-Saxon Chronicle, Peterborough version.

greatness. Harold was the greatest man in England after the king, and in fact he was the actual ruler of England, for the easy-going king was only too glad to get someone to take the trouble of governing for him, so that he might spend his time in prayers and hunting. Of Harold we are told by a writer of the time that 'he was the friend of this nation and of his fatherland, that he filled with earnestness the office of his father, and walked in his steps, to wit, in patience, kindness, and graciousness to all the right-minded. But to the turbulent, to thieves, and robbers, he was terrible as a lion.' In person he was tall, strong, and handsome; in manners good-natured and frank: in temper forgiving. He was a first-rate general, but he was also skilled above other men in his knowledge of English law. He had travelled much, and with more purpose than most men of that time, though the English at all times have been great travellers, and eager observers of foreign customs; but Harold had made a special study of the laws and state of France. With all these gifts of nature and education Harold was not unfitted for the great part he had to play.

His great work during the reign of Edward was the subjugation of Wales. The princes of Wales had been more or less under the yoke of the English kings since the days of Egbert, king of the West-Saxons (828). But they were always ready to throw this yoke off whenever they could. A powerful prince had now arisen in North Wales, Griffith by name, who after much fighting had quelled the other small kings of Wales, and brought the whole country under his own rule. Before this was done, he began to make himself troublesome to his English neighbours. In the year of the banishment of Godwin and his sons, he made an inroad into Herefordshire, and after making great slaughter both of the English 'fyrd' and of the Normans of Richard's castle, he went back with much booty. In 1055, two years after the return of Godwin and his sons, Elfgar, son of Leofric, Earl of Mercia, was outlawed on some charge of treason, we know not what. Elfgar was at that time Earl of East Anglia. He quickly justified the charge by gathering a fleet of Irish Danes, joining himself to Griffith, King of Wales, and invading Herefordshire. This was part of the earldom of the Norman Ralph, King Edward's nephew, who had succeeded

Affairs of Wales.

to Swegen, son of Godwin. The Norman earl marched against Elfgar and Griffith, with the fyrd of the shire; but he made his followers fight on horseback, as the Normans were wont to do, instead of on foot, after the English fashion. This lost the battle; English and Normans fled, and Hereford city was sacked and burned the same day by the Welsh king and the English traitor.

Earl Harold was now sent against the Welsh, with an army gathered from nearly all England. But as winter was setting in nothing could be done that year; Harold entrenched Hereford and made peace with Elfgar, and, as the old chronicler rather bitterly observes, 'when they had done most evil, then this counsel was counselled, that Elfgar earl should be inlawed, and his earldom should be given to him, and all that was taken from him.' We cannot explain all this, but it shows the great power of the House of Leofric, the only family who in any way rivalled the House of Godwin. An irksome warfare went on with the Welsh in the Hereford district, till Leofric, Harold, and Ealdred, Bishop of Worcester, brought Griffith to terms, and he swore to be a faithful under-king to King Edward (1056).

Griffith was not faithful to his oath, and in 1063 Harold went on another campaign, with the determination to end this Welsh rebellion for ever. He invaded Wales by sea, while his brother Tostig, with a Northumbrian land-force, invaded it by land; they ravaged the country mercilessly, giving no quarter. The spirit of the Welsh was broken; they now turned against their own king as the cause of the war, and slew him. Harold brought his head to king Edward. The king bestowed Wales on two kinsmen of Griffith's, who swore oaths and gave hostages to the king and the earl, that they would be faithful in all things, would perform all the wonted services of under-kings, and pay the tribute which had formerly been paid to the English kings. A law is said to have been passed that every Welshman found in arms on the east side of Offa's Dyke should have his right hand cut off.[1] After this the Welsh were quiet for some time.

[1] John of Salisbury says so; but as he lived 100 years later, and those who lived at the time are silent about this law, we cannot call it certain.

Part of what is now Monmouthshire, the country between the rivers Wye and Usk, was yielded to England after Harold's victory. Thus we see the conquest of Britain is still going on. Yet not long after, a discontented Welsh chief made a raid into this very district, and slew a number of workmen, who were building a hunting-seat for King Edward by Harold's orders ; so unsafe were all border-lands in those days, and for long enough afterwards Things were just as bad on the borders of Northumbria and Scotland; it was not so long since King Malcolm himself had made a raid into Tostig's earldom.

And now we draw near to the fateful year 1066, and all the causes which brought about the Norman conquest are running to a point. Tostig, King Edward's favourite among the sons of Godwin, did not do well as Earl of Northumbria. It is true that that province was very hard to govern; the half-Danish people were wild and savage in their manners, and the roads were quite unsafe because of the swarms of robbers. Tostig was resolved to put down this disorder, but he was hard and violent in the means he took, and he was suspected of having caused the death of some Northumbrian thanes only in order that he might get their possessions for himself. In 1065 the Northumbrians revolted, while Tostig was away with the king; they seized his treasures at York, slew his followers, and chose Morkar, the second son of Earl Elfgar (who was now dead) for their earl. Morkar was not at all unwilling to accept the office thus thrust upon him; he marched southward with all the men of the shire, and was joined by his brother Edwin, Earl of Mercia, with the forces of the Mercian shires. The grandsons of Leofric, unstable and selfish men, were ever ready to foster strife, and keep up the old divisions of England, hoping to find their own advantage in renewing the partition of the kingdom; we shall find them playing this game again.

<small>Northumbria revolts against Tostig.</small>

The united hosts marched to Northampton, plundering the country, and even carrying off the inhabitants, 'so that that shire, and the other shires which are nigh, were for many years the worse.' Earl Harold was sent by the king to the rebels at Northampton, to bid them submit their grievance to the decision of the law. They replied by demanding that Tostig should be outlawed from the kingdom, and Morkar confirmed in his earldom. Harold bore back their message to the king. A Wise Men's Meeting was held; many speakers boldly accused Tostig of harshness and greed, while Tostig reproached his brother Harold as having stirred up the strife against him. Harold denied it on oath; but this quarrel between the brothers was never set right, and was the cause of bitter woe to England in the future.

The king was so wrath with the Northumbrians for rebelling against his favourite Tostig, that he wished to march against them with an army, and punish them with the sword. But the winter was coming on; it would be impossible to gather in time an army large enough to cope with the forces of Mercia and Northumbria; besides the thought of civil war was horrible to those men who desired that 'the dear realm of England' (so called in a poem of that day) should ever be one and undivided.[1] Wiser counsellors, Harold no doubt among them, held back the wrathful king. He was persuaded to grant the requests of the rebels, even the banishment of Tostig, and at a great meeting held at Oxford (1065) *Cnut's law was renewed*. This kind of expression, which is often found in the old chronicles, means simply that after a time when the laws had been neglected, solemn promises were made to keep them as they had been kept in the days of Cnut, Edgar, Alfred, or any other king whose reign was looked back to as a golden age of good government. Tostig and his family retired to Flanders. *Witenagemot at Oxford.*

The pang which it cost the king to be forced to repress his rage and do the very thing he most hated, threw him into a sickness from which he never recovered. He had long been very busy in building a splendid monastery and church in honour of St. Peter, on the site of an earlier foundation, on the small island of Thorney in the Thames, a short way beyond the western gate of London. The church and palace of *Westminster* have been entirely renewed since the days of Edward, though some portions of the monastic buildings still remain; but the minster has ever since been the place of crowning, and generally of burial, for *Westminster Abbey built.*

---

[1] The name England appears for the first time after the conquest of the Danish Swegen in 1013.

the English kings, and the Wise Men's Meeting of all England is still held in the palace hard by. The most noteworthy deed of Edward was this removal of the seat of English royalty from Winchester, the old capital of Wessex, to the city, which by its position and its growing influence was fitted to be the capital of the whole realm of England.

<small>Death of Edward.</small> Edward was too ill to be present at the hallowing of his own minster, the last act of the year 1065, and on January 6, 1066, he breathed his last.

The very next day, Edward was buried, Harold was elected king, and crowned in Westminster. The best English <small>Harold king.</small> writers tell us that Edward on his death-bed named Harold as his successor; and seeing that Edward had been under Harold's influence for fifteen years, it is the most likely thing to have happened. But Edward's mere nomination was not valid in English law; therefore the same writers tell us that Harold was chosen king by the chief men of all England, who no doubt were in London at the time, attending the usual Christmas Wise Men's Meeting. Such a choice was certainly a new thing, since Harold did not belong to the royal race of Wessex, the descendants of Cerdic and Woden. The sole male survivor of that race was a little grandson of Edmund Ironsides, known to history as Edgar Atheling, or Etheling. His father, the Etheling Edward, had found a refuge in Hungary from the jealousy of Cnut; there Edgar, and his sisters Christina and Margaret, were born, the children of a foreign mother. King Edward, in the year 1057, sent for this Etheling Edward, wishing, no doubt that he should be his heir. But he died soon after he landed. It was always the custom of the English Wise Men's Meeting to pass by a minor, when there was an abler man to be found of the royal house. Now there was no abler man of the royal house to be found, but there was one man so marked out to reign, a man who had been king in fact for so long, that ancient prejudices about royal blood might well be thrown aside. But when we consider how immensely strong those prejudices were, even in much more enlightened days than those of Harold, we cannot help seeing that some effort, perhaps some pressure, must have been needed to make men throw them aside, and take an English earl for their king. Yet we have no reason to doubt the fact so well asserted, that Harold was formally chosen, and duly crowned and hallowed.

These facts rest on the witness of the most trustworthy English writers; it is only by the Norman writers, the partisans of William the Conqueror, that they are denied. William the Norman maintained that Edward had promised the English crown to himself as his nearest kinsman; that Harold had sworn to support this arrangement, had done homage to William as his lord, and had promised to marry his daughter; therefore Harold was a usurper, a perjurer, and a traitor to his lord. Now it seems most likely that truth and falsehood were cunningly mingled in this charge of William's. It was most likely true that Edward had at one time spoken of William as his successor; it is certain that on his death-bed he named Harold; it is still more certain that he had neither right nor power to dispose of the crown; but the European princes and prelates, whose sympathies William wished to enlist, did not know that the choice of the English king rested with the English people. It was true that William was Edward's blood-kinsman, and Harold was not; but this kindred was wholly on the Norman side, through William's great aunt, Emma, having married King Ethelred, and did not give William the smallest right to belong to the English royal family. Therefore, in truth, William was the usurper, and not Harold. The English writers are almost all silent about the story of Harold's oath, but there are several circumstances which have led the best judges to believe that there was some truth in that story; that at some time in Harold's travels, when accident had thrown him into the power of William, he did promise to marry his daughter, even if he did not become his man, and swear to help him to the kingdom of England. So that here William had a good handle against Harold. For though the sin was often committed, yet no sin was worse thought of in those days than unfaithfulness in a sworn vassal to a lord. If there could be one thing more shocking, it was that Harold had sworn his oath (whatever it was) on the relics of the Norman saints; though some say that this was a trick of William's, who made Harold swear on a chest which he thought was empty, but which William had secretly filled with saintly bones.

It was an unsteady seat to which Harold had climbed. I have noted as I went along, in the reign of Edward the Confessor, that the North and South of England were beginning to feel themselves one nation;[1] but still the fact that the great divisions of the country, Northumbria, Mercia, East Anglia, Wessex, and even Kent, had once been several kingdoms, and still held to their separate customs, hindered the progress of national unity, which was still further hindered by ambitious men who wished that the old divisions should be kept up for their advantage. Though the nobles of Northumbria must have been present at the meeting which chose Harold to be king, and though the Northumbrian archbishop had placed the crown upon his head, the ancient Northern kingdom was not disposed to accept him at first, and it was needful for Harold to go to York in person immediately after his coronation. He took with him his best friend, Wulfstan, Bishop of Worcester, the most saintly Englishman of that day; and by the eloquence and skill of the king and the saint, the Northumbrians were led to submit peaceably to Harold's authority. Edwin and Morkar were still Earls of Mercia and Northumbria, and it would have been well for Harold if he could have removed them, but they were too powerful.

Harold's difficulties.

Harold hastened back from York, to hold his Easter feast in London. Already it had been told him that William the Bastard intended to come hither and win this land. That Easter saw a strange and mighty comet blazing in the sky; a sight which in those days, when the movements of the heavenly bodies were so little understood, was always thought to forebode some coming evil. As the first forerunner of sorrow, came Harold's ill-starred brother Tostig, with ships which he had gathered in Flanders or Normandy (for Tostig had married Judith of Flanders, aunt of William's wife, Matilda) and harried the south coast. But King Harold was busy gathering 'so great a ship-force, and also a land-force, as no king here in the land had before done.' When Tostig heard that Harold was coming against him at Sandwich, he went north to the Humber and harried there. But the earls Edwin and Morkar for once did good service, and drove him out. He went

Tostig harries the coast.

[1] See pp. 92, 94, 99.

to Scotland, and abode with the King of Scots all summer, plotting mischief.

The Norwegian *Saga*, or Story of Harold Hardrada tells us that Tostig went to Norway, and persuaded King Harold Hardrada to invade England. It is more likely that Harold Hardrada was the first to plan the invasion. This Harold is a prince of great renown in Northern history. He had been an adventurer all his life; his exploits in the Mediterranean, where he fought in the service of the Greek emperor, were favourite themes of Northern song. The wondrous treasures he had brought back from these wars, the magic powers of his banner the Landwaster, gave a flavour of romance to his fame. He was as quick-witted in times of difficulty as he was bold in arms, and had won many battles by clever shifts; but 'he was very greedy of power and property.' Just at this time he had made peace with Denmark, after fifteen years of warfare; his hands were therefore free for another enterprise, and he may well have wished to rival the great deeds of Olaf, Sweyn, and Cnut. Whenever it was that he made his alliance with Tostig, in September 1066, Harold Hardrada appeared in the Tyne with three hundred ships; and Tostig joined him with all his followers from Flanders and elsewhere, and became his man. The host was swelled by troops from Orkney and Scotland, and even an Irish king appeared among them.

Invasion of Harold of Norway.

Meanwhile Harold's fleet lay all summer off the Isle of Wight, and the land army watched on the coast, for the coming of William of Normandy; but he was not yet ready. At last, in the beginning of September, provisions were used up, and Harold could no longer keep his forces, but ships and men disbanded. As King Harold arrived in London, it was made known to him that Harold Hardrada and Tostig with all their forces had appeared in the Humber and landed in Yorkshire. 'Then went he northward day and night, as soon as he could gather his fyrd.' But ere he reached York, the earls Edwin and Morkar had been defeated with great slaughter in a battle at Fulford, and York had surrendered to the Norwegians. Peace had been made with the enemy, and the main body of the Norwegian troops had withdrawn to Stamford Bridge, about eight miles from York, to await the hostages which were promised them from the whole shire, intending then to go southwards and subdue the whole land.

At Stamford Bridge, on Monday morning (Sept. 25th) King Harold of England surprised them. Part of the Norwegian army was lying unprepared on the right bank of the Derwent; they were pushed into the river by the sudden onset, and the stream was choked with their corpses. A single Northman kept the bridge against the whole English host, and slew forty of them with his axe, till an Englishman stole under the bridge, and pierced him under his byrnie (mail shirt). The rest of the Northern army had now time to form round their king, whose proud banner, the Landwaster, had never known defeat in any battle. They fought nearly all day, till King Harold of Norway and Earl Tostig were slain, and after a great slaughter on both sides, the Northmen fled from the English. Their overthrow was complete; the remnant who had remained in the Ouse with the ships sued for peace, and Harold allowed them to sail in peace to Norway. Harold gave his much-tried men a brief rest at York; but while he was celebrating his victory, as he sat at the feast, a messenger from the south came hastily in, and announced that William of Normandy had landed on the coast of Sussex.

Battle of Stamford Bridge.

William had not wasted a moment of time since Edward's death. His first step had been to send an embassy to Harold, demanding the fulfilment of his oath. Harold of course refused; according to one writer, he made answer that to break such an oath was a less evil than to keep it, for that without the consent of the English Wise Men's Meeting, he had no power or right to swear away the crown. William at once prepared for war. He had to gain the consent of the barons of Normandy; they were not at first very eager to join in a difficult enterprise, which would make their duke more powerful and troublesome than before. He sent to the various courts of Europe, to plead the justice of his cause, and secure the good opinion of the Continent; but what was most important of all, he gained the Pope over to his side. Already the Popes were setting up claims to decide causes between nations and kings, and already at the papal court a man was to be seen (Hildebrand,

William's preparations.

afterwards Pope Gregory VII.) who did more than anyone to establish these new powers of the Popes. The bait which William offered to Rome was that the English Church should in future be more subject than heretofore to Roman authority. By the influence of Hildebrand, Pope Alexander II. issued a bull declaring Harold a usurper and William the lawful claimant to the English crown. A banner blessed by the Pope was sent to William, to secure success to his army.

Volunteers came from all quarters, especially from France and Flanders. A goodly host was gathered, a goodly fleet was built. They were delayed a month by contrary winds; but at last the south wind blew, and on the 28th of September, 1066, William landed at Pevensey, where stood *He lands in* and yet stands on the gorse-clad downs, the ruins *England.* of a Roman fortress, the last relic of a great city destroyed by our forefathers when they conquered Britain. There was no one to prevent the landing of the Normans; Harold's fleet had gone home, his fyrd was with him in the North. The treason of Tostig, the ambition of Harold Hardrada, had wrought England's undoing as well as their own. But Harold Godwinson's heart did not fail him. With the same speed with which he had marched to York, he marched back again to London, gathering on his way the forces of the earldoms of his brothers Gyrth and Leofwin. He left the North under the rule of the sheriff Merlsweyn, expecting Edwin and Morkar to follow his host. But the traitorous earls, seeing in William's invasion a fresh hope for their own independence, held back from Harold's muster. Harold waited about a week in London, gathering troops. Before fighting, he went to pray at the church of Waltham which he himself had founded, where there was a wonder-working crucifix whose fame had been the first cause of this church of the *Holy Rood*. The awe-struck fancy of a later day has preserved the legend, that when King Harold was leaving the church, as he turned and bowed himself low upon the ground towards the high altar, the Christ upon the Rood drooped his head in sorrowful foreboding, nor ever lifted it again.

It is said that Earl Gyrth, the brother of Harold, tried to persuade Harold to remain in London, and not incur the guilt of fighting against a lord to whom he had sworn homage; but to allow him, Gyrth, who was bound by no oaths, to go forth at the head of the English troops. 'Let not the glorious freedom of England be staked on Harold's life. Let the king wait the assembling of a larger force, and in the meanwhile let him lay waste the whole country between himself and the enemy, that they might find nothing to live upon.' Harold answered that he should be held a coward if he sent his good friends to fight when he dared not go himself; nor would he ever lay waste the houses and villages of his people. 'How can I destroy and harry the folk whom I am bound to care for?' he said. If Harold really uttered these noble words (it is a Norman poet who tells us of them) they show how Norman calumny has deposed him from his rightful place in English history.

Our trustworthy English chroniclers accuse Harold of having fought with William before he had gathered a sufficient army. We know that the Earls Edwin and Morkar did not join Harold. It was in fact the weak point of the Old-English system that there was no defensive force which could be thoroughly relied upon. The fyrd was the great national defence, but through the spread of peaceful habits the fyrd had become a gathering of half-armed peasantry, a clumsy weapon in the hour of danger; besides, the fyrd was always a local force, and the kingdom was not united enough to make it truly national. Hence the kings were driven to rely on their own immediate followers and the followers of the great nobles, house-carls as they were called, it being the custom of both kings and nobles to keep about them bands of retainers, trained and armed at their own expense. It was therefore a serious thing when great nobles like Edwin and Morkar held back from the muster. What was wanting in the Old-English system was that the holders of property should be compelled to perform their services to the State, especially the service of defence; and we shall see later on that the Norman conquest made a change in this respect. It appears from the ground which Harold chose that he intended to take up a defensive position, for which a small force might be deemed enough. Yet if I rightly understand the story of the battle, it was by numbers that the English were at last overpowered, though we have no certain estimate of the numbers on either side; each party exaggerates the numbers of the other. There can be no doubt that the

Normans were better disciplined and better armed. Harold, however, could no longer wait in London, but marched against William, with a force which he doubtless deemed sufficient for the ground he had in view.

William had advanced from Pevensey to Hastings, and had pitched his camp on a hill above the town. On the evening of October 13, Harold arrived within seven miles of Hastings, and took up a strong position on the hill of Senlac, which was steepest towards the south, the Hastings side, and defended on either flank by a stream and swampy ground. Harold further secured it with a threefold hedge of stakes and wattles, and a ditch. It is said the night was spent by the English in drinking and singing, by the Normans in confession and prayer.

The next day (Oct. 14) the Norman army marched up from Hastings and attacked the hill of Senlac. The Norman knights were on horseback, after the fashion of the Continent; the English were all on foot, as of old, formed into a thick impenetrable shield-wall. Vainly did the Norman infantry and cavalry dash against their unswerving ranks, which thrust them back as the rock thrusts back the sea-foam. The Frenchmen began to lose heart; the left wing, which consisted of Bretons, fled; the infection spread, and for a moment the whole Norman line gave way. A report flew round that the duke was slain; William uncovered his face, which was protected by a nose-piece fastened to his helmet, and drove back the fleeing with words and blows. The Normans now began a second onset with redoubled eagerness; the barricade was broken through in several places; Duke William slew Earl Gyrth, the brother of Harold, with his own hand, and Earl Leofwin also perished. But still the shield-wall was unbroken. Then the Norman leader bethought himself of a cunning shift to draw the English from their position; the left wing had orders to pretend to flee. The English right wing rushed down upon them with shouts, and left the most accessible side of the hill open to the Normans. The Norman horsemen now rode to the top of the hill, and the hardest tug of battle began. The English shield-wall held so close and firm that the dead alone fell from the ranks. Both leaders shone in prowess, Harold hewing down horse and man with his great Danish axe, then the main weapon of the English soldier. It was now evening, and the battle had been raging since nine o'clock. Then Duke William ordered his archers to shoot up into the air, that the arrows might fall downwards on the English. One of these arrows pierced King Harold in the eye; he fell to the ground in death agony. But still his thanes and house-carls fought unflinchingly round his standard, the Fighting Man, and the banner of England, the Dragon of Wessex, which waved for the last time over the hopes of England. Not till these heroes, the flower of the English nobility, were slaughtered to a man, were the standard and the Dragon overthrown. Then the rest of the army took to flight, and 'the Frenchmen held the battle-field.'

They did not long pursue the vanquished foe in the darkness, for even in the flight the English turned and inflicted loss on their pursuers. William returned to the hill of Senlac, gave thanks to God, and ate and drank among the dying and the dead. Where the down-trodden standard of England lay he ordered his own banner to be reared; and there, a few years later, rose the high altar of a stately abbey, built by the conqueror's care, that cloistered monks might ever offer prayers for the souls of the slain—the Abbey of Battle. William ordered the body of Harold to be buried in a cairn on the sea-shore: 'Let him be the warden of the coast, where before he sat in arms,' said the conqueror, grimly jesting. But it would seem that Harold's body was afterwards taken to his own church at Waltham.

To no man did fate ever give a greater part to play than to this half-Danish Englishman, Harold, the son of Godwin. To be the second man in a great revolution which rid his country of the stranger; to quell the Briton and make England again supreme from shore to shore; to shatter the invading force of Norway under one of her greatest heroes; and, lastly, overborne by the double stroke, to die for his country in a last glorious though mournful struggle—to have done this is sufficient fame for Harold. We do not know what England would have been if he had lived, and been victorious over the Norman. Edwin and Morkar, those unstable men, the want of cohesion in government, the as yet imperfect union of South and North, make the problem a hard one.

But beside Harold's cairn on the sea-shore, we seem to be

standing at the grave of the old England. 'This was the fatal day of England, the mournful death of our sweet country, when she changed her ancient lords for strangers.' 'When the Normans had fulfilled the righteous will of God upon the English nation, there was hardly a noble of English race left in England, but all were brought to thraldom and sorrow, so that it was a disgrace to be called an Englishman.' 'The Lord hath taken away health and honour from the English people for their sins, and hath bidden that they be no more a people.' So wrote the men of the next generation, sad as the Jews by the waters of Babylon. But a day of resurrection is at hand. England will be again a people, and the Normans will become Englishmen. The laws, the language, the liberties of England will rise again, stronger than before. She will become the mother of mighty nations, who will inherit from her the freedom which King Alfred strove for, the freedom which stands in willing obedience to law. And she will bequeath to these nations the deathless song of Shakspere and of Milton, and of the great company who have followed them. The making of the English nation was completed by the suffering of all men of English race together, under the hand of the Norman.

DATES.

Edward the Confessor	A.D. 1042
Earl Godwin outlawed	1051
Godwin's return	1052
Harold earl of the West Saxons	1053
Harold subdues the Welsh	1063
Tostig outlawed	1065
Death of Edward, crowning of Harold, battle of Stamford Bridge, and battle of Hastings	1066

CHAPTER IX.

WILLIAM THE BASTARD, the victor of Hastings, is a man who has left such a mark on the history of England, that it is worth our while to look at him a little more closely. In person he was immensely tall and strong; very stout, too, in his later years; stern and wrathful in his behaviour, though given to grim jokes at times. The English

Character of William I.

chroniclers find two things to praise him for—the support which he gave to the Church, and the good order which he kept. In truth, William was a soldier of order, he hated misrule and savageness; he supported the Church, because she was the greatest help to the cause of order. But there have been great men, such as our own King Alfred, who have fought for the cause of order because they felt it to be a higher cause than their own, and these are the men who have left the noblest names behind them in history. William was not one of these; he had not learned to yield up his own will to a higher law; and therefore, though he was nobler by nature than most men of his time, his stern self-will led him into acts of injustice and cruelty, such as were blamed even by the men of that day. Yet all these acts were done, like his invasion of England, under some legal excuse, for William hated violence, and if he could not always be just, he wished at least to appear just. He had had the very education to make him self-reliant and hard-hearted. He had been left as a boy to fight his own way in life, and make good his position as Duke of Normandy against proud and powerful barons who despised him for his shameful birth, and who were determined that they would not brook his rule. It was a hard life that William had as a young man, and it was a life to make a man hard. Yet it is certain that there were wells of tenderness in William's heart which were never quite dried up; he loved his wife devotedly, and he was an affectionate father till galled by the ingratitude of his children. It is worthy of note that in an age of vice his married life was free from blame. There have been many better men in the world, and there have been many worse, but there have been few that have done more lasting deeds.

The first step taken by the English nobility after the battle of Hastings was to choose a new king. They chose the Etheling Edgar, grandson of Edmund Ironsides, the only remaining prince of the royal line of Wessex. He was very young, and quite unfit to be leader at such a difficult time. And before he was crowned the Earls Edwin and Morkar forsook him and went off to the North. As William of Malmesbury says, all the strength of the land had fallen with Harold; there was now no leader in whom Englishmen could trust. William gradually skirted London with his forces, laying waste the country;

Edgar the Etheling.

Submits to William.

and before long Edgar the Etheling, with the bishops who had made him king, gave up the game as lost, and made submission to William. The City of London was not long in following their example.

William, as soon as he was master of London, though the conquest of England was only begun, took care to secure his position by being solemnly crowned king in West- *William minster Abbey. For the coronation rite was of the crowned.* utmost importance in those days, when all forms were taken as serious matters, supposed to make real changes when they were used. A king solemnly crowned and anointed by the Church was very much stronger than any uncrowned claimant. All the forms which had been used in the choosing and crowning of the Old-English kings were gone through in William's case; the consent of the people was asked, and William swore to defend the Church, to rule his people justly, to uphold right laws, and keep down violence and wrong judgments; or as the Anglo-Saxon chronicle says, he swore that he would rule this folk as well as any king before him had done at the best, if they would be faithful to him.

The first great result of the coronation was that the Earls Edwin and Morkar came and made submission to William. Since they were the Earls of Mercia and Yorkshire,[1] *Submission* their submission was the nominal submission of the *of Earls Edwin and* middle and north of England. Edwin received *Morkar.* the promise of William's daughter in marriage.

But four years of fighting lay before William ere he could call England his own. Had England been united, the conquest might have taken much longer. But not only was there no one leader like Harold able to make all Englishmen trust and follow him, there was not as yet a united English nation. So there was resistance, first in one part of England, then in another, but no united resistance of all England against the Normans. When William made his first triumphal return to Normandy in 1067 he was only master of the south- *Conquest of* eastern counties, including London. Then the suc- *the West and* cessful siege of Exeter, in 1068, made him master *North.* of the West. In the summer of the same year there was

---

[1] Morkar had given the northern part of his earldom, from Tyne to Tweed, to Oswulf. This is the modern county of Northumberland, to which the name Northumberland begins about this time to be restricted. Northumberland is first distinguished from Yorkshire in the 'Worcester Chronicle,' 1065.

a rising in the North, which was the occasion of the conquest of the earldoms of Mercia and Yorkshire. The stiff-necked North, says William of Malmesbury, scorned to be subject to the soft South. The Earls Edwin and Morkar, inconstant to William as they had been to Harold, fell away from their faith. Though the brothers were not men to be trusted, they were highly popular for their beauty and winsomeness, and when they set up the standard of revolt, the nobility and people of Mercia, Northumbria, and even Wales, rallied round them at once. William marched to the North, subduing the counties which lay on his way, and receiving the submission of the inconstant brothers. York yielded up its keys as William drew near, and he at once secured his conquest by building a castle to command the city.

But William did not advance further into the country; he returned to the south, subduing Lincolnshire and Cambridgeshire on his way. When, the next year (January, 1069), he appointed a foreigner, Robert de Comines, as Earl of Northumberland beyond the Tyne, the Northumbrians attacked the new earl in the bishop's house at Durham, to which they set fire. He perished in the flames, and his followers were put to the sword. This was followed by a general rising of the North, and the new castle at York was besieged. But William marched speedily to the rescue, beat the rebels, and built a second castle to hold the Yorkshiremen in check. He then went to hold his Easter feast at Winchester.

First revolt of the North. 1069.

His back was hardly turned before a new revolt in York showed what an unsteady seat the Normans held as yet in the North. This revolt was soon repressed by the trusty earl, William Fitz-Osbern, whom the king had left in command of York. But in the autumn of the same year (1069), a Danish fleet appeared in the Humber. Though the designs of Norway upon England had been quashed by the victory of Harold at Stamford Bridge, Denmark was not yet going to give up her right to meddle in English affairs. Svend, King of Denmark, was the nephew of King Cnut, the Danish King of England; he had some cause to think himself the heir of Cnut; but he appears now to have sent his fleet at the invitation of the English, as a friend of Edgar the Etheling. This Edgar was a weak

Second revolt and Danish invasion.

youth; he had already been mixed up with most of the revolts against William, but William feared him so little that he treated him with indulgence to the end of his life. Edgar, with the earls and thans of the north country and all the landsfolk, joined the Danes when they landed, ' and so they fared with one mind towards York, riding and walking very joyfully, with an untold force.' The Norman garrison sallied forth to meet them, and a battle took place, in which Earl Waltheof, who came of the noblest blood of old Bernicia, and was likewise the son of Siward, the doughty earl of Northumbria, is said to have stood by the gate and hewn down the Normans one by one. The Normans were cut to pieces, only a few being saved as prisoners; the castles were overthrown.

This was the time of greatest danger to William's rule in England. The news of the Danish invasion had caused revolts to spring forth in many parts of England, and William was busy with disturbances at Stafford when the tidings of the loss of York was brought to him. Great was his sorrow and anger, for his commander at York, William Malet, had too confidently promised him that he should be able to hold out for a year. But evil tidings always found William ready, bold, and wary. At every point where rebellion had broken out, the rebels were made to feel the power of his arm. He got rid of the Danes by a bribe to the commander of the fleet. As for the Northumbrians, they had neither leader nor plan; and after their fruitless victory at York, they had returned every man to his own home; and when William entered the ruins of York, he found none to resist him. *William re-enters York.*

But a change had come over William's mood. His invasion of England had been a great wrong, but he had tried to make himself believe that it was a righteous deed, and had tried to act not as a lawless conqueror, but as a just and lawful king. But when a man has once embarked on a great wrong, he cannot prevent its leading him into other wrongs. Now he was sore and wroth because of the repeated risings of the English; to him it seemed mere stiffneckedness and lawlessness that they so hated his rule. When the Conqueror was wroth, he shrank from no deed that was needful to make his will prevail. In *He lays waste Northumbria. 1069.*

I

order then that once and for all North England should know whom she had to obey, and that further struggle should be impossible, he harried the whole region beyond the Humber for the space of a hundred miles, burning all the dwellings, the crops, the storehouses, even the cattle, and slaying all who offered resistance. The blow was so fearful that for nine years the land was untilled; and sixteen years later, the value of land in Yorkshire was only a fourth of what it had been in the time of King Edward. The wretched people lived on the flesh of horses, dogs, and cats, or died by thousands in the roads, and as there was none to bury them, famine was followed by frightful pestilence. Many sold themselves for slaves that they might not starve. Even fifty years later, a writer says that 'the land for more than sixty miles lies bare unto this day, and the traveller groans as he looks upon the wide fields, the flowing rivers, and the ruined cities formerly so beautiful.' Between York and Durham every village was uninhabited, except by wild beasts. And 'Waste,' 'Waste,' 'Waste,' is the entry to place after place in the Conqueror's Survey of Yorkshire seventeen years afterwards. Such a deed as that, even the men of that day thought unpardonable. The historian Ordericus, an Englishman by birth, but brought up in Normandy, and a thorough admirer of the Conqueror, tells the tale with mingled indignation and pity, and adds that 'such barbarous homicide could not pass unpunished, for the Almighty Judge beholds both high and low, scrutinising and punishing the acts of both with equal justice.'

While the ruins were smoking around him, and the cries of the desolate were going up to heaven, William held his Christmas feast and wore his crown at York. But still the conquest was not complete. A band of outlaws held out in a stronghold at the mouth of the Tees. Thither William marched, as soon as his Christmas feast was over (January 1070), and received the submission of the Earls Waltheof and Gospatrick, the two most important men of Northumbria. The land between the Tyne and the Tees was then ruthlessly harried as Yorkshire had been. William's return march to York, through the hills of Cleveland, amidst snow and ice, was rugged and dangerous, and once the king lost his way, and with a few knights was separated all night from his army. But he reached York in

[marginal note: Completion of the Conquest of England.]

safety, restored the castles, and set in order the affairs of the shire. From York another toilsome march through the boggy hills of South Lancashire,[1] in February weather, brought the Conqueror to Chester, the only great city that did not yet acknowledge his sway. Chester fell, and the neighbouring shires were harried with fearful desolation. 'Hence there arose afterwards,' says Orderic, 'such poverty in England, and famine brought the feeble and helpless folk to such misery, that more than a hundred thousand Christian people of either sex, and of all ages, died.' The numbers must not be taken as exact, since tables of mortality were unknown then; they loosely represent the immense sufferings of that time.

Thus the conquest of England was finished. The rest of the acts of William, how he put down the revolts against him, especially that of Hereward in the isle of Ely, and of Ralph Guader in Norfolk, how he shed tears over the murder of Earl Edwin, how he cut off Earl Waltheof's head, and how his later years were saddened by the death of one of his sons, and the bad conduct of another,—these things (and they are deeply interesting) may be read in greater histories than this. What concerns us now is to examine the Norman settlement in England and its effect on the English people.

William, when he came to England, intended to rule as the lawful heir of the English kings who had gone before him. He had no design to overthrow the English laws and customs, and make them after the pattern of things in France. He had one fixed design; that he should be master in England. All the changes which he made were made in order to carry out this plan. At his coronation he had sworn to uphold right law, and the old laws of England, as they had been in the days of Edward the Confessor, were kept up in his reign, with only a few changes. The City of London was confirmed by charter in all its former privileges. The English language was still used in laws and charters,[2] and William even tried to learn English, that he

William no overthrower of English law and custom.

---

[1] Lancashire was not then a separate shire. The land between the Mersey and the Ribble formed part of Cheshire; the land north of the Ribble was reckoned in Yorkshire.

[2] Latin was also used, and in time became more and more used, but there is an English charter to be found as late as 1155. French took

might be a better judge over his new subjects. The Wise Men's Meeting still gathered round the king at solemn seasons, nor did he venture to publish laws without its consent. The courts of the Shire and the Hundred were still held; and the responsibility of the Tithings, even if not originated by the Conqueror, was at any rate enforced with greater strictness.

In what respect, then, did the Norman Conquest bring about a change in the condition of England and the English?

In the first place William had to reward his followers by gifts of English lands. Not that every foreign soldier who fought at Hastings was rewarded with an estate, for before the conquest of England was finished William sent back the hired troops he had brought with him. It does not seem likely that the number of foreigners who remained and settled in England was more than 10,000 males; and of these of course only the nobles received estates. At first the lands of Godwin's family and of others who had fought at Hastings, were sufficient to divide among the conquerors. And now we see William acting upon the idea, which, as I have said, was unknown to the Old-English, but began to creep in in the days of Cnut, that all the land of the country is the king's, and other men only hold it by his leave. All the English, after William's coronation, had to buy back their lands from the king. And it often happened that they were outbid by some Norman, who thus stepped into their possessions. But as all this was done under the form of law, the Norman chronicler is doubtless writing in good faith when he tells us that nothing was given to any Frenchman which was unjustly taken from any Englishman.

Results of the Conquest. The land.

It was only later, when William had found how stiff a piece of work the conquest of England was, and when repeated revolts had given him reasons for fresh confiscations, that the English began to lose their lands on a large scale. Then, by degrees, all the greatest estates in England were given over to Norman owners. But still, in all parts of England, Englishmen were to be found in possession of land, though very often they had only small pieces of the estates they possessed before; or what was still more galling, the land which they had held

the place of Latin in laws and charters from about the middle of the thirteenth century.

before as freemen, they now held by servile tenure of some powerful foreigner. Very often we find King William by his writ *commending* some Englishman to a Norman, making the Englishman the *man* of the Norman, to hold his lands of him and owe him service. We also find him assuming the feudal suzerain's right to marry an heiress or a widow to whom he pleased, so that in this way many estates passed by marriage into the hands of Normans.

This personal change, however, in the position of English landholders, was a slight and temporary thing compared to the great change which the Norman Conquest caused in the relation of all landholders to the State. It is this change which people allude to when they say that William introduced the feudal system into England. Now we have seen (Chapter VIII.) that a loose kind of feudalism already existed in England before the Conquest; what the Conquest did was to introduce a rigid feudalism, while at the same time the type of feudalism was entirely changed by the establishment of a strong central authority. The introduction of a more rigid feudalism was not brought about by any law or ordinance; it was done simply because the men who administered the law were Normans. In Normandy a very rigid feudalism prevailed. The Normans had settled in Normandy as a military colony, and their Duke was their hereditary captain. All Norman landholders held their land under strict condition of military service; the defence of the land was the rigid duty of all who enjoyed the land. The Duke, as captain of this army, settled on the land, had the right of insisting that the land should be held only by those who were capable of defending it. This was the origin of the right possessed by the Norman dukes and exercised by the Norman kings, of ruling the marriages of heiresses, and of guardianship over minors; the right of taking away land in punishment for certain offences; and various other rights, which were before unknown or almost unknown in England.[1] When the Norman duke became king of England, he found the relation of lord and vassal existing on English soil, and what was more natural than that he should suppose that it meant exactly the same thing as it meant in Normandy, and that in England

A new kind of Feudalism introduced.

[1] See Gneist, *Geschichte des Self-government in England*, p. 29.

as in Normandy, the vassal only held his lands on condition of military service.[1]

England made a defensive State. Thus, in course of time, by the mere working of the Norman way of looking at things, all free tenures of land in England (with few exceptions) became strictly feudal, that is, military duty became now the fixed obligation of landed property. The theory henceforth to rule was that all the land in the country belonged to the king, and that all landholders held it of him either mediately or immediately on condition of service, generally of military service. The change was a very valuable one; it made England a defensive state. The military system, which had been the weak point of the old English government, became the strong point of the Norman. It is an important mark of the change that, though fiefs were still heritable, the landholder was no longer able to bequeath his land.

The holders of real property were now strictly responsible for the defence of the country, and could not escape their duty. The service was equally divided according to the amount of property; every five hides must send a fully armed man for forty days' service. This had been a recognised obligation even in Old-English times, but the obligation lay on the landlord rather than on the land; it was not a condition of property, but the personal duty of men occupying a certain extent of country. Besides, the feudalism which existed then was too loose to bind the great landholders to their duties. We have read how in the hour of England's danger, Edwin and Morkar did not join Harold with the fyrd of the shires. In truth, the old Teutonic military system, which required every freeman to fight simply because he was a freeman, having fallen into decay, the new, strictly feudal system became a necessary stage in the development of all European nations, the system, namely, that those who held the land should provide for the defence of the State. No State could exist which was not a fighting State, in that time of universal war; no standing armies could be kept up in times when it was so difficult to get money, owing to the imperfect development of industry. The feudal system, the system of strictly military tenures, secured the safety

---

[1] Compare what Sir H. S. Maine says, in *Village Communities*, of the change which the English have wrought in the working of Indian law, simply by reading it with English instead of Indian eyes.

of the State from external enemies, so long as there was a captain at the helm strong enough to manage his own crew.

And this was the second great feature of William's work, that he secured the position of the captain at the helm. For there was one thing which William was determined that he would not have—he would not allow his vassals the same independence which the great vassals had in France. It is due to his strong will that the worst features of feudalism never prevailed in England. Himself a vassal of the King of France, he often defied his liege lord; but he was determined that none of his vassals should defy him. He had had enough of that in Normandy, where only a hard struggle with his barons had made him supreme; he wished to prevent any such struggle in England. He abolished the four great earldoms, that no earl might rival the king; henceforth, earls were appointed only to single shires, or, if he gave them two, he separated them; and those of his followers whom he trusted most, and to whom he gave largest estates, had these estates scattered in different parts of the country. This putting an end to the great earldoms was a most important stroke; for those great earldoms represented the ancient kingdoms of Wessex, Mercia, East Anglia, and Northumbria, the four pieces into which England was always inclined to fall. Further, lest even the earls of the shires should become too powerful, he took care that the government of the shires should be mainly in the hands of the sheriffs, who were officers appointed by and dependent on himself. And in order that his nobles might never be able to use their own vassals against himself, he established his power over the under-vassals as well, by renewing the custom (as old as the days of Edmund I.) that all landholders, whose men soever they were, should swear him faithful oaths that they would be faithful to him against all other men. By these faithful oaths the throne of William became the strongest in Europe.

The King's supremacy secured.

As he built up the English throne, so did he uphold the English Empire. The King of Scots bowed to him, and became his man in 1072. And it was probably on his victorious return from this expedition that William first acquired a solid footing in Northumberland, Gospatrick, the English earl, being banished. The

The English empire upheld.

Welsh also had to renew their submission (1081). William gave great powers to the border earldoms of Chester, Shrewsbury, and Hereford to extend their dominions at the expense of the Welsh. It was only in cases like these, where the defence of the empire required it, that William allowed powerful earldoms to exist. Kent was one, as the bulwark of England against France and Flanders. But William gave this earldom to his brother Odo, Bishop of Bayeux, who being a churchman, could not found a rival family. In the same manner he gave the management of the earldom of Northumberland to the Bishop of Durham. And no doubt the great harrying of the Northern counties in 1069 had partly as its object to place a desert on the borders of the English and Scottish kingdoms. The authority of William in the extreme North of England was never very firmly settled: and in this part of the country we find more men of native birth in high position than in any other part. The four northernmost counties do not appear in the great survey which William caused to be made of all England. Only a part of what we now call Westmoreland and Cumberland was held by William; the rest belonged to the King of Scots. It was not till the reign of his son, William Rufus, that England grew to her present size on the map.

The Scots and the Welsh were not the only foes to be kept off from the English Empire. England's old kinsmen, the Danes, had still a hankering after her, and she was well disposed to welcome them as friends, and deliverers from the Norman. William used gold more than once to stave off their attacks; but when in 1085 he was threatened by a joint invasion from the Kings of Denmark and Norway (the great-nephew of Cnut and the son of Harold Hardrada), he not only brought a host of hired troops over to England, but ruthlessly laid waste all the land along the sea-coast, that the enemy might find no support in case they landed. On the west, the Norwegians (who held the Isle of Man in those days) gave much trouble to the Norman Earl of Chester; but he was a match for them and for the Welsh too, from whom he wrested much of North Wales and the Isle of Anglesea. But after the reign of William, the Northmen ceased to trouble England any more; the great wandering of the Northern nations was drawing to a close.

Danish invasions kept off.

This was the great work of William, that he made England a solid state, with a central authority; he tightened all the bonds of the state, and drew them up into the hands of the king. By this he has influenced our history ever since, and for this we are bound to reckon the Norman conquest as a great boon, in spite of all the suffering which it caused. Nay, that very suffering, as it was common to all the land, helped to weld all English kin together into one nation. There was now in England what there was nowhere else in Europe, a state, not a bundle of states loosely tied together. And there was order in this state; robbery and violence were put down with a strong hand, and the barons were not allowed to turn the realm upside down by wars with one another.

Not only did the State become organised and strong under William's sway, a like change went over the Church. But this must be left for another chapter.

Feudalism could not be strengthened without altering the character of the old English institutions. The great council of the nation, which had been the Wise Men's Meeting in the Old-English times, now became the assembly of the tenants-in-chief, as those were called who held their lands directly of the king; that is, it became an assembly of Norman barons and prelates. The 'counsel and consent' of the Great Council thus assembled was always asked by the conqueror and his successors; but the asking does not seem to have been much more than a matter of form. *The Great Council.*

If, however, the great vassals were held in strict subordination to their suzerain, on the other hand their feudal rights over their own vassals were strengthened. A feudal system is a system which puts great power in the hands of the nobles; and though in England the nobles had not such power as in France, because of the superior power of the Crown, they had enough to make their position odious to the common people, especially when the difference of race between Norman and Englishman added bitterness to the relation of lord and vassal. Also we cannot doubt that the extension of feudalism under the Conqueror hastened the process which had been going on in Anglo-Saxon times, whereby the common freemen were losing their independent rights in the land, such rights being now held under and by favour of some Norman 'Lord of the Manor.' Never- *Increased power of nobles.*

theless, so strong was the old system of community, so deep its roots, that for many centuries after the Conquest the greater part of the land of England, both ploughlands, pastures, and meadows, was still subject to certain common rights, especially the right of common pasture in stubbles; and separate private property existed only in houses, farmyards, crofts, gardens, and parks.[1]

William secured his conquests wherever he went by building castles. Every large city, every rebellious district, had a castle to hold it in check. Close to the walls of London rose the Tower, so famous afterwards. But unfortunately these castles worked in two ways. They were not only the guardians of William's conquest; they were also strongholds from which the baron could oppress the country round, and defy the power of his sovereign, if the sovereign happened to be weak. Hence by building these castles William prepared the way for that great struggle between the Crown and the barons which our later history will have to relate. William foresaw this struggle, and did all he could to prevent it; but as the Norman nobles were the instruments of his conquest, it was not in his power to cripple them utterly; what he could do and did was to place the power of the Crown on such a firm footing that it should come through the fight victoriously.

Castles.

It was for the welfare of the people at large that there should be a sovereign strong enough to curb the nobles. But nevertheless, the pressure of this authority was felt keenly by the English, and it seems plain from the chronicles that William was more hated as a despot than as a foreigner. Though the good order which he kept, the safety that there was for life and goods under his reign is praised, the extortions of his stewards and underlings are bitterly complained of; and we know that in his absence the affairs of the kingdom were left in the hands of regents much more hard and greedy than himself. But the kind of government which William set on foot was so much more thoroughgoing than what the English were accustomed to, that they resented many measures which were really useful. They resented, for instance, the great Domesday Survey, which William caused to be made, a careful report of the whole land in the country, of unspeakable value to us

William's government unpopular.

The Domesday Survey.

---

[1] Nasse, *Agricultural Community*, p. 50.

now as a source of history, but of the greatest value then in settling taxation, and all other claims upon the land, whether of the State or of private persons. 'There was not a single rood of land, nor was there an ox, nor a cow, nor a pig passed by,' says the chronicler scornfully; 'it is shameful to tell that which he thought it no shame to do.'

A juster cause of wrath on the part of the English arose from William's love of hunting, which led him to lay waste a flourishing district in Hampshire, thirty miles long, full of villages and churches, to make the New Forest. The sorrows of William's later years, the deaths of three members of his family in that forest, were regarded as the judgment of God for this crime. He also was the first English king who made game-laws,[1] and restricted to himself and those whom he favoured the sport which had till then been the right of every man.

<small>The New Forest.</small>

The building of the castles was another grievance which rankled in the breasts of Englishmen. The towns especially suffered from this, since numbers of houses were destroyed to make room for the castles. Consequently the towns in general were great losers by the Conquest; the only towns which flourished under William were the sea-ports leading to the Continent, whose trade was increased.

Injuries like these, which struck home, were resented more bitterly by the English of that day than the fact that a foreign conqueror was ruling over them, and that a stricter account was taken of the murder of a Norman than of the murder of an Englishman. The reason of this was that the sense of nationality was not yet fully grown up anywhere, because the nations were not full grown. It was stronger in England than anywhere else. It was strong enough to make Englishmen feel a pride when William won victories in France with the help of English troops. And Orderic, the Englishman, is proud to tell of those English who, having lost their lands, or being unable to endure the Norman sway, took service with the Eastern Emperor at Constantinople, and were the bravest defenders of his throne. But the monks who wrote the chronicles could find nothing to say about the Conquest, except that 'God would have it so, for the people's sins.' And

---

[1] If, with Mr. Freeman and K. Maurer, we regard the forest laws attributed to Cnut as spurious. See Stubbs, *Const. Hist.* p. 200, note.

no old songs have come down to tell us how the people felt, except part of a ballad which has been put into the Anglo-Saxon chronicle. I will finish this chapter by giving you the picture drawn of William by this chronicler, which is evidently taken partly from some old song made at the time :—

'If anyone would know what kind of a man he was, or what dignity he had, or of how many lands he was lord, then will we awrite [describe] him as we knew him, we who looked upon him, and dwelt once in his court. The King William of whom we are speaking was a very wise man, and very mighty, and more honoured and powerful than any of those who went before him. He was mild to the good men who loved God, and beyond measure stark to those men who withstood his will. On the spot where God granted him that he should win England, he reared a great minster, and set monks there, and gave them much goods. In his days the great minster at Canterbury was built, and also very many others all over England. Also this land was filled with monks, who lived after St. Benedict's rule, and there was such Christendom in his day, that every man, to whatsoever [religious] order he belonged, might live accordingly. Also he was very worshipful; thrice he wore his kingly crown each year, as oft as he was in England, at Easter he wore it at Winchester, at Pentecost at Westminster, at Christmas at Gloucester. And there were with him all the powerful men from all England, archbishops and bishops, abbots and earls, thanes and knights. Such a stark and wrathful man he was, that no man durst do anything against his will. He kept in bonds those earls who did against his will. He put down bishops from their bishoprics, and abbots from their abbacies, and put thanes in prison, and at last he spared not his own brother Odo; he was a very mighty bishop in Normandy, his bishop-stool was at Bayeux, and he was the foremost man next to the king. And he had an earldom in England, and when the king was in Normandy, then was he the greatest in this land; and him the king put in prison. Amongst other things the good peace that he made in this land is not to be forgotten, so that any man who himself were worth aught might fare over the kingdom with his bosom full of gold unmolested; and no man durst slay another man, if he had done ever so much evil against him. He reigned over England, and so thoroughly surveyed it in his craftiness, that there was not a hide in England that he did not know who had it, and how much it was worth, and then it was set down in his writ. Wales was under his sway, and he wrought castles therein; and the Isle of Anglesea was altogether in his power; Scotland also he got under him by his mickle strength; and if he had lived two years longer, he would have won Ireland by his wariness, without any weapons.

'Truly, in his time men had much trouble, and manifold sorrow; he caused castles to be wrought, and did greatly swink poor men.[1] The king was so very stark, and he took from his subjects many marks of gold, and many hundred pounds of silver, which he took either by right and also by mickle unright from his people, and for little need. He was fallen into covetousness, and greediness he loved withal. He made a great deer-frith,[2] and laid down laws therewith, that whoso slew hart or hind, he should be blinded; he forbad [to kill] the harts, and likewise the bears; so much he loved the high deer as if he were their father; and also he set [made laws] concerning the hares, that they should go free. The rich men bewailed and the poor murmured, but he was so stiff that he recked nothing of them all, but they must altogether follow the king's will, if they would live or keep their lands or goods or his peace. Alas! that any man should so swell in mind, and uplift himself, and reckon himself above all men! May Almighty God show mercy to his soul, and grant him the forgiveness of his sins. These things we have written about him, both good and evil, that men may follow after the good, and wholly leave the evil, and go on the way that leadeth to heaven's kingdom.'

DATES.

The West of England conquered	1068
York submits	1068
Rebellion and devastation of the North	1069
Malcolm King of Scots does homage to William	1072
Rebellion of Roger Earl of Hereford and Ralph Earl of Norfolk; for his share in which Waltheof, the last English earl, was beheaded	1075
The Survey made for Domesday Book	1085

[1] From this point the description is actually in rime.

[2] This means literally a great peace, or protection for the deer; it **may** either refer to the New Forest, or to the laws protecting game.

CHAPTER X.

If we would understand the history of the middle ages, we must grasp the position and work of the Church during that time of the childhood of nations. We must remember that these nations, with a few exceptions among their rulers, some of whom understood their business, were composed of self-willed barbarians, who had no thought in life but to gratify the passion of the hour. In the midst of these nations stood the Church, a well-compacted army, the only body of men who had learning and culture, the only power whose aim was a righteous aim, the only power which cared for the poor and the oppressed. All who were good, all who were thoughtful, all who had high ideas, and longed for the kingdom of God on earth, saw no other course open to them than to shave their heads and join the great army of the Church; for in the Church alone was there any hope for the renewing of the world. What an immense power was thus ranged on the side of the Church! It was her office to teach the barbaric feudal world that there was an unseen Power watching all its actions, and to frighten men out of their selfishness by dread of the Judge who would render to every man according to his works. This was the coarsest but the commonest side of the Church's task. She had yet another and higher work—to spread from man to man the longing after goodness, which is the noblest power of the human soul, to teach self-sacrifice for noble ends, to proclaim the brotherhood of all men in God's sight. Since the aims of the Church were so noble, since good men for the most part were wholly on her side, since the world itself acknowledged her superior goodness and loaded her with gifts, what was more natural than that the Church should begin to claim authority to rule the world for God?

The Mediæval Church.

We must not forget that in those days the sovereignty of the Pope seemed to good men to be a short cut to the kingdom of God. Churchmen reasoned in this way: 'The world is very bad; we have to make it good; if men won't do what we tell them, they must be *made* to

The Papacy.

do it. The Pope represents Christ upon earth, and all earthly kings ought to obey him.'

From this point of view, we can understand why all the best men of those days fought hard for the supremacy of Rome and for Church discipline. Depend upon it they were fighting on the right side, whatever blunders they made, and however often they mistook the shell for the kernel. And whether or not the Popes succeeded in establishing the kingdom of God on earth, they certainly did good service to mankind. The Papacy, at a time when society was in a state of wreck, was the only strong central power, binding Europe together. Through it the name of Rome became the watchword of civilisation, and awed the barbarian world. Through it the idea of a great European commonwealth was kept before men's minds. When Europe was in her childhood, she needed a strong nurse to feed and guide her, and teach her the way to go. And in the eleventh century, the Popes did truly represent the tribunal of divine justice, before which wicked kings, whom none other dared to rebuke, had to answer for their sins; and in whom the weak and the oppressed found a protector.

But though the Church was strong by her high aims, and by her close organisation and discipline, good men could not help seeing that her weak point lay in the enormous wealth and worldly power which had come *Simony.* to her in the course of ages. This wealth and power had corrupted the springs of her life, by filling her ranks, from the priesthood to the papacy, with ambitious and worldly men. One of the most crying evils of the day was simony, the sale of church orders and offices. The sacred office of a shepherd of Christ's flock was an object of greed, to be bought and sold for money. It was worth so much in a worldly point of view, that worldly men were eager to buy it, and needy kings or nobles who held bishoprics or livings in their hands, were eager to sell. It was said in praise of William the Conqueror that he was free from the guilt of simony; and when we read the history of the times, we see that it is a very rare praise.

What was worse, these worldly men, when once in possession of benefices, strove to hand them on to their children. In this way a church was often divided among several children, and became a sort of family property.[1] Bishops were known to give away church lands in dowry to their daughters. Had this kind of thing gone on, the only asylum of the serf would have been destroyed. There would have been no more room in the Church for the poor man; an hereditary caste would have taken possession of all the wealth and power of the Church, and those who had entered merely by the door of inheritance, would not have cared to use the power for the defence of the poor and the upholding of right. The salt of the earth would have lost its savour. There would have been no power in any country to work as a balance to feudalism.

Church threatened with feudalisation.

And already the feudal nobles had far too much power in the Church. They put into their own pockets a large part of the revenues of churches. They put their younger sons, and even their small children, into the great offices of the Church. In fact, the Church threatened to become completely feudalised.

Yet if any churchman arose (like Arnold of Brescia at the end of the twelfth century) to propose that the wealth of the Church or the power of the popes should be given up, he was hooted to death; for the spiritual kingdom could not in those days be separated from the machinery of clerical power and wealth with which it was bound up.

What then was to be done in order to preserve the only power which could fight for justice and mercy against the greed and cruelty of feudal kings and nobles?

In the time of William the Conqueror, the Church was ruled by the monk Hildebrand, who became Pope in 1073, under the name of Gregory VII. Hildebrand saw perfectly well the danger the Church was in of becoming feudalised. He sought to meet it in two ways. 1. By purifying the Church herself; 2. By exalting the authority and independence of the Church. The measures which he took were not new; he simply followed out the aims which all strong churchmen had had in view for centuries.

Reforms of Gregory VII.

1. The first end, the purification of the Church, Hilde-

---

[1] See what Giraldus Cambrensis says of the churches of Wales, *De Illaud. Walliæ*, vi.

brand sought to bring about by putting down simony and forbidding the marriage of the clergy. In his war against simony, he had little opposition to fear from good men; the difficulty lay in the wide spread of the sin, of which all orders in the Church were guilty. But the decree against the marriage of the clergy met with a fearful storm of opposition. Gregory's purpose was to take away from the clergy all possibility of founding families, and thus to secure them from the temptation to make the interests of the Church come second to their own. He could see no way of keeping the Church pure except by cutting her off entirely from the world, and building a gate of self-sacrifice for all who would enter her service. *Simony and marriage of clergy forbidden.*

We must take the evil with the good. The good was that the Church, by this great sacrifice, gained an immense moral power which was for a long time wielded largely on the side of right; the evil was that by cutting herself off from human nature, the Church not only put her priests in great danger—a danger which never ceased to work evil—but she became hard and proud, and all the more eager for earthly power because she had given up earthly joy. And there was yet further evil; by pronouncing marriage unholy for priests, the sacredness of marriage was tacitly denied; the position of women was lowered, and religion was divorced from common life.

2. The second way in which Gregory VII. sought to free the Church from feudalism, was by putting all Church offices and property out of the disposal of laymen. He absolutely forbade any member of the clergy to receive investiture (that is, the appointment to any benefice) from the hands of any layman, whether duke, king, or emperor. The free election of the clergy out of their own body was to dispose of the greater Church offices; the lesser were to be in the hands of the bishops or abbots. No layman was to touch the sacred ark of the Church. *Investiture by laymen forbidden.*

But Gregory's purpose reached further than this. He aspired to regenerate the world by making the Pope the supreme ruler of mankind. He saw the selfishness of kings and princes; he judged his own purpose pure; and he aspired to make that purpose prevail by setting his foot upon the necks of kings, and teaching them that the Pope was the sun from whom they derived their light, and to whose throne they must pay obedience.

This claim was not new, though no one had yet pushed it so far as Gregory VII. Already the Popes had interfered in Relations of Church and State. the affairs of kings, very often with good effect; and they did so for ages afterwards. But there were among the rulers of the world men (as I have said) who understood their business, and would not allow the Pope to be lord over them. The German Emperor, in particular, would not allow himself to be likened to the moon, which drew its light from the sun, to wit, the Pope. 'It is all very well,' said those who took the side of the emperor, 'for the Pope to be supreme in spiritual matters, but in secular matters the State must manage her own concerns. The Pope has no business with temporal affairs.' We can very well see how, when the Pope said, 'We priests are too holy for marriage,' he made it easy for laymen to retort, 'Then if you are too holy for the affairs of this life, leave them to us!'

Thus arose the great quarrel between the Papacy and the Empire (though its nominal cause was the question of investitures), which lasted some fifty years. We have now to ask how these decrees of Gregory VII. affected England.

Before the Norman Conquest, the English clergy mixed with the world, and were not marked off by hard lines from their fellow-countrymen; it was said, indeed, that they thought too little of their sacred profession, and that even the monks cared as much as laymen for fine clothes. The priests were husbands and fathers of families. 'God's right and the world's right,' or, as we should now say, ecclesiastic and secular matters were judged in the same shire-moot before the bishop and ealdorman jointly. The State gave the Church power to enforce penances for sin, so Church and State worked harmoniously together, and no English bishop ever dreamed of appealing to Rome against his king.

To the Norman churchmen, whom William brought with him, it seemed that the English clergy were far too free from Reforms of William I. and Lanfranc. discipline. William set himself to alter this state of things. By gradually filling up the English bishoprics and abbacies with foreigners, he made the English Church less national, more ready to accept

Roman rule and discipline. He deposed Stigand, the English Archbishop of Canterbury, and appointed in his stead an Italian monk named Lanfranc, a shrewd and clever man, a faithful and able helper of William in the affairs both of Church and State. Lanfranc was a man of great reputation as a scholar, who had already made the monastery of Bec, in Normandy, of which he had been prior, famous as a school of learning: he had in fact contributed largely to revive and elevate monasticism in Normandy.

With the help of the king, Lanfranc accomplished many reforms in the English Church. He set his face against simony, and he tried to carry out the decrees of Hildebrand forbidding the marriage of the clergy, and to force the English priests to abandon their wives. But it was not found possible to carry out this decree with strictness in England. All that could be done was to forbid any priest to take a wife in future, and to insist that the canons should always be unmarried. In his own church of Canterbury, Lanfranc at last carried out the work of Odo and Dunstan, and turned his cathedral canons into Benedictine monks. He rebuilt the cathedral, he recovered lands for the Church, improved the church estates and looked after the welfare of the tenantry, encouraged education and the formation of libraries, and corrected manuscripts. 'Before the coming of the Normans,' says William of Malmesbury, 'religion and learning had fallen into decay in England;' the clergy were ignorant, the monks made their rule a pretence. But now ' churches and monasteries arose on all sides, and the land rejoiced in fresh worship.' The splendid cathedrals which then began to be built all over England were emblems of the renewed life of the Church. The Church of the North, in the person of its archbishop, was put under the authority of the Archbishop of Canterbury; an important point, seeing that the North was not thoroughly united to the rest of England. A revival of monasticism took place in the North, where, since the harryings of the Danes, there had been no monasteries and not many churches for two hundred years; and the Northerners, says their chronicler, 'began to change their beast-like way of life for a better.'

One great change was made by William and Lanfranc which altered the whole position of the Church of England.

They were shocked that 'causes belonging to the care of souls, should be brought to the judgment of worldly men; and a law was made by William that henceforth all cases concerning the Church or the clergy should be tried not in the Hundred or the Shire Meeting, but before the bishop, and not according to English law, but according to the canon law, whereby the clergy of the Continent were governed. Thus the Church and the State were henceforth to be separate. It may have been a good thing that there should be courts of justice independent of the king or his officers; but it was not good, and it afterwards caused much confusion, that there should be two systems of law in one realm.

Clerical and lay courts separated.

William certainly did not foresee that this separation of Church and State would by-and-by bring them into collision. Though he gave the Church a measure of independence, he had no intention that there should be any power in the kingdom which should be a balance to his own. He established certain rules with regard to the Church, about which we shall have more to say presently, which were capable of being used to strike a blow at the very root of Church power and influence. He would not allow the Archbishop in his synods to make any laws for the Church except what the king had first consented to; and in the time of the quarrel between the Papacy and the Empire, when the Emperor had set up a rival Pope, he would not allow either Pope to be acknowledged by his subjects without his consent, nor any papal letters to be received in England unless they had first been shown to him. You can judge by this, that he was by no means disposed to agree to the universal empire of the Pope, which Gregory VII. wished to bring about, still less to his claims on the realm of England. When Gregory wrote to him, and demanded that William should do homage to him, in return for the blessing which Pope Alexander had pronounced upon his invasion of England, this was William's reply:—' My pious father, thy legate Hubert coming to me from thee has admonished me that I should do fealty to thee and thy successors, and should attend better to the money which my predecessors were accustomed to send to the Roman Church. I admitted the one count, but the other I did not admit; I neither would

William's attitude to the Papacy.

nor will do fealty, for I neither promised it myself nor do I learn that my predecessors performed it to thine. It is true that the money has been collected negligently for three years, while I have been in France; but now that by the Divine mercy I have returned to my kingdom, what has been collected shall be sent by the present legate; and what remains shall be sent by the messengers of Lanfranc, our faithful Archbishop, when opportunity shall occur. Pray for us and for the state of our kingdom, for we have loved your predecessors, and we desire sincerely to love and diligently to obey you before all men.'

The Pope was not in a position to press his claim; and such was his respect for William, as for one who was in general a good son of the Church, that he freely allowed him to do what he fought to the death to prevent the German emperor from doing, namely, to appoint bishops himself to the vacant sees, as the kings of England had always done before him. When a Norman abbot, who had been turned out of his abbey by William, came back with letters from the Pope, William said 'that he would willingly receive the messengers of the Pope, as the common father of the faithful, if they came to speak of faith and of the Christian religion; but if any monk did anything against his sovereignty, he would straightway hang him up by his hood, on the highest oak of the next forest.'

In truth, William, as long as he was king, wielded the powers both of Church and State. He employed Lanfranc to curse his enemies, and Lanfranc was repaid for his willingness to serve the king by the independent position he occupied at the head of the English Church. He was a sort of little Western Pope in the island realm; the bishops of Scotland and of the remotest Orkneys were subject to him through their dependence on the Archbishopric of York, and even the Irish Church (to speak more correctly, the Church of the Danes in Ireland) accepted him as her head. It is plain that Lanfranc was not a strong churchman, that is, a partizan of the undivided rule of Rome, and he was reproached by Gregory VII. for having declined in his feelings of respect towards that holy Church. *Lanfranc's independent position.*

But so long as William and Lanfranc lived, the affairs of the Church in England were well managed, and Gregory had too much on his hands to quarrel with a son who in the main was so well behaved. It was otherwise when William and Lanfranc were dead, and William Rufus sat upon his father's throne. That throne, which the Conqueror had made so strong, was now filled by the worst man whom England reckons among her kings. William Rufus cared neither for God nor man, neither for faith nor law; he scoffed at all holy things, nor was there anything that could restrain his unbridled will, his gross vices, his treachery and violence, except his own self-interest. Instead of order and law, violence and extortion now reigned in England. 'In his days all justice sank, and all unrighteousness arose, before God and before the world.' The poor were crushed with heavy burthens, to furnish money for the king's wars; 'he was ever vexing the people with armies and with cruel taxes.' The rights of the Church were trodden under foot. When Lanfranc died, William seized the property and revenues of the Archbishop of Canterbury into his own hand, and held them for nearly five years. He did the same with other sees and abbacies; or if he did not keep them to himself, he sold them to those who were base enough to buy them, so that the Church was filled with his creatures. At his court, not only was all religion scoffed at, but strange and unheard-of vices showed their heads under his favour, and spread all over the land. The lights in the palace were not lit in the evening, because what went on was too bad to be seen. 'All that was abominable to God and hateful to man was common in this island in William's time; therefore he was hated by almost all his people.'

William Rufus.

But with all his wickedness, the Red-faced King was a man of great ability; he was determined to be master in his realm, and he kept down the barons with a strong hand. Nor would it have been any better for England if they could have shaken off his yoke; they would only have split up England into a number of small feudal tyrannies, instead of one great tyranny. It was not a bad thing that the barons should be kept in check with a strong hand; but the depression of the Church meant the depression of all moral and intellectual influences, and of the greatest check that there was on vice and tyranny. In the middle ages, the synods or great meetings of the clergy were

Depression of the Church.

the chief means of spreading reforms in society. For at these synods it was the custom of the assembled clergy to condemn with solemn curses the vices which were most popular at the time, and to ordain what measures they thought useful in spiritual matters; and these *bans* were then proclaimed in all the churches of England, so that the influence of the synod took effect over the whole country. We must remember that it was the Church's office to punish, with the weapons of penance and excommunication, many sins of which the laws took no account. Therefore the rule of William the Conqueror, that none of his barons should be impleaded or excommunicated by a bishop for any sin without his consent, worked very badly in the hands of a bad king like Rufus, because it gave him power to allow any of his favourites to commit what crimes they pleased unpunished. No synods were held in Rufus's reign; the Church was corrupted and paralysed by reason of simony, the source of moral life was poisoned; and while the Church had no head, no archbishop sitting by the king's side, and influencing his decrees, the spiritual power was unrepresented in the State.

Was there then no one in England in the reign of Rufus who could dare to speak for the Church, for justice, for peace; no power to defend the poor, or to fight against vice in high places? Yes, there was one frail old man, a gentle, tender soul, a scholar who had spent the greater part of his life in the cloister, far from the strife of worldly business, happy among his books and the society of his loving monks;— Saint Anselm of Canterbury.

How such a man as Saint Anselm ever came to be Archbishop of Canterbury is a strange and instructive story. It happened in this wise. In the year 1093, King William II was very sick. Anselm (whose birthplace was in Aosta, at the foot of the Alps) was then Abbot of Bec in Normandy; perhaps he was not then known to be one of the profoundest thinkers of his age, nor was it known that he would leave his mark on theology from that day to our own time; but his fame as a scholar and teacher was already widely spread. It had been the work of his life to think out the deepest questions of faith, and to prove that faith in God is founded on reason—a noble life-work surely.

St. Anselm.

Nor was it only for his intellectual gifts that he was famous; his unselfishness, his wonderful sympathy, his tenderness, his helpful counsel, his power of drawing out what was good in people, and quenching what was bad, had made him everywhere beloved. People felt about Anselm, says his biographer Eadmer, that he himself had eaten of the living bread, and therefore was able to feed others. It happened that just before William's illness, Anselm had come to England on business for his convent, and also to advise Earl Hugh of Chester, who was settling a colony of monks from Bec in his cathedral.[1] On his way to Chester, he had an interview with the king; he took that opportunity to rebuke him boldly for the evil deeds which were told of him; and this duty he thought more important than to ask the king's help for the business of his monastery. History does not say how William took this plain speaking; he afterwards spoke of Anselm with sneers; but when he lay at the point of death, when his barons and bishops were entreating him for his soul's sake to amend some of the evils which were rife in his kingdom, and above all to be mindful of the Mother Church of the whole realm, which had been so long without a shepherd, the king bethought him of the only man who had ever dared to tell him the truth, and with the joyful consent of all present he named Anselm as Archbishop of Canterbury. In vain did Anselm refuse the offered dignity; it was thrust upon him. 'The plough of the Church of England,' said Anselm, 'should be drawn by two strong oxen, the King and the Archbishop of Canterbury, the one with worldly justice and government, the other with Divine teaching and discipline; but ye have yoked a feeble sheep with a fierce wild bull.'

<small>Becomes Archbishop of Canterbury. 1093.</small>

Anselm had perfectly understood the situation; from the moment that the king got well and became his old self again, he and Anselm pulled different ways. The coarse brutal king lived only for his own pleasure and self-interest Anselm lived for the service of God and man. But to Anselm, as to every good man of the eleventh century, this service meant the service of the Church. To the Church Anselm belonged

---

[1] Chester had been an episcopal city at the end of William I.'s reign, but the see was now removed to Coventry.

by his monastic vows, to the head of the Church he owed obedience before any earthly king. In his oath of homage to the king, he always supposed this obedience to be reserved. He became the king's man for the lands which the archbishop held of the king, but he did not cease to be the man of the Pope. Never before had there been in England an Archbishop of Canterbury who thought that the Pope had a higher claim to his obedience than the king. But the rapid growth of the Papal power under Hildebrand, and the separation which William had made between Church and State, made it a matter of certainty that the two swords, the spiritual and temporal, would one day clash in England. When they did clash—when Anselm asked leave to go to Pope Urban for his Archbishop's pall,[1] and William Rufus refused on account of the rivalry which was then existing between Pope Urban and the anti-pope whom the German emperor had set up,—William could appeal to the rule established by his father, that no Pope should be recognised in his dominions except by his command; and William had not yet decided which Pope he would recognise. He intended, no doubt, to drive a bargain between the two; but no good churchman had any doubt that Urban was the true Pope, and the other only the creature of the Emperor. Anselm, before he came to England, had acknowledged Urban, and took care to say that he had done so before he consented to be made Archbishop.

Quarrel of William and Anselm.

Now to all who think that the Pope has no right to any authority in England, it must seem that William had a very good case, when he claimed his right as king of England to allow no power to be acknowledged in his kingdom without his consent. But this is not looking at the question in the light of the eleventh century. The Pope's power was a sacred thing, independent of and above that of kings; it was the guiding power of Europe, and for a king to throw it off was to throw off obedience to God. The contest between the king and Anselm appeared to all to be simply a fight between wickedness and holiness. 'The king wished,' says Eadmer, 'to take away from the archbishop all power of promoting

[1] The pall was a sort of scarf, the badge of an archbishop's office; it was a rule of the Popes that all archbishops should go to Rome to receive it.

Christianity. I speak what was well known; he felt as though he were only half a king as long as anyone in all the land had any possession or power independent of him.' The down-trodden English folk looked upon Anselm as a martyr in the hands of a tyrant, and cheered him by marks of their sympathy and love. 'And we were greatly encouraged thereby,' says Eadmer, 'knowing that the voice of the people is the voice of God.' They knew that one of his first acts after his consecration had been to rebuke powerfully the loose morals and extravagant fashions of the courtiers, and to call (though vainly) for a synod to put down vice and to remedy the grievances of the Church. They knew that he had refused to buy the king's favour with money, as the custom of the other bishops was. Our old English chronicler hardly notices the quarrel about the Pope, but says that Anselm left England 'because it seemed to him that in this nation little was done according to right;' and no doubt that was the true view of the difference between William and Anselm.[1]

For four years Anselm had to endure the insults, the swaggering, and the bullying of the Red-faced King. If he proposed any measures for the good of religion; if he defended his own conduct by appealing to sacred principles of right, 'Stop your sermons,' was all the answer he could get.

The bishops desert Anselm. The time-serving bishops could only counsel him to submit to the king's pleasure in all things. 'We know that you are a religious and holy man,' they said to Anselm, 'and your conversation is in heaven. But we are hindered by our kindred, whom we have to maintain, and by the manifold affairs of the world, which we are interested in, and we cannot rise to the loftiness of your life, nor escape from the world with you.' Anselm stood alone in his fight with a power which seemed the power of evil in person. Yet in the end he was the victor, through the simple power of consistent holiness and gentleness. The king was brought to acknowledge Urban, and to give his unwilling consent that Anselm should go to Rome to consult the Pope. Bishops, who to please the king had declared that they renounced their obedience to the Archbishop,

---

[1] William of Newburgh (a thorough Englishman) gives a similar version, that Anselm was exiled because the king could not endure to be rebuked for his enormities.

came to beg his forgiveness for their desertion. Even the king was softened for an instant when the moment of parting came. Though William's leave to go had been given him with anger and ill-will, Anselm had no mind to sneak out of the kingdom like a thief. He went cheerfully and boldly to the king, and as his spiritual father, as Archbishop of Canterbury, he offered him his parting benediction. 'Thy blessing,' said the king, 'I do not reject.' He bowed his head, and Anselm blessed him. They never met again. Three years afterwards, while William was hunting in the New Forest, the forest which his father had made by the destruction of smiling thorpes and homesteads, the forest of evil omen which had already been a fatal place to more than one of the Conqueror's family, a chance arrow pierced him as he was riding after a stag, and the Red-faced King was carried to his grave.

Anselm leaves England. 1097.

William slain. 1100.

Henry I., surnamed (in later times) Beauclerc, or the fine scholar, who succeeded his brother William on the throne, was by nature not much less cruel, selfish, and vicious than William. But there was this difference between him and his brother, that Henry had had an education. In the first place, he had had an education of troubles and disappointments, which had taught him how to deal with men, and how to be so far master of his bad passions as to cover them with decent self-control when it was needful. He had also had the literary education which won him his surname. His scholarship, in a king, was thought to be quite remarkable. He was fond of saying that an illiterate king is a crowned ass. The mere fact that his mind was cultivated put him many grades above Rufus, and made it impossible that he should scoff at learning, at refinement, at holiness. He knew the value of these things in a worldly point of view; he wished that they should be enlisted in his service, and should swell the glory of his reign. Therefore one of his first acts was to recall Anselm to his archbishopric.

Henry I.

Anselm in the meanwhile had been to Rome and had found how little help there was to be found there for the pure in heart, since according to the saying which is to be found everywhere in mediæval writers, everything in Rome is managed by money. Yet, strange to say, Anselm came back from this seat of corruption a stronger

Anselm in Rome.

Papalist than before. How was this? Because the great idea of the unity of the Church, of the supremacy of the spiritual power, towered above the baseness of the Roman court, and filled the minds of men who like Anselm were open to great ideas; because also Anselm was able to separate the Pope Urban, a man of really high character, from his corrupt surroundings.

Since in 1073 Gregory VII. had made it a law of the Church that no bishop should receive investiture from any layman, it seems rather strange that Anselm should have consented to take investiture from William II., seemingly without making any difficulty. It is true that this decree of Gregory's had never been observed in England, and we may fairly suppose that Gregory's ideas had not fully penetrated to Bec, or at least that Anselm's attention had not been drawn to them. But while he was at Rome, he heard Pope Urban in Council (1099) pronounce excommunication against all who gave and all who received investiture of churches from lay hands, and all those who became the 'men' of laymen for ecclesiastical honours. This sank into Anselm's mind.

Therefore it was in vain that Anselm was recalled to England, and received with immense hope and joy by all the land, and with every honour by King Henry, in vain that all the lands taken by King William II. from the Church of Canterbury were restored; Anselm would on no account do homage to the king, or be invested with the ring and staff by him. The ring was the sign of the Bishop's espousal to his Church; the staff was the shepherd's crook which he bore as a sign that he guided the flock of Christ; Anselm could never more consent to receive these from an earthly king without disobedience to the head of the Church.

Anselm returns to England,

but refuses investiture from Henry.

Henry was greatly annoyed by this refusal of Anselm's, which in fact was a denial of his supremacy in England. But as he could not afford to quarrel with Anselm just then, he sought to gain time, and sent an embassy to Rome to obtain a decision of the question from the Pope. In the meanwhile, Anselm occupied his post as Archbishop of Canterbury, and showed how important that post was to the stability of the realm. He quashed the obstacles which had arisen to the king's marriage with Edith (afterwards called by the Norman name Matilda) daughter of Malcolm, king of Scots, and Margaret, granddaughter of Edmund Ironsides, a marriage which gave great pleasure to the English people, because Edith was 'of the true kingly line of England.'[1] He threatened to excommunicate Duke Robert of Normandy, the king's elder brother, who had invaded England with an army, and by his own faithfulness and energy Anselm held many of the nobles in faith to the king. He held a synod for the correction of the Church and of morals. In this synod the marriage of the clergy was again strictly forbidden; the slave-trade also was forcibly condemned. If mixed up with these weighty matters we find rules about hair-cutting, which appear trivial, we must remember that the clergy of that day fought against extravagant fashions in dress and personal carriage, because they were closely connected with sins of a far deeper dye. The conduct of St. Anselm on this subject has been utterly misunderstood. It is noteworthy that at this synod, by the special request of Anselm, the barons as well as the clergy were present, that the clergy and laity might work together in carrying out what was ruled.

Meanwhile a second and a third embassy went to the Pope, but without effect; 'the Pope would not, to redeem his head,' give up the investitures. The king grew exasperated. 'What has the Pope to do with things that are mine? what my predecessors held in this kingdom is mine!' Anselm was not unwilling to make concessions if the Pope would give him leave, but he would on no account violate his canonical obedience. 'Not to save my head will I break the law which I heard passed in the Roman Council, unless I am absolved from the obligation by the same see which bound me.' Thus the dispute was drawn out for three years. Anselm's constancy at last began to work on the bishops; two whom the king had invested, and whom Anselm refused to consecrate, refused to receive consecration from the Archbishop of York, the king's tool. Finally the king begged that Anselm himself would go to Rome, and see the Pope about the business (1103). Anselm knew that *Anselm* this was a polite way of sending him into exile. *again leaves* He went to Rome, but it was of no use; the Pope *England.* would not alter his decision, nor did Anselm ask it of him;

[1] Anglo-Saxon Chronicle.

his business was to obey, not to advise. When King Henry received Anselm's message, that he still could not comply with his conditions, he seized the revenues of the archbishopric into his own hand, as William Rufus had done on Anselm's first exile. But as during the whole quarrel King Henry had behaved in a very different way from King William, always treating Anselm with outward respect and often with real consideration, so now he appointed two of the Archbishop's own men to collect the revenues, thinking that they would be more merciful to the tenants.

The king now took in hand the work of Church reform, urged not by pious zeal, but by need of money. Like his brother, he was constantly pressed for money for his wars in Normandy, and the chronicles are full of lamentations over his 'manifold taxes,' which weighed on the people the more from the cruel harshness of the collectors. The decrees of the Council of London had fallen into contempt during Anselm's exile, and many priests had taken to themselves wives again. King Henry fined them heavily for this transgression, but as the sum of money thus gotten was not so great as he had expected, he proceeded to impose the fine on every parish priest in the kingdom, married or unmarried. This was the kind of justice that was to be had from a Norman king, not a Rufus, a mere ruffian, but a polished, cultivated Norman gentleman, who read Greek and Latin, and took an interest in natural history; but who did not scruple, in a fit of rage, to order his own grandchildren's eyes to be torn out.

Many like things were done in England at this time, says Eadmer. Even the bishops, overwhelmed by the evils which had come upon the realm, wrote to Anselm, entreating him to come back, and promising that they would follow his guidance from this time forth.

The Reconciliation. 1106.

After three years of exile, reconciliation at last took place between the king and Anselm in 1106, when after long haggling, the Pope consented to allow the homage to be done to the king, and Henry on his part gave up the delivery of the ring and staff, the symbols of the spiritual power. Thus ended this great contest. What was the real result? The spiritual order had been vindicated; Henry had been forced to respect the decree of the head of the Church. The office of a bishop had been vindicated as a spiritual office, at a time when it had almost come to be regarded as a mere piece of worldly preferment, to be given equally to the clerk of the king's larder, or to any other of the king's creatures whom he might wish to reward. From this time (as Anselm writes in a letter) 'the king did not follow his own will in the choice of persons, [for bishoprics and abbacies] but yielded himself wholly to the counsel of religious men.' On the other hand, the State kept its lawful claim to the services which the Archbishop owed for the estate he held. If the Church was to be a landholder, it was not just that the Church should bear no part of the burthen of the State, nor that churchmen should be free from allegiance to the king.

But from this time forward, the Pope has a footing in England such as he never had before. Was that a good thing? Time will show. Anselm, fighting for the kingdom of God, was obliged to fight for the machinery of the Church. In our time, the kingdom of God is no longer bound up with that machinery; like the wind which bloweth where it listeth, it has broken loose, and spread over the world. But we must never forget that in the middle ages, the Church (whatever its mistakes, follies, and sins) not merely pretended to be, but was, the ark of the testimony, wherein the sacred law of right was stored up and kept safe for mankind.

DATES.

William Rufus, king	A.D. 1089
Anselm, Archbishop of Canterbury	1093
Henry I., king	1100
Dispute about investitures settled	1106

CHAPTER XI.

I HAVE told the story of the struggle between Wiliam Rufus and Archbishop Anselm at some length, because of the light which it casts on the history of the Church. I shall not dwell much longer on the reign of Rufus. There is not much to tell about the English people just now. They are in the background, dimly seen, crushed, oppressed; Norman barons fill the front of the stage; their

William Rufus and the English.

wars with the Kelt, their struggles against their kings, make up the English history of the first four Norman reigns. Yet still the English people count for something. Rufus had to appeal to them against his barons. Orderic tells us that the Norman barons who had been enriched by the spoils of England, were filled with pride and insolence, and were indignant to find that William Rufus governed them as a master; so they made a league against him. Then the king sent for the native English, and promised to take away unjust taxes, to give them the right of hunting in their own woods, and to sweep away all abuses. The English rallied round him, and with their help he overcame the barons. But he kept none of his promises, and the English in his reign were much oppressed with heavy taxes, to support the king's wars in Normandy and Maine, and to pay for his splendid buildings. For King William, though a bad man, was not a small man; he had large ideas, not only of his kingly power, but of kingly state; he built the noble hall of Westminster, finished the Tower of London, which his father had begun, and repaired London Bridge. And as I have shown him in the last chapter as a bad man fighting for his own self-will against the good, it is only fair to show him as king who knew how to curb the unruly, and who in fighting against the *unlaw* of his barons, really defended the interests of his people at large.

Robert Mowbray, earl of Northumberland, had robbed four merchant ships from Norway which fell into his hands, and had stripped the peaceable traders of all that they possessed. The merchants went to Court, and complained to the king; William immediately ordered the earl to restore their goods to them, but the order was treated with contempt. William then made good their losses out of his own treasury, and as the earl refused a summons to appear and answer in his Court, he marched against him, and Robert was taken prisoner, and kept in the pit of Windsor Castle for thirty-four years. So that we can to some extent believe what Orderic says in another place of Rufus, that robbers and thieves felt the terrible weight of his power, and that his efforts to keep the peace throughout his dominion were unceasing.

<small>William's justice.</small>

The work of conquest over the Kelt went on in Rufus's reign, but of that I shall speak in another place.

When William II. was slain in 1100, his brother Henry, who succeeded him, had to make good his hold of the throne against the eldest brother, Robert, Duke of Normandy. He therefore began his reign by a solemn promise 'to God and all the people, before the altar at Westminster, that he would abolish the unlaw which prevailed in his brother's time, and that he would observe the most righteous of the laws established in the days of any of the kings before him.' Every English king, indeed, since the time of Ethelred at least, had been made to swear at his coronation that he would protect the Church and all Christian people, would put down all iniquity in every rank, and would observe just judgments and mercy. This coronation oath was first drawn up by Archbishop Dunstan, and it expressed the idea that the king was bound to his people by solemn duties, that he held his office in trust from the Divine justice, and was answerable to it and to them. *Henry I.*

King Henry, however, did more than this; he gave a charter in which he solemnly promised to amend those things which were found most grievous by the clergy, the barons, and the people. This charter of liberties was even more important for later times than in Henry's reign. It was not made solely for the benefit of the barons; the under-tenants were to share in the reforms, and the king promised to restore the good laws of the time of Edward the Confessor, the time which the English people looked back to as a golden age. The fact was that it was necessary for King Henry, as it had been for his brother William, to court the English people, in order to get their support. The English were full of hope at the beginning of Henry's reign. A reign of good law, they thought, was going to begin. Anselm had come back amongst them. Another great cause of joy to them was that the king, as before mentioned, had married a wife 'of the true royal line of England,' (as the English chronicler proudly says) Matilda, the daughter of Margaret, queen of Scotland, Edmund Ironsides' granddaughter. *His charter.*

To a great extent these hopes were blighted. Although there was peace in England during Henry's reign, there was almost endless war in Normandy, between Henry and his brother, between Henry and the king of France, between Henry and his nephew, Duke Robert's son. *Sufferings of England.*

These wars could not be kept up without money, and this money had to be wrung from the English people. *Taxation* in those times was a rude affair, in which there was not much regard to justice or mercy; the king simply tried to squeeze as much out of his subjects as he could get. It is true that in England all dues were fixed by either law or custom, and the king could not just ask for whatever he would; yet there were many ways in which he could extort money unjustly; and the chronicles are full of almost yearly bewailings over 'the manifold oppressions and taxes.' 'The miserable folk is oppressed with all unrighteousness; first men are bereft of their property, and then they are slain.'[1] Poor people who had nothing to pay were driven out of their cottages, or the doors of their houses were torn off and carried away, or all their little furniture was seized.

There was another abuse from which the people in certain districts suffered much. In those days, when there were not such means for sending provisions from all parts of the country to the capital as there are now, it was not the custom for the king always to hold his court at one place, but he used to move about, now to some of the great towns, now to some hunting-seat on his own estates. This had been the custom from the earliest days of the monarchy. These royal movements, though first undertaken from economical reasons, were also travelling courts of justice, and means of extending the king's personal authority in different parts of the kingdom. Wherever the king went, his whole court went with him, and as long as they stayed they lived upon the neighbourhood, and their followers were quartered upon the people. 'In the time of the king's brother,' (Rufus) says Eadmer, 'the multitude of those who followed the king's court had this custom, that they seized everything they could spoil, and as there was no discipline to restrain them, they laid waste all the country through which the king went. Another evil was added to this, for many of them, intoxicated by their own wickedness, when they had found in the houses which they had invaded anything which they could not carry away, would make the owners take it to market to sell for them, or would even set fire to it, or if it were drink, would wash their horses' feet with it, and pour

Abuse of Feorm.

[1] Anglo-Saxon Chronicle, 1124.

the rest of it on the ground. And what insults they did to the families I am ashamed to tell. From these causes, wher⋅ the king's coming was known beforehand, the people left their houses, and fled with their families and what they could carry to the woods and other hiding places.' King Henry tried by severe punishments to put a stop to these acts of oppression.

It was not King Henry's wish to let injustice go on, unless it was to his own advantage. Like his father and his brother, he was determined to be master, and to hold his barons in check. There was a certain Norman, named Robert of Belesme, who was Earl of Shrewsbury in Henry's time, who seems to have been the very model of a wicked feudal baron, a man whom the earth could hardly bear for his lawlessness and cruelty. He was said to have torn out the eyes of his little godchild with his own hands, for some slight offence of its father's; and in war, he preferred torturing his prisoners to getting ransoms for them. This man was not only bad, but able, and was marked out by King Henry as one dangerous to his crown. Being summoned to appear before the king's court, Belesme refused, and open war broke out between him and Henry, the only war in England in Henry's reign. Henry was successful; but the earls and barons of the realm, seeing that, if the king crushed Belesme, their own turn might come next, tried to reconcile the king to him on easy terms. But the king's English troops, who had heard of the nobles' plan, cried out, 'Henry, lord king, trust not these traitors. Let justice be done, and we will stand by you.' Henry took the advice of his people; Belesme was driven out of the kingdom, and for many years was the scourge of Normandy; but at last he was taken prisoner by Henry, and thrown into a dungeon, where he languished until his death. For the rest of Henry's reign, that is for thirty-three years, there was no disturbance whatever in England.

Henry and the nobles.

1102.

1112.

The *King's Court*, before which Robert of Belesme was summoned, was a thing which had grown up under William the Conqueror. When the king was away in Normandy, he left behind him a chief justice or *Justiciar*, who managed the kingdom in his absence, and was a sort of prime minister when the king was at home. The

The King's Court.

king's clerks or chaplains formed a body of secretaries under the Justiciar, the chief of them being called the Chancellor, who kept the king's seal. In Henry I.'s time, the Chancellor and the other great officers of the king's household, with some barons chosen for their knowledge of the law, formed a standing council called the King's Court, which now managed all the carrying out of the laws. But the power of making the laws still rested with the king and his Wise Men's Meeting, now called the Great Council.

This King's Court (*Curia Regis*) was the chief court of appeal in matters of law. When it had to deal with finance, that is, with the money affairs of the realm, it sat in a chamber called the Exchequer, and was hence called the Court of Exchequer. The old courts of the Hundred and the Shire were still going on, and an ordinance was issued by Henry to strengthen their authority; for he did not wish all the justice of the country to be in the hands of the nobles in their feudal courts. From time to time the Justiciar's staff went down into the country, and held sittings there; once in Henry's reign they hanged forty-four thieves in one place. The justice of the King's Court was not always to be trusted in those days; nevertheless, these visits of the King's Court into the country were the beginning of that system of justice which is now perhaps the best in the world. Thus we see in Henry I.'s reign the first germs of an organised central government in England.

<small>Court of Exchequer.</small>

The Justiciar, Chancellor, Treasurer, and other important officers were not generally nobles; they were often men of low birth, who had risen through their industry or servility. But (with perhaps two exceptions) they do not seem to have been Englishmen at this time; in Henry I.'s days the English were still a conquered race. Eadmer particularly tells us that no virtue could make an Englishman worthy of any honour; the king always appointed foreign abbots to the monasteries; it is no wonder, he says, if they turned out to be rather wolves than shepherds.

<small>Englishmen not promoted.</small>

Nevertheless, in the next reign, the unhappy reign of Stephen, the English looked back to the reign of Henry as a time of peace and order, simply because he had kept the barons down. 'He was a good man,' they said, 'and great was the awe of him; no man durst ill-treat another in his time.' We should hardly call a man a good man who could order the eyes of his own grandchildren to be torn out because their father had offended him. And though we may be glad that feudal anarchy was kept down in Henry's time, it is certain that it was not love to his people, but his own interest, which was his motive. The order of his reign rested only on his own will, and when he died the order fell.

Many towns obtained charters of privilege from Henry I., the citizens of London, for instance, being set free from tolls throughout the kingdom, and from the jurisdiction of any courts but their own. The king's need of money was his reason for granting these charters; they were paid for by the citizens.

The only quarter from which there was ever a righteous resistance to the king's will was from St. Anselm. The Church alone made a stand for justice, and gave the people lessons how to fight for freedom.

King Henry's only lawful son was drowned in crossing from Normandy to England in 1120. Henry then sought to make his daughter Matilda the heiress of his kingdom, and many years before his death he made his barons swear that she should be their queen after him. Matilda was then a widow, having been married to Henry V., emperor of Germany. The barons were not much pleased when in 1127 her father gave her in marriage to Geoffrey, count of Anjou, as they thought they ought to have been consulted about the marriage, and many of them made this an excuse for breaking their oath to Matilda when Henry died. As soon as the king was dead, his nephew Stephen, count of Blois, whose mother was a daughter of William the Conqueror, came to England. Being received *Accession of Stephen. 1135.* by the citizens of London and Winchester, and greatly helped by his brother Henry, Bishop of Winchester, he was chosen king, and crowned by the Archbishop of Canterbury. He was supported also by the Pope, who perhaps was not sorry to have an occasion of having a hand in English affairs. Stephen was not a bad man; he had a great deal of generous feeling, and his manners were very popular; but he was utterly unfit to cope with the strong monster, feudalism; he was far too easy, and allowed the barons to have whatever they asked for. As soon as the late king's treasures, which Stephen scattered with a too liberal hand, were spent, the barons began to falter in their troth, and Matilda found supporters to her claim to the crown. The powerful Earl Robert of Gloucester, one of King Henry's many unlawful children, brought his sister Matilda over from Normandy, and for thirteen years England was scourged by a most cruel civil war.

Civil war.

None of the nobles of England (except Robert of Gloucester) cared very greatly about either Stephen or Matilda; what they wished for was to make themselves independent of any rule at all. It was seen then what feudalism meant, when there was no State, no strong hand above the nobles, to hold the turbulent to right. Castles rose in every part of the country, and every castle was the abode of a little king, who coined money, levied tribute on the surrounding country, and did what was right in his own eyes entirely. The rivalries between the owners of different castles added a host of private wars to the great civil war. Moreover, both sides employed hired soldiers from Flanders and Brittany, who showed no mercy to the country folk, and when the barons who employed them were not able to pay them their hire, they allowed them to ransack the country, driving off the flocks and herds, carrying off the yeomen as prisoners to be ransomed, and even violating the churches. The churches were places of refuge in those days, and had a sacred right of protection; the poor country people, in times of danger, used to carry all their little property into the churches; sometimes even they made booths in the churchyards and lived there for days. But these robbers paid no respect to the churches; they plundered and burnt them; it was an added horror of war in those days that the victors ruthlessly set fire to buildings when they left them. The prisoners who were carried away were often tortured with the most frightful cruelty in order to extort money from them. Famine and pestilence spread over the land; whole villages stood empty; and in some places the crops were whitening in the fields where there was not a man left to gather them in. Hear the picture which the Peterborough chronicler draws of this time :—

Horrors of Stephen's reign.

'Every rich man built his castles, and defended them

Horrors of Stephen's Reign.

against him [Stephen], and they filled the land full of castles. They greatly oppressed the wretched folk by making them work at these castles, and when the castles were finished they filled them with devils and evil men. Then they took those whom they suspected to have any goods, by night and by day, seizing both men and women, and they put them in prison for their gold and silver, and tortured them with pains unspeakable, for never were any martyrs tormented as these were. They hung some up by their feet, and smoked them with foul smoke; some by their thumbs, or by the head, and they put burning things on their feet. They put a knotted string about their heads, and twisted it until it went into the brain. Some they put into a crucet-house, that is, into a chest which was short and narrow, and not deep, and they put sharp stones in it, and crushed the man therein, so that they broke all his limbs. There were hateful and grim things called sachenteges in many of the castles, and which two or three men had enough to do to carry. The sachentege was made thus: it was fastened to a beam, having a sharp iron to go round a man's throat and neck, so that he might no ways sit, nor lie, nor sleep, but he must bear all that iron. Many thousands they exhausted with hunger. I cannot and I may not tell of all the wounds and all the tortures that they inflicted upon the wretched men of this land, and this state of things lasted the nineteen years that Stephen was king, and ever grew worse and worse. They were continually levying an exaction from the towns, which they called tenserie, and when the miserable inhabitants had no more to give, then they plundered and burnt all the towns, so that well mightest thou walk a whole day's journey, nor ever shouldst thou find a man seated in a town, nor its lands tilled.

'Then was corn dear, and meat, and cheese, and butter, for there was none in the land; wretched men starved with hunger; some lived on alms who had been erewhile rich; some fled the country; never was there more misery, and never acted heathens worse than these. At length they spared neither church nor churchyard, but they took all that was valuable therein, and then burnt the church and all together. Neither did they spare the lands of bishops, nor of abbots, nor of priests. If two or three men came riding to a town, all the township fled before them, and thought that they were robbers. The bishops and clergy were ever cursing them, but this to them was nothing, for they were all accursed, and forsworn, and reprobate. The earth bare no corn, you might as well have tilled the sea, for the land was all ruined by such deeds, and men said openly that Christ slept and his saints. These things, and more than we can say, did we suffer nineteen years for our sins.'[1]

The only part of England where there was peace was in the three northern counties, Northumberland, Cumberland, and Westmoreland, of which David, king of Scots, had taken possession. The king of Scots supported the party of Matilda (who was his niece by her mother), and his Scottish garrison at Carlisle made cruel raids into England.

But let us pass over this hideous reign, a time in which our England was as though she were not, her laws all sunk, her people a prey to robbers. It would be a waste of time to follow all the turnings of the warfare between Stephen and Matilda; how first one side triumphed and then the other. When the young earl Henry, Matilda's son, was grown to be a man, he married a wealthy heiress, Eleanor of Aquitaine, who made him lord of half the south of France. He had inherited Anjou and Maine from his father, as well as Normandy, which his father had won from Stephen, so that his dominions stretched from the English Channel to the Pyrenees. He now came to England with a large force, and the war threatened to take a new lease of life. But Stephen was tired of fighting; his son was dead, and he was willing to recognise Henry as his heir. This peace (of Wallingford, 1153) was sealed by the death of Stephen in 1154.

Peace of Wallingford. 1153.

The reign of Henry II. is one of the most important in the history of England. The crisis was this; England had already passed through the great change from clanhood to feudalism more successfully than any other country, because she had almost always had kings who were able to govern. But feudalism was only valuable as a transition to a better form of government, and the danger for England was, lest this transition should not be quickly made. For while the authority of the central government

Reign of Henry II.

[1] Anglo-Saxon Chronicle, Peterborough continuation, 1137.

rested on no secure basis, it could be overthrown under any weak king like Stephen, and then the country became a prey to all the evils of feudalism without any hope of deliverance except in a despotism. But what was needed was not a despotism like that of the Conqueror and his sons, but a government which should draw out all the best elements of the national strength, and use them as a balance and guarantee against the encroachments of the nobles. Henry was the man fitted both by circumstances and nature to curb the power of feudalism, and to make sure for the future the framework of government.

The great wealth and power which his marriage with Eleanor had brought him, his sovereignty over all the Western half of France, gave him a position such as no English king had had before him. And in his strangely mingled nature he had the gifts necessary for his situation; he had a brain capable of conceiving great plans, and an energetic will which would not flinch in carrying them out. Besides, he had the mind of a lawyer, a great fondness for business, and an inborn love of method and order.

His first work was to straighten the confusion created during Stephen's reign, and to carry out the peace of Wallingford. The hated mercenary troops from Flanders and elsewhere were driven out of the country, and disappeared like a dream. Henry ordered all the castles which had been built in Stephen's reign to be destroyed, except a few which he kept in his own or in trusted hands. The few barons who tried to resist this measure were brought to submission by arms. The people rejoiced greatly to see these strongholds of tyranny demolished. Those estates of the crown which Stephen had heedlessly given away to his supporters Henry took back because the wealth of the crown was diminished by the loss of them. The Scots and Welsh had to do homage. Malcolm IV., king of Scots, consented to exchange the three northern counties for the earldom of Huntingdon, and thus the northern boundaries of England were fixed at last. Against the Welsh Henry led an expedition in person, and brought them to submission. And he put an end to a cause of confusion which had existed ever since ancient Anglo-Saxon times by striking a uniform coinage for the whole kingdom.

His first reforms.

1157.

All this was a good beginning, and the English people began to have great hopes of their new king, when they saw his prudence and his zeal for justice. But in Henry's brain there was already planned a wider task than this: to place the government of England on such a sure foundation that no future commotions should shake it down; to organise that government itself; and to make it supreme both in Church and State.

Now in those days, when representative government and free parliaments were yet unborn, secular government was a thing which could be thought of only under one form, the power of the king. The teaching of the Church to some extent favoured this power. To some extent, I say; for though the Church looked upon kings as divinely ordained for the maintenance of order, she always insisted on the duties of kings to their subjects; and besides, there were certain levelling doctrines belonging to the Church, which, though kept rather in the background just then, did make themselves heard from time to time. An influence far more powerful in promoting ideas of kingly authority was the study of Roman law, which had been revived in Europe during the twelfth century, and had come to Oxford University in the reign of Stephen.

The Royal power.

We must pause a moment to consider what is meant by the revival of the study of Roman law. The Romans, great as they had been as conquerors, had shown themselves even greater as governors, and their law was the greatest and most lasting monument of their strength. That law is still studied by those who wish to master the principles on which law ought to be composed, and the *Corpus Juris*, or body of law drawn up into a code under the Emperor Justinian in 529, has been the model not only of the laws of many European nations, but even of some of the newest States of America. And even where, as in England, its decrees have not been copied, their influence has been enormous. We may say, speaking roughly, that in the twelfth century people began to think; that is to say, thought or what is called *theory* began to exercise a marked influence on the course of affairs. A hunger of the mind had been awakened, and for this hunger there was no food so grateful as the study of Roman law. For this law was a very different

Roman law.

thing to the rude codes of the Teutons; it was the work of some of the greatest minds of the past; it was written in a spirit of clear, wide common sense, and was expressed with force and elegance. For these qualities alone it was fascinating to the awakening minds of the twelfth century, and it became the object of ardent study. Moreover, as the shadow of the Roman Empire had not yet passed away from Europe, the written laws of that empire were not looked upon as dead laws; those who studied them venerated them as something still binding. And though the law of England is much freer from this Roman influence than the law of any other European state, it is nevertheless true that the writings of English lawyers have been strongly influenced by the study of the Corpus Juris.

What has now to be pointed out is the favour which the study of Roman law gave to the doctrine of the sovereign right of kings. The Roman code was compiled at a time when the authority of the Emperor was at its height, and the checks which feudal customs put on the power of kings were unknown; consequently, this law was favourable to despotism, and to the spread of the notion that a king was a sort of little god upon earth, whose will no one had any right to gainsay. Thus there was at hand an influence, a prevailing opinion, to back Henry up in asserting his royal authority, and in trying to establish a system of settled justice and legal order.

What is the chief business of government? A little thought will show that it falls mainly under two heads; keeping order and paying the expenses of order. We should say now-a-days, that government exists for the sake of public order and benefit, and that taxation is needful only in order to pay the costs of order. *The ends of government.* This, of course, was not exactly the view of a king of the twelfth century. To him the chief business of government did not appear to be in the keeping of public order, but in the working of that business in a manner profitable to himself. This was his chief concern, to get as much money as he could. If he bestowed any thought on the keeping of order, as a business worthy of care in itself, he must have been a very good king for the twelfth century. And therefore we may say that Henry II. was on the whole a very good king, though he was anything but a good man. Nevertheless we must bear in mind that in his time order existed for the sake of revenue, and not revenue for the sake of order. But both these branches of government were reformed and organised by Henry, and placed on such a sound footing that by the end of his reign a settled system of finance and a uniform system of justice existed already; in fact, the outline of an orderly modern State was complete. A government by the king and his ministers was established, and guaranteed, as we shall afterwards see, by the development of popular institutions and a national army.

All seemed to go well with Henry; the mercenaries were cleared out, the castles destroyed, he was the most prosperous sovereign in Europe, and no one seemed in a better position for carrying out reforms in the law and administration of his country. But unfortunately, while he was trying to fix the framework of public justice on a better foundation than before, he came into collision with the Church.

Henry's collision with the Church.

I have already tried to sketch the position of the Church in the middle ages, and have related the contest between William Rufus and Anselm, which gave to the world a picture of saintly heroism struggling with brutal violence. Every such picture added to the Church's gallery was an additional strength to her, endearing her more and more to the hearts of mankind. In the days of Anselm, a revival of religious feeling had taken place, which had shown itself most markedly in the Crusades and in the founding of the Cistercian order of monks, events which led to a great increase of the power of the Popes and the influence of the Church. Of the Crusades I shall speak afterwards. The Cistercian order was founded by pious men who desired to revive the strictness of monastic rule, and find a higher saintliness through a more rigid asceticism. The order spread rapidly, and during the troubled reign of Stephen, when monasteries were the only havens for peace-loving people, between thirty and forty Cistercian abbeys were built in different parts of England, among them such noble foundations as Fountains, Tintern, and Furness. We are told that more monasteries were built in Stephen's reign than during the last hundred years. 'As the barons built castles,' says

Growth of Monasticism. The Cistercians.

William of Newburgh, 'so did the heavenly King build monasteries, to fight against spiritual wickedness.'

When Henry II. came to the crown, the grave had just closed over the greatest of the Cistercians, the greatest monk of the age, the man in whom monkhood had produced its perfect and crowning flower, St. Bernard of Clairvaux. St. Bernard: This man, a frail worn-out ascetic, had been the master-spirit of Europe during the whole of Stephen's reign. Some wonderful influence dwelt in him, which made all men bow before him. For in him was incarnate the best and highest spirit of monasticism; he was the perfect type and image of the man who has died to self, died to nature even, that he may become the servant of God and man. Whatever faults St. Bernard had, (and we can see in him most of the great faults of monkhood,) he had this reality of self-devotion, and by this he ruled the minds of men. He showed them self-devotion in a form which they could understand and reverence. And because he was the man who perfectly fulfilled the best ideal of his time, his influence was unbounded. 'By him the sorrowful were comforted, those in trouble helped, the sick healed, the poor relieved. He made himself as much the servant of all as if he were son to the whole world; yet he took care of his own conscience in such freedom from outward things as if the keeping of his own heart were his only care.'

In England, during the struggle between Stephen and Matilda, the power of the Church, and of the Pope as head of the Church, had increased immensely. Both parties frequently sought the help of the Pope. The Pope gave his sanction to Stephen's coronation; *Growth of Papal and Clerical power.* and from the Pope the Earl of Gloucester got leave to break his oath to Stephen. The Pope was induced to forbid the crowning of Eustace, the son of Stephen. Thus the Pope's right to interfere in the affairs of the nation became a settled thing. In a quarrel which Stephen had with the Pope, Stephen was worsted, for the Pope laid the first interdict upon England, and Stephen was only too glad to submit, that he might have it taken off. Meanwhile the clergy, though obliged to take sides with either Stephen or Matilda, tried to hold aloof as much as they could. They were the only men of peace, the only men whom the nation trusted.

When Stephen in 1139 ventured to arrest the Bishops of Salisbury and Lincoln for treason to himself, though the character of these bishops was by no means high, public feeling was entirely against him for this outrage on sacred persons, and the clergy took advantage of the general indignation to call a council at Westminster (1142) and pass a decree that no laymen should lay violent hands on a priest or a monk under pain of excommunication. What was still more important, they succeeded in exempting all clerical persons from being tried for any offence whatever in secular courts of justice; the Church alone was to have the right to judge her own sons. This must have been carried in Stephen's reign; at least King Henry declared that it had not been the custom in his grandfather's reign, and the clergy did not contradict him;[1] though it is difficult to understand this, as by William the Conqueror's law all church causes had been taken out of the lay courts into the separate courts of the Church.

'Benefit of clergy.'

But when it came to the knowledge of King Henry that owing to this freedom of the clergy from secular judgment, thefts, murders, and other crimes were done by wicked priests almost with impunity, because the bishops were too lazy to visit them with due punishment, he was very angry. He was told that more than a hundred murders had been committed by clergy during his reign; and some cases which came under his own notice, showing the inadequacy of the ecclesiastical courts to punish offences, roused a more personal feeling, and made him determined to put an end to this abuse of privilege on the part of the clergy.

Henry opposed to it.

Perhaps to the successful young king of England, who was lord of the goodliest half of France, who had defied the king of France, and received the homage of the kings of Scotland and Wales, it seemed a light thing to try his strength against the Church. If so, he had not reckoned the forces which were against him. Let us try to understand what the feelings of common men towards the

Influence of the Church.

[1] Some indeed denied that Henry's customs had ever been customs at all, as Fitz-Stephen, 'Vita Becket,' p. 216, and Becket himself, according to Benedict of Peterborough, though never in his letters; but the ground ordinarily taken by the clergy was to rest their claim for immunity not on custom, but on inherent right.

Church in the twelfth century were, by looking at her through their eyes. The Church was imposing enough in her outward splendour, her wealth and lands, her cathedrals and monasteries, her gorgeous hierarchy, her universal dominion. But all these temporal thrones, dominations, princedoms, powers, were only the vanguard of the great army of the Church; in the rear was the glorious company of apostles, prophets and martyrs, the whole hierarchy of heaven, stretching upwards to the throne of God himself; and this unseen host (it was believed) was constantly interfering in human affairs, smiting the evil-doers, helping the humble and the poor. And this great Church, so vast and awful as a whole, was not too far off to be loved. If the Father was unapproachable in his infinity, if the Son was too dreadful when thought of as the coming Judge, the mild-hearted mother of God was easy to be entreated. Her lovely image kept alive in the people's mind the idea of Divine goodness and mercy. Moreover the Church was the sympathising companion of every man and woman from the cradle to the grave. Her magic tokens were needful at every crisis of life, to bless the infant, to hallow the marriage, to help the passing soul through the gates of death, to give the corpse quiet rest in the grave. Though even in those days there were some who doubted, and some who mocked her spells, none dared to go entirely without them. Even amusements were blessed by the Church; she opened her sacred buildings to Christmas shows and religious plays. Every monastery was a school, a dispensary, a hospital, a hostelry. The legends of the Church were the one imaginative influence which the poor of the middle ages knew; for the old legends of heathendom had been taken up by the Church, and woven into her own tales.

Besides, however many bad priests there might be in the Church, the ideal of what a priest ought to be was ever present in the middle ages, and was from time to time more or less realised in some man who, like St. Anselm or St. Bernard, looked on himself as not born for himself, but for all those who needed his help; whose very stole signified the yoke of Christ, and who had put off the secular man that he might put on Christ;[1] and such an ideal

The true priest.

[1] See FitzStephen, 'Vita Becket,' pp. 203, 206.

commanded the allegiance of all hearts. And the common people had good reason to be grateful to the Church. In the wars between Stephen and Matilda, when bands of cruel mercenaries were scouring the country, where could the poor villagers with their wives and children and their little bits of furniture take refuge, except in the neighbouring church? How often had they sat cowering in the sacred place, blessing the saint who had provided their only refuge, until the band of bloody men had passed away! And though there were among the nobles of that day some men so abandoned that they paid no respect even to churches and monasteries, had not the judgment of God been shown in terrible ways upon these very men? Again, who was it but the Legate of our Lord the Pope who had made David, King of Scots, promise that he and his barons would leave off their horrid habit of killing women and children and defenceless persons on their raids into England? And had not the clergy in council at London, in Stephen's reign, ordained that the plough and the husbandman in the fields should enjoy the same peace as if they were in the churchyard? Who but the Church cared to protect the poor and the defenceless?

What had the king to set against this? The king of the twelfth century was chiefly known to his subjects as a hard exactor of money. If any reverence attached to his office, it was chiefly because the Church had anointed him, and he was in some sort the servant of the Church. It was his part to do the coarse work which the Church's hands were too fine to touch. The old tribal feeling of respect for the head of the race was dead long ago; the Englishman felt no national enthusiasm for his Norman or Angevin[1] king. The feeling of feudal attachment and faithfulness existed only among those who were personally bound to the king; but the enthusiasm, the loyalty of the masses, turned towards the Church. The men of the twelfth century were quite able to separate the Church as an institution from the clergy as individuals. They were quite aware of the worldliness, greed, and uncleanness of priests; no more bitter things were ever said

The King's position.

---

[1] Henry was an Angevin, being descended by his father from the Counts of Anjou.

against the clergy than were said (and sung) in the twelfth century: but though men found fault with the clergy, they were quite satisfied with the Church as she existed in idea; it had not occurred to any but a very few thinkers that there was anything wrong in the programme which the Church put forth, any mistake in her claim to enforce on the world the law of God. 'The kingdom of God is within you' is a truth that mankind has been slow to learn.

Henry had not reckoned on these strong tendrils of affection and gratitude which held together the fabric of the Church's power. Still less had he reckoned on finding a stout champion of the Church in Thomas Becket, Archbishop of Canterbury, whose history must now be told.

DATES.

William Rufus	1089
Revolt of Mowbray, earl of Northumberland	1095
Henry I.	1100
Rebellion of Robert Belesme	1102
Henry wins Normandy from his brother Robert	1106
Henry's only son drowned	1120
Stephen	1135
David, king of Scots, who had invaded England on behalf of his niece Matilda, defeated in the Battle of the Standard	1138
Peace of Wallingford	1153
Henry II.	1154

CHAPTER XII.

THOMAS BECKET was the son of some respectable citizens of London, of Norman race. It was possible even then to rise from the humble rank of a citizen to the high position of an archbishop; for even in those aristocratic times the Church could not wholly forswear the essentially democratic nature of Christianity; and when in later years Thomas the Archbishop was taunted with his lowly origin, he answered in quite a republican spirit: 'I had rather be one made noble by a noble mind, than a degenerate slip of an ancient house.' Becket received a good education, and studied for some time in Paris. His father had influen-

Thomas Becket.

tial friends, through whose introduction the young man, after serving some time as clerk to the sheriff of London, was received into the household of Theobald, Archbishop of Canterbury in Stephen's reign.

Becket was then a tall handsome young man of very pleasing manners, an excellent companion, and a first-rate man of business. He was eager to get on in the world, and the natural force of his character gave him ascendancy in every society in which he moved. He used his opportunities whilst in the Archbishop's household to make progress in his literary studies, in which he became fairly accomplished. He spent a year at Bologna, and a shorter time at Auxerre, in the study of law, the sure path of advancement for a churchman. He rose in the Archbishop's favour, was ordained a deacon by him, and preferment flowed in upon him. Before he was ordained he appears to have held two livings and two prebendaries, and shortly afterwards he was made Archdeacon of Canterbury, the highest dignity in the English Church after the Bishops and Abbots. *Pluralism* (the holding more than one living at once) had indeed been distinctly condemned by canons, with which Becket must have been familiar, but though he was afterwards the stout champion of the Church's privileges, he never aspired to the office of an ecclesiastical reformer.

His next step on the ladder of advancement was the Chancellorship of England. The Chancellor was the second officer in dignity after the king (the Justiciar being the first); he kept the king's seal, was present at all the royal councils, and had the charge of all the vacant bishoprics and abbacies. It was the Archbishop himself who recommended Becket to Henry II. He had employed him already in more than one difficult mission to Rome, and proved his skill in conducting delicate matters, and he thought that Becket would not only be a useful servant to the king, but a useful friend to the Church, constantly at the king's side.

Made Chancellor. 1155.

Such an accomplished man as Becket, a man of superior education and manners, lively and witty in conversation, extremely skilful in business, and at the same time excelling in all manly exercises, such as hunting and falconry, was a companion just suited for the clever young king. They soon became great friends; the king delighted in Becket, and Becket threw himself with zeal into the king's service. One biographer claims for Becket a large share of the useful measures which were taken for the peace of the kingdom, such as the banishment of the mercenaries, and the destruction of the castles. 'Thus by the diligence and advice of the Chancellor,' says Fitz-Stephen, 'the clergy and barons helping, the noble realm of England begins to thrive as with a new spring; holy Church is honoured; the vacant bishoprics or abbacies are given to honest priests without simony; the king thrives in all his affairs; the realm of England waxes rich; plenty empties on it her full horn; the hills are tilled, the dales abound with corn, the pastures with herds, the folds with sheep.'

The Chancellor kept a splendid house, to which the noblest barons of England were proud to send their sons to be educated, as the custom of that time was for noble youths. The table was open to all frequenters of the king's court; the floors were daily strewn with fresh straw or hay in winter, with fresh rushes or leaves in summer, so that the multitude of knights, for whom there were not benches enough to sit upon, might not dirty their fine clothes by sitting on the ground. A company of invited nobles dined every day with the Chancellor. Often the king himself would call in a friendly way; sometimes he would drink a cup of wine, sometimes he would leap over the table, sit down, and eat. When serious business was over, the king and the chancellor used to play together like two boys. There never were two greater friends in Christian times, says the chronicler. And another says that the Chancellor's will was law throughout all the king's dominions.

The king placed his own son in Becket's household, and Becket was his envoy to Paris in 1158 when he desired the hand of the king of France's daughter for this son. Becket astonished the capital of France by the magnificence of his train, his carriages, horses, dogs, birds, and apes, his splendid plate and furniture. 'What must the king of England be,' cried the Frenchmen, 'if his Chancellor is so rich!' Not long after, the king of England was at war with the king of France. Becket brought to France a chosen force of 700 knights out of his own household. He appeared in arms, took three formidable castles, and unhorsed a French knight in single combat.

When after the death of Archbishop Theobald in 1162, Henry sent a mandate to the monks of Canterbury, requiring them to elect Becket for their archbishop, Becket was chiefly known as a brilliant courtier, warrior, and statesman. It was true his liberality to the poor had been noted; and it was known that he used to submit himself to private floggings for the good of his soul. His moral character was free from blame; nevertheless the Church did not expect to find a saint in him, and there were some murmurs against his appointment. Foliot, Bishop of London, said afterwards that it was an unheard-of thing that one who to-day was a steward of the court, should to-morrow be a steward of the Church, and from dogs and falcons and courtly games should pass to the altar and administer the spiritual things of the whole realm. Moreover, no one expected to find a strong Churchman in the man who had advised the king to tax the clergy for the war of Toulouse in 1159.

Archbishop of Canterbury. 1162.

Without doubt the king's idea was that with Becket as Archbishop, both Church and State would be governed by his will. On the other hand, Becket, it was said, had prophesied that if ever he were made Archbishop, discord would arise between him and the king. In the middle ages, Church and State were divided under two separate heads. The king was the head of the State; the Pope of the Church. Becket, as Chancellor, not yet in priest's orders, had been the king's servant; as Archbishop of Canterbury he became the Pope's servant. Though scarcely a religious man, he was an honest man; he had served the king to the best of his power; he resolved to be equally faithful in his new service. His biographer, Grim, represents him as reasoning thus with himself: 'Thus far I have lived for the world, I have striven for earthly things; now I have reached the summit of my desire, and shall I seek to rise higher? Nay, this height which I have gained will drag me down to hell, unless I redeem the time, while the patience of God allows me to repent. If I do not care for my own salvation, let me at least beware that I be not a cause of ruin to others with myself. Let me listen to the

Mediæval theory of Church and State.

voice which says, "Whoso will come after me must deny himself, and take up his cross, and follow me; for what shall it profit a man, if he gain the whole world, but lose his own soul?" Therefore let my light shine before men, that those committed to my care may profit by me.'

This was Becket's attitude of mind; he had sufficient greatness of soul to respond to what seemed a nobler calling than the king's service, and to embrace it at all risks; but his conceptions of that higher service were influenced by his narrow intellect and overbearing character. The change which had come over his spirit was soon apparent outwardly. He now aspired to be a saint, and in all the outward fashions of saintship he was soon perfect. He limited his diet, he shortened his hours of sleep, he was constant in prayer and reading, admirable in groans and tears. He was regularly flogged by his chaplain three or four times a day, and wore a hair shirt next his skin, which he only changed once in forty days, and which was a continual torment to him from the vermin with which it swarmed. The innate vulgarity of his idea of saintship is shown in this last detail; St. Bernard, that perfect model of monkhood, had said that dirt was a sign either of carelessness or of spiritual vanity. Every evening he privately washed the feet of thirteen beggars. He threw a veil of concealment over his rigidity, for over his hair shirt he wore costly garments, and his table was still splendid and abundant. He now passed a large part of his time in the cloister, sitting with the monks and reading some useful book; he visited the sick monks and supplied their needs. He was more careful in the administration of justice, scorning all bribes (an unusual thing even in an ecclesiastical judge at that day), and paying no respect to persons. His contemporaries thought it a piece of truly saintly liberality that he gave a tenth of his income to the poor. He at once took a decided attitude as a protector of the rights of the Church, and tried to reclaim with a strong hand all possessions which had been unrightfully alienated from the Church in the time of his predecessors. The pleasing manners, the tact which had hitherto secured him success in life, were thrown to the winds; perhaps it was not without a sense of relief that he felt he might now, in the cause of God, give full swing to a naturally overbearing will. He did not hesitate to take away churches from priests who were careless in their office, even when they were members of the king's court; and thus he raised up for himself a host of enemies, who were not slow to warn the king that his royal authority was in danger from this overbearing priest.

Becket himself speedily made known his change of mind to the king by resigning into his hands the office of Chancellor. This was a plain declaration that he meant to be the servant of the Church only. From this time he did not hesitate openly to oppose the king when the king's policy was in any way adverse to the interests of the Church. On one occasion, he resisted an unjust tax which the king was about to lay on church and other property, whereby he gained no little popularity, though he lost ground with the king.

Becket resigns the chancellorship

The king soon became aware that the archbishop was another man than the chancellor, and that he had been deceived in his hope of reigning over the Church through Becket. But he did not give up the plan he had long entertained, of bringing the clergy under the jurisdiction of his courts. The precedent to which he appealed (for to propose anything quite new in those days would have been to shock everybody) was the state of things which he asserted had existed in his grandfather's time. But he forgot that (as a chronicler says) 'the strength of the Church had grown since then.' Even Becket's biographers give the king credit for a sincere zeal for justice. But his natural self-will was rendered more violent by success, and he was as little disposed as Becket to carry on the controversy in a mild and conciliatory spirit. He may well have said then what he said six years later: 'I, who can take two strong castles every day, cannot I crush one priest who chooses to resist me?'

In this spirit he summoned a great council at Westminster in 1163. To this assembly he complained that the peace of his kingdom was disturbed by the crimes of the clergy, and that these criminals escaped punishment through the privilege of their order. He earnestly requested the bishops that they would allow what had been the custom in the days of his grandfather, that clerks convicted of crime, after being degraded, should then be subjected to the punishment of his court like laymen.

Council of Westminster

Great was the discussion on this proposal among the assembled bishops. Some were of opinion that it was just that clerks after degradation should receive condign punishment from the secular arm. But the Archbishop of Canterbury, taking his stand on the canons of the Church, declared that a double punishment was iniquitous; those who had been degraded once by the Church should not receive a second punishment from the secular arm. By these arguments he overcame the hesitation of the bishops, and as their spokesman he made answer to the king: 'Holy Church has her own laws, given her by the apostles and their successors, and you, O king, have no right to ask of us any new custom, nor we to grant.' 'I do not ask anything new,' said the king, 'but only what was observed in the time of my predecessors, by holier archbishops than you, who made no difficulty about it.' The Archbishop answered: 'If former kings presumed to introduce any customs contrary to the canons of the Church, and if these customs were observed for a time out of fear of those kings, they ought not to be called customs, but abuses. If the holy bishops of that time were silent, they must answer for it; their authority has no influence over us, that we should allow anything contrary to God and our order and our duty to be done in the Church divinely committed to us.' He therefore refused, and through his influence the other bishops refused with him to promise anything without the reservation of 'saving our order.' The king was furious, and swore 'By God's eyes, there shall be no mention of your order;' but he was obliged to dismiss his council without effecting his purpose, and he left London in anger.

Becket opposes the King.

He then had a private interview with Becket in a field outside Northampton. He reminded him of all the benefits he had conferred upon him, and offered to exalt him yet more highly if he would do his will. The archbishop declared his gratitude and devotion to the king, but protested that he was bound by allegiance to a higher Lord, to whom they must both answer at the great day of judgment. The king grew angry and cried, 'I won't be preached at by you. Were you not the son of one of my clowns?' 'It is true,' replied the archbishop, 'I am not descended from ancient kings, but neither was the blessed Peter, to whom were given the keys of the kingdom of heaven.' 'True,' said the king, 'but *he* died for his Lord.' 'And I too will die for my Lord,' answered Becket, 'when the time shall come.'

After this, the king tried to gain over the bishops, and was more successful with them; he dealt with them singly, and promised that he would require of them nothing to the prejudice of their order. Thus the archbishop was isolated from his natural allies. Still his resolution abode unshaken, until a certain abbot, Philip of l'Aumône, along with the Count of Vendôme, was sent to him, bearing letters from the Pope and cardinals, entreating him to submit to the king's will. They reminded him of the perilous position of the Church, which was again divided at that time between two rival Popes, and counselled him to bend before the present storm, lest by his resistance he should bring a worse storm upon the Church; for the Pope's constant fear was lest his rival, Octavian, the Pope of the German emperor, should find a supporter in the king of England. The envoys added that the king had solemnly promised them that he would never require of the archbishop anything contrary to his duty or his will; they assured him that his consent was desired only as a matter of form, that the king might not appear dishonoured by his refusal, and that if he would give in now, no further mention would ever be made of the customs. Swayed by the persuasions of this abbot, and still more by the apparent mandate of the Pope, Becket at last gave way; he went to the king, and offered him the long-sought promise. But now the king declared that, as the archbishop's refusal had been public, his consent must also be made in public for the king's honour.

In 1164 a great council met at Clarendon, and a list of the customs for which the king demanded the assent of the bishops, was read aloud; these were the famous *Constitutions of Clarendon*. The aim of these Constitutions was to strike a death-blow at the existence of the Church as an independent State within the State. Journeys to Rome without special leave from the king were forbidden, in order that appeals to the Pope might be prevented; the king was henceforth to be the supreme appeal. 'Benefit of clergy' was put an end to, as the king's court was to have jurisdiction over the clergy in all cases which it should deem to belong to its jurisdiction. The king's tenants-in-chief were not to be excommunicated without his leave. Archbishops and bishops, as they held their lands in barony, must pay all services and payments required of other tenants-in-chief. The revenues of vacant sees were to be in the king's hands, and an end was put to the Pope's power to call the king or his barons to right.

Most Englishmen are agreed now that no privilege of holy orders or anything else should exempt a man from the laws of his country; and that the Sovereign, and not the Pope, should be the supreme authority in England. Why then did the twelfth century condemn the Constitutions of Clarendon with one voice? Not one of the chroniclers of the time defends them; those who are most dispassionate make excuses for the king, and say he was justly incensed by the crimes of the clergy; they lay the blame on the bishops, for not being strict enough in the punishment of guilty clerks, but they consider that the king's zeal went beyond bounds. None of the bishops who afterwards sided with the king against Becket, dares to defend the Constitutions; Becket's most bitter enemy, Foliot, Bishop of London,[1] says that they were contrary to the liberty of the Church and faithfulness to our lord the Pope.

<small>Why condemned by the age.</small>

There are certain facts to which we must turn for an explanation. First, the general fact, (already dealt with at length) that the twelfth century was firm in its belief in the Church's right to rule, and its trust in the Church's will to use that rule for good. Then, it seems probable, as far as we can make out, that the Church courts were juster and more merciful than the king's. Henry's great judicial reforms had not yet been carried out, and from what we know of royal courts of justice in the twelfth century, they seem to have been venal, tardy, and cruel beyond all belief. The charges of venality and tardiness were brought against the Church courts also; but the horrible mutilations which were inflicted in the royal courts were unknown to those of the Church. These punishments were not only cruel, but disgusting and degrading. And since it was not only offending clerks, but those who committed any offences against clerks, who were tried by the Church, and thus escaped mutilation,

[1] Ep. 194.

it is no wonder that the Church courts were popular. Moreover, the Church had taken under her jurisdiction many cases of which the civil law took no cognizance, especially cases of personal trusts, contracts, and the execution of wills; and in doing so she had taken under her protection the classes least able to protect themselves, widows, orphans and the poor. The sympathy of the oppressed was always with the Church. And the Constitutions of Clarendon struck a blow at the greatest hope of the serf by their last article, which ruled that the sons of villeins should not be ordained without the consent of their lords.

When these Constitutions were read aloud before the Archbishop at Clarendon, he found that his promise involved *Becket is overcome.* much more than the abbot of l'Aumône had led him to expect, and he refused to give his assent. The king stormed, the bishops trembled, the nobles entreated with tears, but for a long while the archbishop was inflexible. At length he was overcome by entreaties and assurances that the consent required was only formal. He promised, and made the other bishops promise also. It is not wonderful that at the beginning of this struggle Becket should have shown himself weak and wavering. The feeling of chivalrous feudal devotion to the king his lord had been very strong in him; he could not get rid of it in a moment. He was as yet new to his part. His conduct at Clarendon was looked upon both by himself and his friends as a sad fall; but from that fall he *But repents.* rose stronger than before, and more determined not to keep the promise he had made. He suspended himself from saying mass until he should receive the Pope's absolution for what he had done. He tried to leave the kingdom, in direct violation of the Constitutions of Clarendon, but he was driven back by contrary winds.

A struggle now went on between the king and the archbishop, the one trying to carry out the Constitutions, and bring clerks to judgment in secular courts, the other to resist them. The king accused the archbishop of sheltering thieves and murderers; the archbishop accused the king of conspiring against the liberties of the Church. The question had another complication, that the fees and fines of courts of justice were an important source of revenue, and either party could accuse the other of acting from greed of money.

The king, finding he could not bend the archbishop, resolved to crush him. He was ordered to appear before a great council, held at Northampton in October, 1164, to answer various charges brought against him. The heaviest was that he was called to give account of the revenues of vacant sees and abbeys which had passed through his hands while he was Chancellor. The council lasted a week, and the archbishop delayed his final answer until the last day. Some advised him to throw himself wholly upon the king's mercy; others exhorted him to stand firm, as he could not lawfully be called to account for the chancellorship, since he had received a quittance of all claims on his election to the primacy. Some of the bishops advised him to resign his see. To this his answer was: 'I received the archbishopric, not that I might give it up, but that I might give up myself for it.' It was hinted to him that the king had the darkest designs against him, if he did not submit; that he would be thrown into prison, and his eyes put out. He fell ill from anxiety of mind; but on the last day of the council he summoned all his strength, and rode to the king's castle. Crowds of the common people met him on the way, weeping, and kneeling to ask his blessing; for it was rumoured on all sides that he was to be slain that day. He rode into the courtyard of the castle, and heard the gates locked behind him; dismounting, he passed through the crowd of barons and knights, and taking in his hands the pastoral crosier, he entered the hall. The Bishop of London, looking on the crosier as a sign of battle, tried to snatch it from him, and an unseemly struggle followed, in which Becket came off the better. 'You had better put up your sword,' said the Archbishop of York, 'the king's is sharper than yours.' Becket answered: 'The king's sword pierces the flesh, but my cross strikes the soul; yet God forbid that I should bring it against the king as a sword, for the cross brings peace.'

Becket sat in the great hall and waited, attended only by one or two of his most faithful followers, while the bishops went into an inner room where the king was with his familiars. Messengers went to and fro, angry voices were heard, and Becket was told that the king was thinking of putting him to death. But Becket remained unmoved all day. He refused to submit to the judgment of the king's court; he denied the right of the secular power to judge him, its father and lord, and he appealed to Rome. The bishops abandoned his cause and appealed against him to Rome; because after having made them promise at Clarendon to obey the Constitutions, he now forbade them to observe them. The king and his nobles passed sentence upon him, that he should be imprisoned for refusing to submit to the judgment of the court, and the Earl of Leicester was sent to read the sentence to him. The earl began to read, but the archbishop refused to hear, since he had appealed to Rome. 'How can you refuse the judgment of the king's court?' said the earl; 'you are the king's man; you hold your farms and castles and estates of him in fee and barony.' 'I hold nothing in fee and barony,' cried the archbishop, 'but whatever the Church holds, she holds in perpetual freedom, as a free gift, free from all claim and service to worldly princes.'

Becket condemned.

The earl returned to the king; the archbishop arose, and carrying his cross passed out of the hall. 'As the athlete of God went out of the council of the malicious,' says a biographer, 'curses and taunts arose on all sides, many crying, "See, the traitor is going."' Becket's proud temper flashed out in indignant words: 'If it were lawful, and I were a knight, I would prove thee a liar with my own hand,' he said to one of those who insulted him, and at another he hurled foul names. Some threw straws at him, and a noise arose as if the whole city were on fire. The archbishop would scarcely have got out, but that the king who, however passionate and violent he might be, was too shrewd to have really plotted Becket's death, sent orders that he was to be let out unhindered; and afterwards issued a proclamation that no one was to lay violent hands upon him. The keys of the castle were found hanging near the door by the archbishop's attendants, and Becket rode forth. He was again followed by an admiring crowd, and had to stretch his hands to right and to left to bless the people. He returned to the monastery where he was lodging, and finding that scarcely any of his followers were left, the rest having fled through fear, he ordered the refectory table to be filled with poor folk. He sat down among them, and was cheerful and affable. He exhorted his followers to patience and silence from bitter words, saying, 'It is the part of a higher mind to bear such things; of a lower one to do them.'

That night, in the midst of a storm of wind and rain, the archbishop left Northampton secretly, attended by only two monks and one servant, and rode northward towards Lincoln. He remained three days concealed in a hermitage in the fens; then by a roundabout route he made his way to the south coast, and escaping the vigilant watch which the king had set at all the seaports, he crossed over to the Continent.

Flight of Becket.

Pope Alexander III. was then at Sens, an exile from Rome, where he had been unable to abide in consequence of the successes of the emperor Frederick I., and of the antipope Paschal III. Alexander was bound to support Becket, the defender of the privileges of the Church; but he was in a very difficult position. It was essential to his cause to have the support of the powerful king of England; he dared not offend Henry, lest he should go over to the anti-pope. Alexander was a politician and not a hero; he was not prepared to defy all risks for the cause of the Church; hence his conduct towards Becket was pitiably wavering. He helped him as much as he dared; but whenever he was hard pressed he sacrificed him. He would have been thankful if Becket would have been quiet, and ceased talking of his wrongs. But Becket was not quiet an instant; from his retreat in France he never ceased to press his cause in a stream of indignant and eloquent letters. His one great aim is that the Pope should bring Henry to reason by holding over his head the threat of excommunication. All the impetuosity and violence of Becket's character are poured forth in these letters. He lectures the king of France, the empress-mother, the Pope and the cardinals, on their duty. 'Draw the sword of God and St. Peter, avenge the wrongs of Christ and his people, let your eye spare no one; this is the way to follow the footsteps of Christ.' He tells them that attempts to cajole a man like Henry are useless; he must be driven, not led. When, at Henry's urgency, the Pope for a while suspends Becket's power of excommunicating, he is heartbroken. He writes to the Pope: 'You ask me to have patience for a little while. You do not see, father, how disastrous to the Church is this little while, how injurious to your good name. For this little while the king uses the revenues of vacant sees and abbeys for his own abuses, and suffers no pastors to be ordained to them. For this little while he and the other persecutors of the Church do exactly as they like. .... Soon we shall stand before the judgment-seat of Christ, by whose majesty and awful judgment I adjure you as my father and lord, and as supreme judge on earth, that you do justice to his Church and to me, concerning those who seek her soul to destroy it.'

But if there was little of saintly patience in Becket's conduct, the king's was conspicuous for violence and trickery. *The king's reprisals.* When he heard that Becket had been received with the greatest favour by the Pope at Sens, while the Constitutions of Clarendon were condemned, and his envoys dismissed without success, he was furious, and ordered that Becket's property and the revenues of his see should be confiscated, and that every man, woman, and child of his kindred should be stripped of all they possessed, and driven out of the kingdom, having first been made to swear that they would go to the archbishop and show him the spectacle of their misery. This measure of Henry's was barbarous in more ways than one; it was a return to the principle of the Clan-system which made all the members of a family responsible for the act of one. It was opposed to all the principles of the Church, which sought to establish a wider brotherhood along with individual responsibility; and it was keenly felt by Becket. He took care to make use of it against the king, and it was one of the circumstances which greatly helped to make the king's side unpopular.

And there was a grandeur in Becket's position of which neither king nor pope could boast. He felt that he was suffering in his own person for the whole Church. He always prominently brought forward his own sufferings, but he never forgot that he was not fighting for himself alone. 'The cause between the king and me,' he writes to the Roman cardinals, 'is really your cause; the health of the whole Church is involved.' To the English bishops who had deserted him he writes: 'Ye who persecute me, who forsake me, it is for you I suffer. .... By the mercy of God the confusion of the Church shall not be extorted from me.' The ennobling thought that by his struggles and sufferings he was averting evils from posterity was ever in his mind. 'The outcome of this controversy will be felt to all future times.' He had entire confidence in the justice of his cause. 'Truth may halt and be bound, but cannot be conquered.' And because he had this faith in his own cause he felt the ground firm under his feet, he was always true to himself, always said the same thing, and scorned all temporising and dissimulation. He told the cardinals: 'The Church is not to be ruled by trickery and cleverness, but by justice and truth, which deliver those that keep them from all danger.' To those who blamed him for want of tact and patience he wrote: 'The ship of the Church is shaken by a tempest; I hold the helm, and you call me to sleep!' And again: 'Ye say the times are evil, as if a good God did not dispose them, and as if those were not blessed who do judgment and justice at all times.'[1]

We ought not to look upon these words as mere high-sounding talk, uttered as they were by a man who was ready to seal them with his blood. Self-willed and proud as Becket undoubtedly was, he was faithful to the principles which he believed in; and it is by such faithfulness to principle in the midst of a corrupt society that the world has grown better.

It is not to our purpose to follow all the history of Becket's six years of exile. In 1166 he began active measures against the king of England by solemnly excommunicating some of the king's most trusted councillors. This drew forth letters of remonstrance from the bishops of his diocese, who had now made common cause with the king, and who feared that the same sentence was hanging over themselves. These letters are very clever, but they are quite without that honesty and singleness of purpose which marks the letters of Becket. They none of them dare to defend the Constitutions of Clarendon, but they make excuses for the king, saying that he was moved only by zeal for justice and desire for the suppression of crime. But they blame Becket's way of conducting his cause, his violence, his want of charity and fairness. The opinion of prudent Churchmen seems to have been that Becket ought never to have allowed a quarrel to

Becket excommunicates the king's friends.

---

[1] See Epistles 29, 123, 33, 78, 29, 130, and 153.

grow up between himself and the king; all trials of strength between the Church and the secular power were to be avoided. Foliot, bishop of London, the chief of Becket's opponents, in a long and wily letter says that there are some who maintain that the king ought to have jurisdiction over his prelates in certain cases, because as barons of his realm they owed him the military and other services due from the lands which they held of him; and further, that the sacred chrism with which the king was anointed gave him a kind of priestly character which they might reverence. Foliot does not commit himself as to whether this was his view, and in his earlier days he had been a stickler for benefit of clergy; but he speaks of it as an opinion which had a good deal to say for itself. But it was an opinion which was three centuries before its time, and it had been distinctly condemned by Becket at the council of Northampton.

Meanwhile the unfortunate Pope was between two batteries. Henry, dreading the sentence of excommunication upon himself, or of interdict upon his people, ceased not to send embassy after embassy to Rome, whither the Pope had returned in 1165, urging him to pay no heed to Becket, and backing up his request with substantial help much needed against the emperor Frederick, and gold freely scattered among the Roman cardinals. Becket, on the other hand, kept up an unceasing fire of letters, demanding judgment on the enemies of the Church, and his cause was warmly supported by the king of France, who found it an excellent opportunity for annoying his brother king of England. The Pope's only resource was to send commissioners to investigate the matter, and try to bring about a reconciliation. If the commissioners accomplished nothing, at least they gained time, and thus the Pope three times staved off the ban which Becket was preparing for Henry. But meanwhile the sympathy of Christendom was almost wholly in favour of Becket, and this temporising conduct of the Pope lost credit for Rome with all true lovers of the Church. The following passage from one of Becket's letters will serve both to explain his own view of the struggle and the general feeling of the time about it. In 1167, when Henry's envoys had succeeded in obtaining from the Pope a suspension of Becket's power of excommunicating, and a special exemption for some of his councillors, Becket wrote to one of his clerks:—

'If these things be true, beyond a doubt the Pope has suffocated and strangled not only our person, but himself and all the ecclesiastics of either kingdom, in fact the whole Church, as well the Gallican as the English. For what will not the other princes of the earth dare against the clergy through this abominable example? And to whom will they fly? How shall they trust the Roman church, which thus deserts and strips us, who are fighting for her even unto blood? . . . . And what is worse, other princes through this example will extort like privileges, whether the Church will or no, and thus all liberty of the Church will perish, and all episcopal power and jurisdiction, for there will be none who will be able to hinder or chastise the crimes of tyrants, whose whole intention is now to attack the Church of God and his servants.' (Ep. 90.)

The king of France and some of the French bishops wrote in the same strain to the Pope, and one plainspoken friend told him that the odour of his name was beginning to grow vile in Christendom. This pressure of opinion was not without effect. When the second papal commission returned to Rome in 1169 without having effected a reconciliation between Henry and Becket, and one of the commissioners declared that the king was so deceitful that he ought to be hateful to God and man, Becket was again allowed to excommunicate the king's councillors, and to threaten the kingdom with interdict; the letters publishing the interdict were actually written. Henry now prepared for the worst; he set a strict watch at all the seaports of England to prevent any letters of interdict from being brought in; and he ordered all his subjects to swear that they would not receive the letters or observe the interdict of the archbishop. But he could not induce his bishops to take this oath, nor could he prevent zealous churchmen from sending help in money to the archbishop.

In July 1170 he caused his eldest son Henry to be crowned by the Archbishop of York. As it was the special privilege of the archbishops of Canterbury to crown the kings of England, this was an invasion of the rights of the Church, most abhorrent to the feelings of that age. The Pope had written letters to forbid this violation of the rights of the see of Canterbury,

Coronation of the king's son.

but these letters were not allowed to arrive. He was now at last roused to threaten Henry with an interdict. A final commission was appointed, and Henry was glad to avail himself of it. His recent experience had shown him that a hand-to-hand struggle with the Church was impossible. An interdict was a dreadful thing, as it meant the suspension of all religious rites except the baptism of infants and the extreme unction for the dying; the church bells were hushed, the church doors closed, the dead buried without rites, the people deprived of the magic ceremonies without which life was dangerous. Even Henry dared not incur the odium of bringing this upon his kingdom. So peace was made at last between the king and archbishop, very suddenly, and not a word was said about the 'customs.' Becket and all those who had been exiled on his account were to return to England, and their property was to be restored to them. But the king laid himself under a suspicion of insincerity by refusing to Becket the customary kiss of peace, and Becket's own mind was full of foreboding when at last, after much delay, he set out for England. ' I return to my church,' he wrote, ' if not to reform and re-establish her, at least to die with her.'

The reconciliation. 1170.

The champion of the liberties of the Church was received with rapture on his return to his see; everywhere the people flocked in crowds to see him, crying 'Blessed is he that cometh in the name of the Lord'; his progress was like a triumph. But it was in no spirit of peace and forgiveness that the archbishop had come back; he was burning to avenge the insult done to his see. Letters had been sent to him from the Pope, by the hand of the lately-sent commission, suspending the Archbishop of York, and excommunicating the Bishops of London and Salisbury, for having taken part in the coronation of the younger Henry. It was probably intended that these letters should not be used if Henry could be brought to make peace; but Becket chose to interpret according to his own will a vague promise he had received from the king that his wrongs should be avenged, and before he crossed the channel he sent the letters on by a trusty messenger.

Becket's return.

On receipt of these letters the Archbishop of York and the Bishops of London and Salisbury were thrown into great consternation, and after much consultation they crossed the channel to see the king, who was then in Normandy. On hearing of what Becket had done, the king fell into a storm of rage. Some who were present stimulated his fury by telling him he would have no peace so long as Becket lived. 'A lazy and wretched set of men have I fostered in my kingdom,' cried the king, 'who bear no faith to their lord, but allow him to be shamefully mocked at by a low-born clerk!'

These words were taken to heart more seriously than the king intended by four knights of the king's household who were present. They at once set out for England, and arrived at Canterbury on December 29, 1170. They were admitted into Becket's apartment in the monastery of Christ Church, and rudely demanded that he should recall his sentences against the bishops, and make atonement to the king for his offences. Becket, whose conduct throughout was stately and proud, refused, saying that the bishops having been excommunicated by the Pope, the Pope alone could absolve them. An angry altercation followed, and the knights then proceeded to close the gates of the monastery. It was already dark, and the terrified monks had begun the vesper service. The archbishop's companions hurried him through the cloisters into the church. He refused to allow the church doors to be locked. He was on the steps leading to the choir when the murderers rushed into the church, crying, 'Where is Thomas Becket, the traitor to the king and the realm? Where is the archbishop?' Becket answered boldly, 'Here I am, no traitor, but a priest; why do ye seek me?' 'Absolve those whom thou hast excommunicated,' cried the knights. 'They have made no satisfaction, and I will not absolve them,' answered Becket; 'I am ready to die for my Lord, that the Church may have peace and freedom through my blood; but I forbid you in God's name to hurt any of my people.' They tried to drag him out of the church, but he clung to a pillar; a faithful monk, who alone stood by him, holding him up in his arms. But they fell upon the archbishop with their swords, and blows on the head at last ended his life. They then plundered his palace and fled.

No more deadly blow could have been dealt to the king's

cause than the murder of Becket. While he was living enthusiastically sympathy had been felt for him throughout Christendom, and his death called forth a tempest of admiration for the martyr, of indignation against the king. The horror felt for the murderers was so great that it was said and believed that the dogs would not eat of their food. The King of France, and all Henry's enemies, sought at once to make capital out of the affair, and wrote indignantly to the Pope. The Archbishop of Sens, one of the last commissioners whom the Pope had sent, pronounced an interdict on Henry's French dominions. The Pope confirmed this sentence, and forbade Henry to enter a church; the entreaties of Henry's envoys at last persuaded him to send two cardinals to make enquiry into the matter. Henry had to bow before the storm in the most abject manner; he swore that he had not had any hand in the murder of Becket; that he would serve for three years against the Saracens; that he would allow appeals to Rome; that he would give up all customs hurtful to the Church which had been introduced in his time. Yet the artful king contrived so to word these promises as to leave still open the points which had been in dispute between him and Becket.[1]

Its results.

The Pope was appeased; but popular feeling was still bitter against Henry. Every day the fame of the saint and martyr was growing; miracles were being wrought at his tomb; pilgrims flocked to Canterbury from all parts of the world; and St. Thomas became the great popular saint of England. Henry himself, at a great crisis in his history, four years after Becket's death, had to make a humble pilgrimage to the martyr's tomb.

But for all this, the 'damnable customs' (of Clarendon), or at least some of them, continued in force in England, and all those councillors of Henry who had been his chief instruments against Becket, and had been again and again excommunicated by him, were rewarded with bishoprics in England. A writer towards the end of Henry's reign complains bitterly that all that had been gained for the Church by the constancy of Becket had been lost by his successors.

What was the ultimate result of the struggle? Though there is some uncertainty as to the extent to which the Con-

[1] Fol. Ep. 385.

stitutions of Clarendon were carried out, it is certain that the Church did not succeed in upholding the entire exemption of the clergy from the jurisdiction of lay courts. Moreover, the long discussion of the question must have awakened thought, and shown that there was much to say on both sides. And undoubtedly Rome lost credit through the very contemptible part which the Pope had played in the affair. It was plain that Rome was not the quarter from which to expect the defence of the ideals which the best spirits of the middle ages so passionately cherished.

DATES.

Thomas Becket, Archbishop of Canterbury . . . 1162
Constitutions of Clarendon 1164
Murder of Becket 1170

CHAPTER XIII.

'THE reign of Henry II. saw the end of Feudalism, as far as it had ever prevailed in England as a system of government,' says Professor Stubbs.[1] Henry's great object was to make the government of the king and his ministers supreme over all classes of society. He did this by organising a system of justice, and by placing the royal supremacy on a basis so firmly guaranteed that feudalism should never be able to overturn it. *Importance of Henry II.'s reign.*

We have already seen the origin of a systematic government under the first Norman kings, especially under Henry I.; how the government in the king's absence was vested in the Justiciar or the Chancellor, that is, in ministers trained to their business; and how the Curia Regis or King's Court arose as a supreme court of appeal. We have seen in the last chapter how Henry's attempt to bring the clergy under the law of the realm was balked by the resistance of Thomas Becket, and by the feeling of his time which forbad 'that the rights of the realm and of the priesthood should be confounded.' But during the struggle with Becket, the king carried out his most valuable reforms in the administration of justice.

The great measure which marks his reign was the insti-

[1] Preface to *Benedict of Peterborough*, p. xxxvii.

tution of itinerant justices. This was not wholly new; royal commissioners had been sent into the country by Henry I. for purposes of justice and finance, but in Henry II.'s reign they began to be sent regularly, and in 1176 the kingdom was divided into circuits, and eighteen judges appointed to go the rounds. At first these justices were usually the sheriffs of the counties; the meetings which they held were the county courts in a form which more completely represented the country than ever before, since no class was exempt from the jurisdiction of the court. The king reserved to himself the right of hearing any cause which he chose to summon to his court.

Judicial reforms.
The Justices in Eyre.

The results of this institution were of the greatest importance—1st. It undermined the judicial power of the nobles: no franchise was allowed to exclude the authority of the king's justices; and the royal justices were ordered to make an enquiry by jury into certain cases where the feudal lord withheld from his vassals their rights. 2nd. It undermined (eventually though not immediately) the old barbarous fashions of judicial procedure, compurgation, trial by ordeal and battle.[1] The Grand Assize, another of Henry's measures of judicial legal reform, allowed a man whose title to land was in question to choose between trial by battle and examination of his claim by a body of twelve sworn knights or freeholders. Trial by ordeal had already been condemned by the Church; it was formally abolished by Henry III. in 1220. 3rd. Though at first the sheriffs acted as justices, Henry afterwards restricted their authority, and sent officers of his own court on the circuits. The administration of justice was thus put into the hands of a class of instructed judges, who, as they were trained in one system of law, administered one law throughout the country, and helped to extinguish those local differences of custom which were a hindrance to national unity. 4th. While the authority of the feudal courts was diminished, the ancient co-operation of the people in the administration of justice was retained by Henry II. By the Assize of Clarendon it was ordered that in every shire and every hundred, twelve

The Grand Assize.

---

[1] Compurgation and trial by ordeal have been described in Chap. VII. Trial by battle was introduced by the Normans: the accused had to fight with his adversary either personally or through a champion.

sworn men of each hundred and four men of each township should present all criminals from their respective districts before the justices.

This is a step in the direction of trial by jury. When William the Conqueror caused his great Doomsday Survey to be made, jurors had been sworn in from every manor and township to make a true report of the extent, value, and obligations of the lands with which they had personal acquaintance. This system of enquiry by jury appears to have been a relic of the legislation of Charlemagne, brought into England by the Normans.[1] It was applied by Henry II. so much more extensively than ever before, that he may almost be called the inventor of the jury. Perhaps its most important use was for purposes of taxation, when a sworn jury of the neighbourhood was called to declare the liability of each man. In this case, since the jury represented the country, it might almost be said that the country taxed itself: it was at any rate an important step in training the country for self-government. It did this in another way, by extending the principle of *representation*, already known to the English by the representation of every township at the shire and hundred meetings by the reeve and four men. But the jury as judges in criminal or civil suits, remained undeveloped in the time of Henry II.; it was not till the reign of Edward I. that the jury as judges of the evidence became separated from the witnesses.[2] *The Jury.*

Since Henry's attempts to submit the clergy to royal justice had roused so much ill-feeling against him, it was not likely that the feudal nobility would regard with indifference his measures for bringing them equally under the law of the realm. When he came to the throne the nobility had been so decimated by the wars of Stephen's reign, that they were too weak to offer prolonged resistance to the kingly power. But their discontent smouldered slowly, and after the ill-repute into which Henry fell through the murder of Becket, his enemies gradually banded themselves together against him, and the baronage found *Revolt of the baronage. 1173.*

---

[1] Stubbs, *Const. Hist.*, vol. i. p. 613.
[2] The accusing jury, as it appears in Henry II.'s legislation, had its foreshadowing in Old-English times. In the laws of Ethelred we find that the twelve senior thanes of each Wapentake are sworn to accuse none falsely.—Ethelred. iii. 3.

themselves strong enough to break out into open rebellion in the year 1173.

Henry had many bitter enemies. Louis VII., King of France, his suzerain and jealous rival, was one of the bitterest. But his foes were also those of his own household. He had behaved badly to his wife, and had not brought up his sons well. He had made a great mistake in having his eldest son Henry crowned as king. The vain and self-willed lad was vexed when he found that he had not all the power of a king, and the King of France (who was his father-in-law) did all he could to stir up his resentment, telling him that he ought to require that his father should give up to him either Normandy or England. A slight pretext was made an excuse for an open quarrel with his father, and the rebellion of the younger Henry was joined by two of his brothers, and by all the nobles on both sides of the channel who were discontented with Henry's rule. The King of Scots was enticed into the confederacy by a promise from the younger king of the county of Northumberland.

This was the time when Henry's sovereignty was in greatest danger. In June 1173 Normandy was invaded by the Earl of Flanders from the east, and by the King of France from the south; while in July the Earls of Leicester, Chester, Derby, and Norfolk kindled revolt in the east and north of England. But Henry was not found unprepared for the storm, and never was he more resolute or more successful. Before Christmas he had reduced the King of France and the younger Henry to begin negotiations for peace, and had completely subdued his enemies in Bretagne and Anjou. In England his shield and defence were not only Richard de Lucy the Justiciar and some other faithful nobles, but also all the smaller nobility of recent origin who were free from Norman influence, and the mass of the English people, including the towns. The Earl of Leicester, who had been harrying the county of Norfolk with an army of Flemings, was defeated at Farnham, and the country folk slaughtered the Flemings with flails and pitchforks (October 1173). But the decisive moment of rebellion was in 1174, when the King of Scotland invaded Northumberland with a large army, and was joined by the Bishop of Durham, the most powerful potentate of the north of England; while the Earl of Norfolk was ravaging Norfolk with a fresh host of Flemings, and the younger Henry, with the Earl of Flanders, lay at Gravelines with a large fleet and army, waiting for a fair wind to invade England. It was the faithfulness of the English people which saved Henry at this crisis. The forces of Yorkshire rallied round the king's captains and surprised the King of Scots as he was sitting before Alnwick. He was defeated and taken prisoner.

<small>Battle of Alnwick (1174).</small>

Henry had crossed over to England on hearing of the great danger of his kingdom. He seemed to be then expiating the offence of having had his son crowned by the Archbishop of York in defiance of Becket. Whether to win over the opinion of his time, or to satisfy a secret uneasiness of his own heart, he undertook a pilgrimage to the shrine of Becket. He walked with bare and bleeding feet through the streets of Canterbury, clothed only in a woollen shirt and rough rain-cloak; he kissed the stone on which the martyr had fallen; he submitted to be scourged by the abbot and monks; he watched all night on the hard pavement by Becket's tomb, and vowed an annual payment of forty marks to keep lamps burning there. Then he went on to London, and not unnaturally had a fever after his cold watch and excitement. But he was soon relieved by the joyful tidings from the north. After the fall of the King of Scots the other rebels lost heart, and made submission one by one. The last struggle between feudalism and royalty in England was over. The king returned to Normandy to complete his victory by driving the French king from Rouen, and taking castle after castle from his son Richard in Poitou, till he brought him to abject submission. The peace of Sept. 30 closed the war. Henry used his victory with such mercy as to win the praise even of his bitterest foes.

The valuable help which the forces of the shires had rendered in suppressing the rebellion was not likely to pass unnoticed by so sagacious a man as Henry, and it probably suggested to him the measure which he took in the year 1181 to organise the old national force on a better footing. The Assize of Arms in 1181, ordaining that all freemen should provide themselves with arms on a scale proportioned to their income, was in effect a revival of the Old English *fyrd*, and the origin of our present

<small>The Assize of Arms.</small>

militia. It had existed from the most ancient times, and in many important crises the Norman kings had found their best aid in these levies of the shire. The feudal forces were not to be trusted by the kings, and already in 1159, King Henry, by allowing his military tenants to exchange their service for a fixed payment called Scutage, had both damped the warlike tendencies of feudalism, and provided himself with money for the hire of those mercenary troops of Flemings and Brabançons which were found much more serviceable than the feudal hosts. For it is easy to see that an army of trained soldiers fighting simply because it was their trade, would be a better weapon of war than a host of nobles with their personal followers who would probably share the jealousy, pride, and insubordination of their lords. This weapon was freely used by Henry in taming rebellious nobles in his French dominions. But the mercenaries had made themselves so hated in England during the reign of Stephen that it would have been difficult for Henry to use them there. One of the conditions on which he received the crown was that they should be expelled from the kingdom, and once only, in the extreme peril of 1173, did he venture to introduce them. By the Assize of Arms he hoped to create a force which should be a balance to the feudal power, and a more trustworthy army for the defence of the realm. For every freeman thus armed was made to swear fidelity to the king.

This was one of the ways in which Henry's legislation developed the English people by making use of them. Exercise is as necessary to the political growth of a people as to the development of bodily strength. Henry used the people yet further in this new arrangement, by making them the judges who were responsible for the service of the militia; the oath of the men of the hundred or the borough was to declare who had an income of ten marks or more. This was the same principle of *inquest by jury* which Henry applied so extensively in other matters.

After the suppression of the great rebellion of 1173, Henry took into his own hands all the castles in England and Normandy, and demolished most of them. Those which he allowed to stand were compelled to receive garrisons of royal troops, and it was made part of the

The Castles.

duty of the travelling justices to inquire into the wardenship of castles.

Thus Henry disarmed the nobles by allowing scutage and by keeping hold of their castles, while at the same time he armed the English people. In this manner he based his system of government on sound guarantees.

The Forest Laws are the only part of Henry's legislation which is at all oppressive. Even before the Conquest the forests had been regarded as outside the scope of the common law of the realm, and Henry I. had claimed supreme jurisdiction over them, whether on his own lands or not. Henry II. put them under a law of their own, and appointed special justices for them. He forbade anyone dwelling in his forests to have bows, arrows, or dogs, without special warrant; none were to touch his wild beasts; no benefit of clergy was to save a priest who was found hunting in his forest; and the master forester had power to summon all the neighbouring nobles to a forest-court. But still he did not deny to the common people their ancient right of *estovers*, that is of cutting wood in his forests, provided it were done without damage, and under the oversight of the foresters; and he forbade his foresters to vex his knights or other honest men. *Forest Laws.*

Henry II. is described to us as a man of middle height, strongly made, and corpulent. He was fair-haired, and his otherwise handsome face was too red. His eyes seemed to flash fire when he was angry, and his anger when roused was furious. He was a man of powerful character, with naturally strong affections and passions, a character capable of much good, but which when thwarted turned to evil. His fatal marriage with Eleanor of Poitou, while it laid the foundations of his wealth and outward greatness, also prepared the way for the miseries of his later life. Eleanor was the divorced wife of Louis VII., king of France, and therefore the marriage was regarded even in that day as an iniquitous one, nor did men fail to trace its unhappy results to the wrong which it was in itself. It was a marriage of interest, and the king ceased to care for his wife, neglected her, and led an immoral life. Whilst passionately fond of his children, he spoilt them, and, as might be expected in such a union, they grew up without reverence *Personal character of Henry II.*

for him, and at last broke his heart by their unfilial conduct.
Yet though during his long reign the evil side of his character
seemed to develope, Henry remained to the last a man in-
tellectually superior to most of his contemporaries. His
ceaseless activity, when not employed on the affairs of his
dominions or seeking recreation in hunting, found exercise
in discussing knotty questions with learned clerks, or in
reading history. Though generally very successful as a soldier, he disliked bloodshed, and always avoided war when he
thought negotiations could serve his end. William of Newburgh says of him that he was a most earnest maintainer of
the public peace ; a faithful defender of ecclesiastic properties
and liberties ; a faithful guardian of widows and orphans ;
and that he never imposed any heavy burden on England or
his transmarine dominions, except on the occasion of the
Saladin tithe which he imposed for an intended crusade in
1188. Writing in the reign of his son Richard, he says that
this man who when living was hated by almost all, is now
called an excellent and useful sovereign ; for the excessive
exactions of the following reign have made his burthens seem
small.

When we read Henry II.'s life, we cannot refrain from
the judgment that he was a very bad man, selfish, violent,
cunning, licentious, faithless, cruel at times. Yet when we
look at the works which he left behind him, the system of
justice organised, the guarantees of orderly government established, we are obliged to say that few English kings have
done so much good. The contradiction is illustrated by what
we see in other walks of life. We see sometimes a splendid
poet or painter, whose private character is disgraced by the
worst vices ; yet these drunken and dissolute men have an
irresistible instinct of art working within them, which enables
them to bring forth enduring creations of loveliness in spite
of the forces which are ever dragging them downwards. In
like manner Henry II. was an artist of justice and order.
The power of governing, of arranging, worked in him like a
persistent instinct, which even his violent passions could
not quench. He had genius ; and while as a mere man he
lived for base personal ends, gratifying his passions ruthlessly,
not ashamed of any means of extorting money, nor shrinking
from any devices, base or violent, to gain his ends, his

genius made him the watchful guardian of his people, the organiser of a systematised justice to supersede the feudal jurisdictions, the contriver of guarantees against the power of the nobles, the builder of dykes to hold back the noisome inundations of the Loire. In 1170, when he removed all the sheriffs from office, he consulted his people's interest as well as his own, for not only was it chiefly in consequence of their complaints that the matter was inquired into, but the outgoing sheriffs were obliged to make satisfaction to the parties aggrieved; a fact which shows that Henry did care for justice in itself.

As we see Henry II. playing off the English people against the nobles, we want to know whether English and Normans still form two distinct nations, as they did in the days of William I. We have some evidence that the higher nobility still gloried in their Norman descent, and nourished feelings of contempt towards the common people. *Fusion of English and Normans.* They wished Battle Abbey to be maintained as a sign of their triumph over the English. On the other hand we are told on very good authority, toward the end of Henry's reign, that the English and Normans had now dwelt so long together, and intermarried so frequently, that it was almost impossible to say of the younger generation whether they were Norman or English. Thus the fusion of the two races as a whole was being accomplished; and so was the long delayed fusion between the different parts of England. After the accession of Henry II. we hear no more of the old threefold division of England into Wessex, Mercia, and Danelaw. But this fusion of England into one nation did not yet express itself by a fusion of language. Let us briefly glance at the history of the English language.

In the lips of our fathers, before the Norman Conquest, the Old-English language had been a noble instrument of poetry; in it had been sung the great events of English history, the glory of her kings and warriors, and the best wisdom of English common sense or English piety. *The English language.* For many centuries there was a standard literature, which fixed the grammar, so that the written language underwent no important changes. But even before the Conquest, signs of change began to show themselves.

The English language, thanks in great measure to the impulse given by King Alfred, had become a cultivated book-language sooner than any other European tongue. But this premature blossom was doomed to wither before the overwhelming influence of the Latin language, then the language of European literature, science, and history, and of the Church. When English was banished from the Norman court, it was no longer able to make head against the tide. It fell back into obscurity and localism. English historians and men of science wrote in Latin for the learned; English poets who aspired to court favour rimed in Norman French. Nevertheless, for at least a century and a half after the Norman Conquest, the English language had an independent life of its own, almost unaffected by French influence. The old national legends were still sung in the streets and at the alehouses; and there were men who collected and wrote them down. The monks of Peterborough steadily carried on their chronicle in English up to the accession of Henry II. Priests went on preaching their sermons in English, and making English versions of the Gospels and English lives of the saints, that unlearned men might understand them. And about the end of the twelfth century, the English priest of Arley-on-Severn, Layamon, chaplain to the good knight of that place, must needs translate into English the fashionable poem of the day, the already twice-cooked romance in which the Norman poet Wace, translating from the Welshman Geoffry of Monmouth, had rimed a cock-and-bull history of Britain, in which Layamon's own ancestors were made to cut but a sorry figure, and to be always running away from the victorious Britons. But this book was in fashion, and even Arley-on-Severn must follow the fashion.

The English history, sermons, and poems of the twelfth century which have come down to us are all written in different dialects. There is no longer a standard English; each county is going its own way, developing its own dialect in its own fashion. But though differing in many things, these dialects are all alike in two. They are all still unmixed with French words; the well of English is as yet undefiled; and they are all more or less careless about the inflectional changes. This carelessness was already beginning to appear before the Norman Conquest. In the older and purer English, which we now call Anglo-Saxon, the endings of words were all important to the grammar and to the sense. All nouns and verbs had their fixed changes, inflections as we call them. In the case of nouns we have kept only a remnant of an inflection, the plural in *s*, and a few survivals of plurals in *en*; and we have either dropped or in great part changed the old inflections of the verbs. This is a change which nearly always takes place in a language as it grows old. People get careless about the endings of words, and they drop them and use other words to make their meaning clear. The Norman Conquest, therefore, was not greatly to blame for the changed English of the twelfth century; the change would have come even without the Conquest, though it was doubtless hastened by the loss of an English court, a centre and standard of English.

It was not till the close of the thirteenth century that any real fusion began to take place between the language of the conquerors and that of the conquered. To trace the history of this fusion, and the rise of modern English, would therefore carry us beyond the limits of the period which now occupies us. The English writers of the end of the twelfth and beginning of the thirteenth century, such as Layamon and Orm, are not heralds of the future as regards their language, but echoes of the past.[1] The old native English had to accept an immense infusion of foreign words, to its great gain in some respects, its great loss in others, before the language which we now speak could grow up.

In a literary point of view, the English writers of the twelfth century scarcely call for mention. Layamon's version of Wace is spirited, sometimes nervous and rhythmical; he makes many additions of his own, English literature. and shows a thoroughly English tendency to moralise and improve the occasion. But he is far below the standard of Anglo-Saxon poetry. A poem on the Grave, supposed to have been written in the twelfth century, has much more of the weird and solemn ring of Teutonic genius. We cannot say that no good English poetry existed in the twelfth century because so little has come down to us; for we know that the English originals of many romances, such as 'Horn,'

---

[1] See Morris's *Outlines of English Accidence*, p. 358, for the very small infusion of words of Romance origin in Layamon.

'Havelock,' and 'Engel,' are lost; but we know of no great English poet before the middle of the fourteenth century.

We must now sketch the progress of the English empire under the Norman kings. In a former chapter I said that the English conquest went on for four or five hundred years, and that during that time the English were ever struggling with the Kelts, ever pressing them farther to the west. And, in truth, this warfare went on, and must needs have gone on, till the English were supreme in these islands.

The English Empire.

Undoubtedly we have here the saddest chapter in English history. It may have been needful for the welfare of these islands that the Englishman, with his love of order, his power of making the best use of nature's gifts, his energetic purpose, should hold supreme sway throughout them, instead of the clever but fitful Kelt. But that this sway should have been brought about by so much wrong and bloodshed; that the Kelt should have been trampled down for so many centuries; that for centuries we should have been building a barrier of bitter hatred between ourselves and the kindly, bright, quick-witted natives of Ireland; this ought ever to be a great sorrow to us, and should stimulate us with desire to undo as far as we can the wrongs which our fathers did.

The Norman Conquest was not an event which was likely to alter the relations of the English and Keltic peoples. On the contrary, Norman pride of rank and chivalry was now added to English pride; Norman ambition and love of adventure to English spirit of predominance; and the Normans have not been settled here long before we find them aggressive on all sides, towards the Welsh, Cumbrians, Scotch, and Irish.

I have mentioned the homage of the Welsh to William I. The Norman lords whose estates lay on the frontier or march of Wales, and who were hence called Lords Marchers, held from the king the right of conquering as much land as they could from the Welsh; and very cruel wars went on incessantly on the border. The English historian Orderic is filled with indignation when he tells of these unrighteous wars, and of the cruelties which were done to the Welsh, especially by Robert of Rhuddlan,

I. The Welsh.

lord of the Northern Marches. Some were butchered without mercy like herds of cattle, others thrown into dungeons, or sent into cruel slavery. It is not fit, he says, that Christian men should so oppress their brethren who have been baptized into the same faith. The Welsh were a constant source of trouble to William Rufus during his whole reign, and he did not meet with good fortune in his expeditions against them, though in other wars he was so successful. 'That wild land that Welshmen love' (as our English poet Layamon calls it) was a difficult country for an invader. Wars continued during the reign of Henry I., and the Normans completed the conquest of South Wales, not without frequent bloody reprisals from the natives.

The Welsh, in fact, were as little inclined to keep quiet as the English to leave them alone. A writer of the twelfth century, himself half a Welshman, has left us an interesting description of the Welsh. One cannot doubt that they were a fine people. Henry II. himself took note of their great courage. They were also, like other Keltic peoples, noted for their eloquence; their sonorous and expressive language lent itself readily to the orator. They were a clever race, and quick to learn anything they applied themselves to. Giraldus says they were vehement either for good or evil, and while in no country were holier hermits to be found, yet the Welsh generally were notorious for lying and thieving. The truth was that, hemmed up in those wild mountains, they had not acquired the arts of even that stage of European civilisation; they had not the skill to make the most of their naturally wild country, and hence it did not produce food enough to support them; they were driven to make raids on their neighbours for the sake of a livelihood. They were still in a state of clanhood, and their primitive customs were the constant source of barbarous feuds. One of these was the custom of putting out children to be fostered, in which case it became the duty of the foster-father to back his nursling against the other brothers, and the ties between the nursling and his foster-family were stronger than those which bound him to his own family. Another was the ancient custom of blood revenge, which bound a family to avenge the death of one of its members. Wars were so frequent and violent in all parts of Wales that very few of their kings died natural deaths.

It happened more than once that the Welsh recovered whole provinces which the Normans had conquered. But Wales itself was not a united country. It was split up into three small kingdoms, which were only occasionally joined together under some more able ruler; and Henry I.'s policy was to set one chieftain against the other. Henry led two expeditions into Wales, and he planted a colony of Flemings in Pembrokeshire, to hold the natives in check, and also to get rid of the Flemings, who had swarmed into England in the Conqueror's reign, and had become troublesome. The Flemings were a brave and industrious people of the same Low Dutch stock as the English; but they were hard neighbours to the Welsh, and Orderic says they butchered them like dogs wherever they could trace them out in the woods and caves in which they lurked. Such was the sad lot of the beaten Kelts. They were in fierce rebellion when Henry I. died in 1135. Stephen sent three unsuccessful expeditions against them, but the troubles in his own kingdom obliged him to leave them alone. The Welsh profited by the general anarchy to recover some of their lost lands. It was the policy of Henry II. to avoid fighting as much as possible, and to endeavour to extend his influence over Wales by means of the Church. The Church of Wales already acknowledged the supremacy of Canterbury, and Norman bishops were appointed to it who were wholly in Henry's interest, and were armed by the Pope with the power of excommunicating those who rebelled against Henry. This was one of Henry's attempts to convert the Church into a tool of his own power. He was, however, obliged to lead frequent expeditions into Wales, more than one of them unsuccessful. In one of them (1165) it is said that he 'did justice' on the children of Rhys ap Griffith by tearing out the boys' eyes and cutting off the girls' ears and noses. On the whole, the English ascendency over Wales was maintained, and the very king whose children had been so cruelly treated did homage to Henry in 1171, when he was about to sail for Ireland, and did valuable service for Henry in the rebellion of 1173.

II. *Cumberland.*—William Rufus drove out Dolfin (son

of the banished Northumbrian earl Gospatrick), who governed Cumberland for the king of Scots, and restored the city of Carlisle, which had lain waste ever since the Danish invasions. There he planted a colony of English from the south, thus securing the possession of the country. To this colony may be due the extinction of the Keltic element in Cumberland, if it had not been extinguished long before by the settlements of the Norsemen.[1] It survives to-day only in a few names of places. Yet even in later reigns, especially if the king of England were weak, the Scotch kings frequently laid claim to Cumberland, North Lancashire, and even Northumberland and Durham. It was not till the year 1237 that the disputes concerning the English frontier were finally settled.

III. *Scotland.*—The Conqueror, as we have seen, enforced the old homage due from the king of Scotland to the king of England. It must be remembered that the kingdom of Scotland was scarcely to be called a Keltic kingdom. Scotland south of the Forth, the part anciently called *Lothian*, was inhabited by a purely English race. Even Strathclyde, now part of the Scottish kingdom, had been colonised by Danish and English settlers. And although the kings of Scotland were descended from the old Keltic kings, it was this English part of Scotland which gave laws to the rest. Malcolm Canmore, the contemporary of William the Conqueror, married Margaret, the granddaughter of our king Edmund Ironsides, and sister of Edgar Atheling. Scotland became the refuge of the noble English exiles who were driven out by the Norman conqueror. They received lands in Scotland, and founded families there. Swarms of English peasants were driven into Scotland by the calamities which Northumbria suffered in William's reign. Malcolm, in his numerous raids into England, carried off hosts of others to serve as colonists. Nor were the settlers only English; Normans also came in great numbers to Scotland. Queen Margaret had lived ten years at the court of Edward the Confessor; her husband had been brought up there; they were familiar with the French speech, which Edward loved; they liked the ways of the English court, its civilisation, its splendour, and they tried to make their own court

[1] Palgrave.

and kingdom copies of what they had seen in England. They endeavoured to reform the Church. Margaret chose Archbishop Lanfranc for her spiritual father; English clergy were sent for to Scotland, and the Benedictine monastic system was introduced there by the foundation of the abbey of Dunfermline. The very laws of England were copied. Under the children of Malcolm and Margaret feudal law was gradually adopted in Scotland. The laws and customs of feudal England triumphed in great measure over the patriarchal customs of the highland clans. This revolution was not accomplished without opposition. More than once did the genuine Scotch, the Highlanders, rebel, and insist that no more English or French should be brought into the country. But it was in vain; under David, son of Malcolm and Margaret, the feudal system was completely established in Scotland. The clans lived on in the mountains, but Scotland was theirs no longer; English influence ruled the land, though the day had not yet come for England to rule in outward sway. Homage was paid by the kings of Scotland to the kings of England, but it was not until the capture of William the Lion at Alnwick, in 1174, that the Scotch barons as well as their king were forced to do homage to Henry II., the Scotch clergy compelled to acknowledge the supremacy of Canterbury, and the most important castles of the Lowlands obliged to receive English garrisons. These hard-wrung concessions were sold back to the king of Scots by Richard, the son and successor of Henry, when he was raising money for his great crusade.

1124-1153.

IV. *Ireland.*—Both William the Conqueror and his son Rufus had cast ambitious eyes towards Ireland. 'Had he lived two years longer he would have subdued Ireland,' the Anglo-Saxon chronicler says of the father. The son looked at the Irish coast from St. David's, and said that he would build a bridge of boats across. Henry II. obtained from the Pope Adrian IV. a bull, authorising him to undertake the conquest of Ireland, the Pope assuming that all islands were in the disposal of the successor of St. Peter.

Ireland was a purely Keltic country, with the exception of the settlement made by the Danes on the eastern coast. In all Keltic Ireland the clan system prevailed, and the laws and customs were those of clanhood. Some progress indeed had been made from the primitive state; a judicial system had made considerable development, and the position of women was singularly unfettered. Although most of the evils of clanhood were to be found in Ireland, yet the minuteness with which every custom was regulated prevented a wholesale oppression of the people by their chieftains, whose position was already passing into feudal suzerainty. The Brehon law (law as taught by the Brehons, or literary class of Ireland, who were probably the successors and heirs of the Druidical priesthood) is a remarkable monument of the clan system, and throws much light on the transition from that to the Feudal system. From these laws, in spite of progress in some respects, we can discern a low state of civilisation in the lax relations of the sexes, and the prevalence of payments in cattle instead of money. There seems to have been no coin in the island. Giraldus (who wrote a description of Ireland as well as of Wales) says there were no manufactures or commerce, and that even agriculture was little practised, the Irish having scarcely advanced out of the pastoral stage. The trade with England, though so important as to give the English a hold on Ireland already, was carried on by the descendants of the Danish settlers in the maritime cities. Although private property in land was not unknown, the prevailing rule was the joint property of the Sept,[1] and at the death of every male member of the Sept the chief made a fresh distribution of all the lands among the survivors. Such a system could not give sufficient encouragement to industry, and in fact the most fertile parts of Ireland were a desert at the time of the English conquest.

The island was divided into four kingdoms, Ulster, Connaught, Leinster, and Munster, which ceaselessly struggled with one another for supremacy, a struggle which plunged the country in endless bloodshed.

Even the Church shared in the general decline of the country. When the rest of Europe had been struggling in the chaos which followed the overthrow of the Roman Empire, Ireland, which had never formed part of that Empire, enjoyed a palmy time, in which Christianity, lately introduced into the country, caused a new life to spring up, and the island became famous throughout Europe for her churches, her schools, her learning, and her devotion. As has been

[1] The Sept was a smaller body than the clan, a larger one than the immediate family.

already told,[1] the Scoto-Irish Church in the seventh and eighth centuries threatened to be a dangerous rival of the rising Church of Rome. But every institution in Ireland was formed on the model of the family, and it is always fatal to the Church when family influence becomes supreme in it. The kindred of the founder had the preference in elections to abbacies; we are told that the archiepiscopal see of Armagh had been hereditary in the same family for fifteen generations. A Church so degraded could not do much to raise the tone of morals or to diffuse learning. But it is fair to state that Giraldus praises the chastity and devotion of the Irish clergy, and their regular performance of their duties.

The settlement of the Danes in Ireland, and their conversion in the tenth century, probably by English missionaries, gave an opportunity for Romish and English influence to gain a footing in the island. Lanfranc and Anselm ordained the bishops of the Danish cities, which acknowledged the spiritual supremacy of Canterbury. In 1139 the Archbishop of Armagh, St. Malachi, went to Rome for his pall; he laboured to introduce the Roman ritual and discipline into Ireland. In 1151 all the four archbishops of Ireland received palls from the Pope. Thus the Roman conquest of Ireland preceded the Norman. But it was not complete; Ireland did not pay the Peter's pence, which was regularly contributed by England; and the want of this may have influenced Pope Adrian IV. to give his sanction to Henry II.'s designs of conquest in the bull mentioned above. This bull was confirmed by Pope Alexander III., and Henry received a general commission to reform the Church of Ireland, and root up the vices of the people.

But the internal discord of Ireland brought about the ruin of her independence before Henry was able to carry out his plans. Dermod, King of Leinster, whose misconduct had lost him his throne, called over to Ireland an army of English and Welsh adventurers, headed by Robert FitzStephen and Maurice Fitzgerald, to reinstate him in his kingdom. They seized Wexford and massacred the clans of Ossory. They were followed by Richard of Clare, Earl of Pembroke, surnamed Strongbow, a wild adventurer who had already forfeited his lands to King Henry, was

1170.

[1] See Chapter III., pp. 22, 23.

plunged in debts, and reckless enough to defy the king's express command by sailing to Ireland. Waterford and Dublin fell, Hasculf, the last Danish prince, fled, and Strongbow married the daughter of Dermod. The attempts of Roderic O'Connor, the nominal king of Ireland, and of Hasculf who returned with a large Norwegian force, to recover Dublin, were both foiled by the steadfast valour of Miles de Cogan, who commanded the Norman garrison. Strongbow had to appease the wrath of Henry by surrendering his conquests to him.

In 1171 Henry himself came to Ireland with a small army and received the homage of Strongbow for the kingdom of Leinster, and that of several Irish princes in Munster, and even of Roderic of Connaught, the nominal king of all Ireland, who promised him tribute. He held his Christmas court at Dublin, in a temporary wooden palace; the Irish bishops did homage to him, and he directed a reform of the Church in a synod at Cashel. But the difficulty he was in with regard to Becket's murder obliged him to hurry back to Normandy to meet the papal legates before the conquest of Ireland was completed. The princes of Ulster still defied him, and though a part of Ulster was afterwards conquered, the English *Pale* (as it was called) included little more than half the island (Munster, Leinster, Down, and Clanboy). Within this Pale the laws and customs of England, courts of justice and sheriffs, on the English model, were introduced. English colonists from Bristol were placed in Dublin. Hugh de Lacy was appointed justiciar of Ireland.

But it was quite obvious even to contemporaries that the conquest of Ireland was not a complete success. They even foresaw that it would be a perpetual cause of conflict and bloodshed in future, and prophecies said that scarcely before the day of judgment would Ireland be fully subdued by the English. Giraldus gives a picture of the unhappy state of Ireland in 1185; complaint and mourning on all sides; no security for life; and the uncertain tenure of the English conquest announced by daily rumours. It was no doubt a great misfortune that the conquest was not completed, for even a Norman tyranny would have been better than the division of the island between two opposite factions, whose hatred by race was to be intensified by years of warfare. One of the great evils of the partial conquest was that the Norman colony, being penniless and ignorant how to develope the resources of the country, had to live by plundering the natives.

The conquest of Ireland may be compared with the Norman conquest of England, to bring out the points in which it failed. The latter was undertaken by a prince of high though stern character, sufficiently able and politic to use the adventurers who followed him as instruments to establish his rule, and, though ambitious, desiring to reign as a lawful king. The conquest of Ireland was undertaken by a handful of needy adventurers who had already ruined themselves by their previous lives, and had nothing to recommend them but their bravery and their acquaintance with border warfare. They were hired by a native king of bad character who betrayed his country, a barbarous wretch who tore with his teeth the face of a conquered enemy. They had no idea of showing either justice or mercy to the natives. When it was a question whether to slay or to spare seventy citizens of Waterford, who had been taken prisoners in an attack on the Norman camp, Hervey of Mountmaurice, one of the Norman leaders, said, 'If we mean to indulge in pity for the natives, we may as well go back to England.' The half-Norman, half-Welshman Giraldus, several of whose relatives were among the band of conquerors, could not hope that the result would be good, since out of the bloody conquest, obtained by the slaughter of the people, the conquerors had given no part to God, but had even robbed the churches of their lands and privileges. King Henry, who stepped in to secure the fruits of the conquest, was perhaps an even abler politician than William I. Had he been able to give his full attention to Ireland, and to carry out its conquest, he would no doubt have established a firm, if harsh, government there. But he was called off by the pressure of other affairs, and his son John, whom he sent to Ireland in 1185, proved utterly incapable, and alienated both the native Irish and the Anglo-Norman conquerors. The Church had been made a tool in the whole affair; Henry got the papal legate in 1177 to publish the Pope's confirmation of his right to Ireland, and to threaten to excommunicate all who should rebel against him; yet we learn from Giraldus that nothing was done for the Church, nor was Peter's pence paid to Rome, so that the conditions on which the popes had given their sanction to the conquest remained unfulfilled.

DATES OF HENRY II.'S REIGN, 1154–1189.

Malcolm of Scotland surrenders the northern countries to Henry	1157
Beginning of the quarrel with Becket	1163
Constitutions of Clarendon	1164
Assize of Clarendon. First commission of itinerant justices	1166
Strongbow invades Ireland. Becket's return to England, and death	1170
Revolt of the princes and disaffected barons	1173
Settlement of Ireland	1175
Council of Northampton; six circuits appointed for the Justices in Eyre	1176
Henry arbitrates between the kings of Castille and Navarre. The Welsh kings swear fealty to him at Oxford	1177
The Assize of Arms	1181

CHAPTER XIV.

'IN spring,' says an Old-English poet, 'the glades blossom with flowers, towns look fair, beautiful appear the plains, the world hastens on; all these things stir up the prompt of mind to go on a journey; those who so think, on the floodways far depart.'[1]

When our Teutonic forefathers had adopted a settled life and become Christians, and given up their summer expeditions after plunder, the old wandering instinct found scope in pilgrimages to the shrine of some distant saint. *Pilgrimages.* Such journeys indeed were often undertaken as a penance for some great sins; but it may be questioned whether the pilgrims were not repaid for the hardships and perils of foreign travel, by the gratification of their love of adventure and their taste for strange sights. From the earliest days of the conversion of Europe, pilgrims from the West had been drawn to the tomb of Christ. The great saints of the fourth century found reason to lift up their voices against

[1] The Seafarer, in the *Codex Exoniensis.*

the tide which had set in, when they observed the temptations to which pilgrims to the Holy Land were exposed, and the sins into which they often fell. 'Why seek ye the living among the dead?' was the note of their exhortations. 'God will come to you wherever you are, if you prepare a tabernacle fit for him.'[1] The gate of heaven is as near in Britain as in Jerusalem.'[2] But the words of Christian common-sense could not stay the passion for religious adventure; pilgrimages to the Holy Land went on increasing.

In the seventh century Arabia saw the rise of that religion which was destined to be the great rival of Christianity in Asia and Africa. Its creed was summed up in the words of its founder, 'There is one God, and Mohammed is his prophet.' The followers of Mohammed, inspired with a fiery enthusiasm, rapidly spread their religion with the sword over the western countries of Asia, over Egypt and North Africa. Their victorious hosts crossed the Straits of Gibraltar, conquered Spain, and threatened the rest of Europe. But they were met and checked in their career by the founders of the Frank Empire. Defeated and thrust back, they harried the coasts of southern Europe, and it was the work of centuries to eject them from Spain. They were looked upon as the natural enemies of Christendom; and in truth, we owe a great debt to Charles Martel and Charlemagne for having raised a barrier which shut out the Saracen from the sovereignty of Europe. For though in arts and sciences the Saracens were superior to the Franks who followed Charles Martel on the field of Tours (732), and though in later times the scholars of Christendom had to go for instruction to the Saracens of Spain, yet the religion of Mohammed would have brought a lower morality to Europe, and by its selfish and sensual views of women would have kept one-half of mankind in slavery and debasement.

Rise of Mohammedanism.

When these enemies of Christendom had conquered Syria and were masters of Jerusalem, they still allowed free entrance to Christian pilgrims, for the trade which naturally followed the pilgrims was a useful source of revenue. The Christians of the Holy Land, it is true, were exposed to as many changes

---

[1] St. Gregory of Nyssa.
[2] St. Augustine.

of fortune as there were changes of government in the Mohammedan Empire; but their lot was not such as to move the compassion and indignation of all Europe until the end of the tenth century, when the Fatimite caliphs of Egypt having obtained possession of Syria, a new spirit of persecution arose with the fanatic Hakem, and the Christians of Palestine had to suffer cruelly. Their rites were forbidden, their churches turned into stables. Yet, at the risk of their lives, pilgrims from Europe still journeyed to Jerusalem. The end of the world was generally expected in the year 1000; crowds hastened to the land where the Sovereign Judge was expected to appear. Their custom was to visit the church of the Holy Sepulchre wrapped in a winding sheet, which they were careful to carry back to their native land, that they might be buried in it after death.

The hostility of the Fatimite caliphs relaxed so far as to allow the admission of Christian pilgrims into Jerusalem on payment of tribute. But in 1076 a new Mohammedan conquest of Jerusalem took place, which brought in its train fresh sufferings for the Christians. *The Turks conquer Syria.* The Turks, a savage people from the wilds of Asia, having overrun Persia, and embraced the religion of Mohammed, undertook to conquer Asia for the caliphs of Bagdad. Not only Syria, but Asia Minor, the route by which Christian pilgrims were accustomed to reach the Holy Land, fell into their power. Though the Turks did not absolutely stop the entrance of pilgrims into Jerusalem, their insults and outrages made it more perilous than it had ever been since the days of Hakem.

How deeply Europe had been moved by the tales of suffering which the returning pilgrims brought back from the East, was shown by the fact that the eloquence of one man, a poor rough-looking pilgrim of obscure origin, *Peter the Hermit.* was able to rouse high and low to the arduous enterprise now famous as the First Crusade. This preacher, Peter the Hermit, does not seem to have had any gift but eloquence and the enthusiasm of his subject; he had no great force of character, as events afterwards showed; but he spoke to an audience full of sympathy for his words; he was as a spark to a mass of cotton that has long been drenched in oil; he spoke, and Europe was in a blaze.

There were many reasons to enlist the sympathies of Europe in the eleventh century with the first crusade. Religious feeling was appealed to; and reverence for holy places and holy things formed a large part of the religious feelings of that age. Men's deepest feeling would be thrilled now by the sight of the grave where Christ lay, and the hallowed earth which his feet had trod; but in an age which deemed that earth to be hallowed, not only by memory, but by a certain imparted virtue, it seemed a horrible sacrilege that the sacred grave and the Holy Land should be in the possession of infidels. Compassion for the sufferings of their fellow-Christians was another generous feeling to which the enterprise of Peter the Hermit made appeal; and this compassion continued to be a powerful motive till it was weakened by actual contact with Eastern Christians. The passion for war and the love of adventure were addressed. The men of the eleventh century were still barbarians, whose normal state was a state of war. The Church had for ages been struggling to bridle their warlike instincts; now she turned face, and invited them to fight! A delightful vent for the warlike passion! And then the adventure of it! The East was a fairy land, where the strangest sights might be seen, where the most romantic deeds might be done, and where prizes were to be had such as the West could never offer. A safe place in heaven was made sure by the Pope to every crusader who perished in the holy war; and there were also rewards to be had of a more tangible nature, in the plunder of eastern cities, and the sovereignty of eastern kingdoms.

The call to the crusades thus appealed to all the mingled high and low motives which were strongest in ordinary human nature at that day. No wonder the preaching of Peter met with such a widespread response. As the hermit went from town to town, preaching in the churches, the highways, and the market-places, he was followed by crowds who wept passionately over the tale of sorrow which he bore from the East, and vowed to give their lives for the deliverance of the Holy Land. When the enthusiasm was at its height, Pope Urban II., who had all along been the patron of Peter's cause, summoned a great council at Clermont, in Auvergne. The sovereign pontiff of Christendom and the poor hermit appeared side by side, and before a crowd of illustrious prelates

Preaching of the First Crusade.

and princes, repeated the story of the sufferings of the Syrian Christians, and the profanation of the holy places, and exhorted the warriors of the West to hasten to the deliverance of the Holy Land. The key-note of Urban's address was noble: ' Ye ought to lay down your lives for the brethren.' 'Warriors who listen to me, ye who search unceasingly for vain pretexts for war, rejoice; for here is a lawful war. The time has come to show if you are inspired by true courage; the time has come to expiate your many violent deeds committed in time of peace, your many victories stained by wrongs. You who were often the terror of your fellows, or who sold your arms for base hire to serve the fury of others ; now, armed with the sword of the Maccabees, go to defend the house of Israel, which is the vineyard of the Lord of hosts. It is no longer a question of avenging the wrongs of men, but those of God; it is no longer a question of attacking a town or a castle, but of conquering the holy places. If you triumph, the blessing of heaven and the kingdoms of Asia will be your portion; if you fall, you will have the glory of dying where Christ died, and God will not forget that he has seen you in his holy army.'

When Urban had finished speaking, the whole assembly rose to their feet, crying, ' God wills it ! ' And in this spirit of enthusiasm the First Crusade was resolved upon by nobles and people, the richest and the poorest alike. The enthusiasm was soon carried to all the countries of Europe. Everywhere intending crusaders flocked to the priests who distributed the crosses, which were given with these words: 'Receive this sign of the cross in the name of the Father, the Son, and the Holy Ghost, in memory of the cross, passion, and death of Christ, for the defence of your body and soul, that having accomplished your journey you may by divine grace and goodness return to your own people safe and better.' In like manner when they brought their arms to be blessed, the priest said: ' Use this sword for the triumph of the faith ; but let it never shed innocent blood.'

There can be little doubt that a strong religious passion, however mingled, was touched and roused by the proclamation of the first crusade. The Europe which arose at the voice of Peter the Hermit was a fervent, artless child, changeable as a child it is true, and easily diverted from its higher aims by golden baits, but still

The First Crusade (1096).

sincere in its bursts of feeling. This childlike character of mediæval Europe is very evident in the first crusade. Not only the troops of villagers with their wives and children who were led by Peter the Hermit, and the miscellaneous rabble who afterwards set out under the guidance of a goat and a goose, but even the host of knights and barons that formed the real army of the crusade were very like a multitude of big children. They were childish in their ignorance, their hatred of the enemy, their quarrels with one another; childlike in their trust, their quick feelings, their sudden repentances, and generous bursts of enthusiasm. They took no thought for the morrow, carried no provisions with them, and rushed recklessly into dangers which a little forethought would have avoided. They had no discipline; its place was taken by knightly honour; it was considered disgraceful for a knight to flee even when the numbers were three to one. What did such odds matter when they saw the knights of heaven, St. George and St. Demetrius, fighting for them in the air? The poetry of Christian legend constantly came to their rescue in the hour of need, inspiring them with fresh courage by rekindling their active imaginations. They perpetually lost sight of their aim under the pressure of some present calamity, or the enjoyment of some present good; then, roused by the voice of their teachers, or by some vision, or judgment, they passed quickly into passionate repentance; they forgot their quarrels and embraced each other; they fasted, prayed, and communed; and, inspired with invincible enthusiasm, they won victories which were little short of miraculous, such as the defeat of the Turkish army by the emaciated troop of Christians who were on the point of starving to death in Antioch. Their emotion at the sight of holy places, as, for instance, when they first saw Jerusalem, was profound and real; they threw themselves on their knees, they kissed the ground, they stretched out their arms towards the holy city, and renewed their vows for its deliverance. Yet with all this devotion they committed the most horrible cruelties on their enemies, and thought no more of slaughtering them in cold blood than children do of killing flies. In the pitiless massacres which often took place they would cut open the Saracens simply to find if they had concealed money by swallowing it. The chroniclers describe the horrible carnage which followed the storming of Jerusalem by saying that the blood was knee-deep. Godfrey of Bouillon, the leader of the Flemish contingent, whose virtues had given him the chief place among the leaders of the various nations who formed the army of the first crusade, was the only one who abstained from slaughter; his absorbing desire was to pay his devotions at the Holy Sepulchre. In the evening of the day on which the holy city was stormed, the rest of the crusading army followed his example, and then (says a modern historian of the crusades) 'the crusaders showed such a lively and tender devotion that one would have said that these men, who had just taken a city by storm and made an atrocious massacre, had come out of a pious retreat and a long meditation on the Christian mysteries.'

Among this childish troop there were no doubt many cunning ones, like the wily Norman, Bohemond of Tarento, or Baldwin of Boulogne, the brother of Godfrey, who had no aim but their own interest. No one knew better how to speak the language of enthusiasm, and play upon the chords of generous feeling, than Bohemond. But unless the majority had been generously and childlikely sincere, they would never have endured what they did, and still have pressed forward to the end.

The effect of such a wave of intense feeling passing over Europe, carrying her out of herself into real sacrifice, must have been elevating. I believe that the most valuable influences of the crusades on Europe were of this intangible kind. A thrill of unselfish sympathy passed over all countries, binding all Europe together, and lifting men for awhile out of the little selfish rut of their daily lives. And not only were the sympathies roused, but the imagination was kindled. An English writer of the time exultingly calls the first crusade the most glorious subject presented to the poets and writers of any age. A new world was opened to the gaze of Europe; the East with its different life, its different thoughts; and this was an influence of incalculable magnitude. *Influence of the crusades.*

Our own country felt the thrill of these new impulses as much as any other. There was a very great stir in this land, says the Anglo-Saxon chronicle. Numbers of English followed Duke Robert of Normandy, the oldest son of William the Conqueror, to the first crusade. In *England and the Crusades.*

the miserable reign of Stephen, so many barons who were sick of their own crimes went to the Holy Land that one writer says you would think England would have been emptied. The whole English people passionately desired that Henry II. should march to the relief of Jerusalem; and after the preaching of the third crusade such was the enthusiasm 'to revenge the injuries of the Saviour' that very few men were to be seen in any public assembly who were not signed with the cross.

Our country therefore partook of all the healthy effects of the Crusades, the elevating enthusiasm, and the mental stimulus which resulted from the contact of East and West. England shared with other countries in the privilege of getting rid of some of her most restless spirits. The knowledge of the East did not fail to bring in time many important discoveries and inventions to the West. At first, the crusaders were too bigoted and too ignorant to be able to learn anything from the Mohammedans; but in the course of years they learned to respect their enemies, and in the third crusade (1189) we find the Christian and Saracen princes exchanging acts of politeness in the spirit of chivalry. Europe had much to learn from the East, which was then far before her in many of the arts of civilised life; and it is said that the compass, printing, and gunpowder came to us from the East, and are to be traced to the intercourse brought about by the crusades. A more certain good effect of the crusades was that the lord and his vassal were then thrown into close contact, and that the sufferings and dangers they endured together could not but bring about sympathy with each other, and tend to soften the hard lines which separated the noble from the serf. Tancred of Sicily, one of the most famous of the leaders of the first crusade, used to say: 'My men are my fortune and my glory; let the gains be theirs, I reserve for myself the cares, perils, and fatigues, the rain and the hail.' In a time of famine, he swore to drink no wine, and to reduce his table and clothing to the same state as those of the poor, until the distress was over. Often, too, the serf was able to distinguish himself by his valour, and prove that as a poet of the twelfth century sang, 'Better is a villein who is brave and wise, than a weak and good-for-nothing gentleman.'

So much for the good side of the crusades; but there was a darker side which must not be passed over. The Church, in summoning the chivalry of Europe to conquest over the infidel, sanctioned the spirit of religious war, which, once evoked, could not be satiated with fighting against the Turks abroad; it next turned to fight against heretics at home. The crusades opened the door to wars of religion, the most hideous wars by which this earth has been desolated; wars by which slaughter and fire and torture have been carried into innocent and happy countries in the name of the God of love, and in which man's hatred and rapacity have veiled themselves in the holy garb of zeal for religion. That spirit, once allowed, was fatal to the true life of the Church herself. The twelfth century was the culminating period of her influence. After that time we find her taking a decided position as a persecuting church, and the same date marks the beginning of the decline of her sway. I do not say that other influences were not at work; but there can be no more deadly worm at the root of a church than the persecuting spirit, which was admitted by the crusades, and sealed by the great crusade against the Albigensian heretics of France, undertaken by Pope Innocent III. in 1209.

Darker side of the Crusades.

The first crusade was the only one in which the flame of religious enthusiasm burned comparatively free from the vapours of human greed and self-seeking. In the other crusades, as they follow one after another during the twelfth and thirteenth centuries, we see human ambition coming more and more into the foreground, until the design to recover the sepulchre of Christ is almost forgotten in schemes of conquest and plunder. And as religious enthusiasm was the only bond which united the motley host of crusaders, so when that enthusiasm began to abate, and selfishness to prevail, it became impossible to carry out any well-combined plans. The first crusade was also the most successful. It did at least recover Jerusalem from the Turks, and founded in Palestine a feudal kingdom, which though weak and disunited, did for nearly ninety years serve as a barrier against the further advance of the Turkish power. And in the important check given to that power, which had been and was yet again to be so threaten-

1099-1187.

ing to Europe, is to be found one of the most weighty results of the crusades. But individually, these expeditions present a sad history of misery, folly, and failure. The Christians set the Turks the example of breaking treaties, and reaped the fruits of their own bad faith. Nevertheless, for more than two hundred years, the crusades were in the eyes of Europe holy enterprises, the first duty of the Christian warrior; and through the twelfth and thirteenth centuries, she did not hesitate to send her bravest sons to perish in the East.

The crusades sprang from chivalry, but in their turn they reacted upon chivalry and gave it an immense development.

Chivalry. Chivalry was so important and noteworthy a blossom of feudalism that it demands our careful study, for the influence which it exercised on the twelfth and following centuries was enormous.

To trace chivalry to its source, we must go back to the primitive times when our forefathers were still in their German forests, and when clanhood was in full vigour. The bearing of arms was then the badge and the right of every free man; and the most important event in the life of a youth was the day when he was deemed old enough to carry arms. These were solemnly bestowed upon him by the chief of the clan in a public assembly; he received the shield and the lance, and was henceforth a full freeman of the clan. I have already tried to show how, when the Teutonic nations conquered Europe, and feudalism succeeded to clanhood, an artificial image of the clan gathered round a noble instead of a patriarch. The noble in his castle, surrounded by his followers and the young men who came to be trained in his household, carried on the life of feasting, fighting, and amusement, which had been led by the chief of the clan in the German forests. The band of chosen companions who had held themselves ready to accompany the chief to the wars, were represented in feudal times by the host of young men who came to the feudal castle, as to a school, to learn the profession of arms and the manners of a gentleman. The solemn ceremonies which had been anciently observed when these youths became of an age to carry arms, were still enacted, but a new and deeper significance was given to them, for they passed under the transforming touch of the Church.

The Church was trying to preach a religion of peace and love to men whose chief amusement and chief business was fighting, and in a state of society so unsettled that constant fighting was scarcely to be avoided. And the Church did the best thing that could be done in such a difficulty; she tried to consecrate and sanctify the profession of arms. She found that loyal service to the master whom they had chosen was regarded as an honour and glory by the young men who gathered in the feudal household. She laid hold of this idea of service; and by her influence the investiture of the young man with arms came to be regarded as his initiation into a service which was as sacred and binding as the orders of priesthood or monkhood; and thus arose gradually a new order, that of chivalry or knighthood. *Fusion of barbarism and Christian ideas.*

'As the priesthood was instituted for divine service, so was knighthood for the maintenance of religion and justice. A knight ought to be the husband of widows and father of orphans, the protector of the poor, and the prop of those who have no other support; and they who do not act thus are unworthy to bear that name.' These words are put in the mouth of a Portuguese king of the fifteenth century, and the idea they express was that which the Church sought to impress on the young warrior. The solemn religious ceremony of reception into the order of knighthood took the place of the old Germanic admission to arms. After a long education in the feudal household, first as page, then as squire, where he learnt the profession of arms by close attendance on his lord, and after he had shown by his conduct that he was worthy of the honour which he sought, the young man who was about to be knighted, having bathed and dressed himself in new white clothes, watched all night in prayer in a church, in the morning confessed and received the communion, and then in solemn assembly, either in the church or in the hall of the castle, his lord dubbed him a knight in these or similar words: ' I make thee a knight in the name of God and my lord St. George, to maintain the faith and justice loyally, and defend the Church, women, and orphans.' The young man vowed to fulfil these conditions, and even when in after times the oath of service to the *The order of knighthood.*

Church was dropped, it was considered to be fully implied by the offering of his sword upon the altar.

Whatever evils chivalry may have brought in its train, we cannot doubt that an immense step forward was taken when the sword was claimed for the service of God and man. Above all, it was a step forward because it was an earnest attempt to unite Christianity and common life. The priest, the monk, and the nun were too much the ideals of Christian life; the ideal of the Christian soldier was one which made ordinary men feel the possibility of serving God as laymen.

The crusades gave an immense stimulus to this ideal and to chivalry in general. The notion of using the sword for God's service laid hold of men's minds with increasing power. New orders of knighthood arose, more rigid and more akin to the monastic orders, the principal ones being the orders of the Templars and of the Hospitallers. *Templars and Hospitallers.* The knights who sought admission into the order of Templars were addressed by the chief of the order in these words: 'The rules of the order are severe; you expose yourself to great labours and eminent dangers; when you wish to sleep you will have to watch; when you wish to rest you will have to labour; to suffer hunger and thirst when you wish to eat and drink; to go into another country when you wish to stay where you are.' The candidate who took upon him the vows of this hard service, swore never to flee even if his enemies were three to one. This exaggerated bravery of the Templars was the cause of many a misfortune in the Holy Land.

There were, however, other influences at work in the development of chivalry besides the direct hand of the Church and the traditions of Germanic times. *Education in castles.* The castles with which Feudalism had covered France, and with which it covered England after the Norman Conquest, had an important effect on the lives of those who dwelt in them. A castle would have been a very dull place if the owner had lived alone in it, but it was rendered lively by the household of young people who gathered round the noble owner to learn chivalry at his court. But in order that his castle might be chosen as a school of chivalry, the owner must distinguish himself as a courteous and liberal knight, besides making himself famous for feats of arms. No man would send his sons to a churlish and barbarous noble for their education. Children were received into these noble households as soon as they were seven years old. They became pages, and fulfilled the ordinary offices of servants. Even when they became squires (after a seven years' service as pages) they still performed most of the duties which in the present day devolve upon servants. They made the beds, laid the table, served the dishes, carved the meat, brought water for the guests to wash their hands, dressed and undressed their lord, and looked after his horses. Thus they learned that no kind of honest work is degrading; personal service, indeed, was deemed ennobling, because of the nobility of him to whom it was rendered. Before they were admitted to knighthood, they were expected to distinguish themselves by some feat of arms, to win their spurs in fact, and thus they grew up under the wholesome idea that neither birth nor wealth availed without merit acquired by labour and valour. The ladies in the castle took great part in their education, endeavouring to form them in gentle manners ; and here we must speak of the great and important change which feudalism brought about in the position of women.

This change was simply the introduction of the *home life* ; a quiet but enormous revolution, to which it is difficult to fix any precise date, but which M. Guizot says was accomplished between the ninth and twelfth centuries. Many causes contributed to it. The position of women had been raised by Christianity, which had proclaimed their equality with men in the sight of God. The noble, shut up in his castle, was thrown much upon the society of his wife and children, and so the tenderer side of his character was drawn out. When he was away, his wife took his place as commander of the castle, and acquired a new dignity. The separation of classes which was brought about when feudalism displaced clanhood, whatever evils it caused, brought about this good, that refinement could be developed when the more refined lived apart from the vulgar. Then, too, the worship of the Virgin lifted before the minds of men an image of womanly purity and goodness which they did well to reverence. In the person of the Virgin, all motherhood was redeemed and glorified. From all these various

Position of women.

causes, the lady of the feudal castle occupied a far more important position than the chieftain's wife in the Teutonic clan. And parallel with the idea of serving God with the sword, which the Church was so anxious to inculcate, sprang up the idea of devoting it to the service of some noble lady, of doing great deeds and undergoing great hardships for her sake, and deeming no toil too hard for the precious reward of her love. This chivalric woman-worship was often carried out to a ridiculous extent, as might be expected when it was taken up by idle people who had no judgment; but at the same time it marks an important change in the relations of men and women. These relations lie at the foundation of our social life ; for until there is sanctity, permanence and equality in marriage, civilisation rests on an unsound basis. Now the poets of chivalry, though they too often profaned the name of love, did do something to raise it out of the sensuality of paganism by the very importance which they gave to it ; and some of them rose to really noble ideas of the elevating power of a deep and true love ; as Christian of Troyes when he sings: 'He who has a fair lady for his sweetheart or his wife, must learn from her to become a better man.' And one of the first maxims of chivalry was 'He who pays no honour to ladies is dead to honour himself.'

It was in these feudal castles that a school of poetry and romantic fiction arose, destined to exercise a great influence on the literature of future ages. The baron's court was as much the resort of the gleeman and the story-teller as the chieftain's hall had been in ancient times. The exploits of Charlemagne and his Paladins were the delight of the knights who followed William of Normandy to the conquest of England. But a new impulse was given to this kind of poetry in the twelfth century, by the discovery or the invention of the history of King Arthur and the knights of his Round Table. The rough outline of some of these legends may have been preserved in Wales or in Bretagne, but it was in the twelfth century, and largely at the court of Henry II., that they were worked up into chivalric poems and romances, which became the fashionable literature of the age, and the recognised guides to all courteous and knightly manners. Every country in Europe began to ring with songs of the glory of Arthur's court, the matchless prowess and wonderful adventures of his knights, the loveliness and tenderness of Enid and Elaine. In these fanciful tales of Arthur and his court, the twelfth century read its own life reflected, and its best ideals held up for imitation. Arthur was the perfect model of knighthood, and his knights were his devoted followers at various degrees of bravery and purity. The portrait of a knight, as drawn by the poets of chivalry, is no unworthy ideal. The true knight must not only be valiant, but courteous, gracious, and eloquent; not only accomplished in all bodily exercises, but a hater of injustice and of all who take part in it. He must be liberal and open-handed with his wealth; and the poet, who had to live by what he could get, generally took care that this particular trait of knightly character should be prominently brought forward. He must be modest and eschew all vainglory; must ever keep his word; must be temperate and chaste; and his courtesy must extend to both high and low equally. While many of the romances of chivalry are only tales of gallantry, not by any means moral, those of Arthur and his knights are eminently pure, some of them even religious in tone, representing the life of the true knight as a career of toil and effort in which he is purified by suffering and temptation until he arrives at perfection.

Thus far I have tried to show the best side of chivalry and the chivalric literature, the high ideals which it held up to men of a life of noble and toilsome effort for the service of others, rendered beautiful by courtesy and refinement. *Hypocrisy of middle ages.* But alas! the very age which thus sang of faithfulness and nobleness and purity was venal, selfish, and unclean to such an extent that these tales of chivalry which it delighted to honour seem only to add to its other sins the guilt of hypocrisy. Never indeed was the contrast between high ideals and base conduct so great as in the middle ages. And yet after all perhaps this was not wonderful. Christianity had brought into the world the highest ideals, and she had to try to stamp them upon men who were still barbarian and animal at heart. They were men enough to recognise the commanding beauty of these ideals, but the force of animal habit was still too strong to allow them to be reduced into practice. Consequently the middle ages were the most hypocritical ages that have ever been. Lofty words were ever on their lips; and the lofty words were often followed by the vilest deeds. But let us not think, because of the crimes and disorders of the middle ages, that it was all in vain that their poets sang the high ideals of true knighthood. As M. Guizot has well remarked, theory must sooner or later take effect upon practice. And to a great extent the theory of the twelfth century as to what a gentleman should be, a *Value of ideals.* man courteous to high and low, who never breaks his word, who never shrinks from any noble deed, who protects the weak and reverences women, has been wrought into the actual character of the English gentleman of to-day.

Besides, I have already pointed out that the song of the *Trouvère* (as the Norman romancers were called) did a great work in lifting the relations of men and women into a higher and nobler light. The Church alone could not have created the home life; for though by making marriage a sacrament and by preaching the equality of all human souls before God the Church had done much to raise the position of women, it was nevertheless impossible that the true sacredness of marriage could be recognised as long as the Church proclaimed by the celibacy of the clergy that the unmarried state is the holiest. Nothing can be more coarse and degrading than the way in which many churchmen of the twelfth century speak of marriage; the sacredness of the home, that most powerful institution for the regeneration of society, is a thing they utterly fail to recognise. Nor could the sacredness and purity of the home life be fully declared until the Reformation had abolished the celibacy of the clergy. In the meanwhile, the Trouvères, by glorifying human love, did much to nullify the degrading influences of asceticism.

There were, however, some evil influences exerted by chivalry and its literature which we must not overlook. *Darker side of chivalry.* There was a glorification of display and useless splendour in dress, festivals, pageants and tournaments. To maintain all this magnificence, and to give away freely in the open-handed style which the Trouvères took care to insist upon, the feudal noble was often driven to acts of extortion. Besides, the glorification of feats of arms tended to keep up the love of fighting which the Church was so anxious to put down. Tournaments, those games of war which did so much to keep up the love of war, and were themselves often so fatal, were in vain forbidden by the Church. Henry II. put them down in England, as they did not suit his schemes of order, but his son Richard I. revived them, and they were continued until the end of the sixteenth century. Reading the romances of chivalry led many weak minds astray, and even the strong mind of our Edward III. caught from them an infatuated desire to be distinguished as a matchless warrior, which led to the weary wars with France, prolonged for nearly a hundred years. Chivalry had so many fascinations that it dominated men's minds long after its power for good was ended; it was good only for a period of transition, but it was prolonged when ideals more suited to a peaceful and industrial state of society ought to have taken its place, and thus it degenerated into a false ideal, more powerful for evil than for good.

The worst evil which arose out of chivalry was the class spirit which grew up along with it. Pride of birth indeed was a thing as old as the clans from which our Teutonic ancestors sprang. We know that the Old-English kings boasted their descent from Woden. But it was not until the separation of classes brought about by the building of feudal castles, which in England was contemporaneous with the separation of race between the Norman noble and the English peasant, that the low-born man was looked upon with bitter contempt. This, indeed, was not the spirit of the early Trouvères. In the twelfth century the calling of the husbandman was honoured. Some of the early Trouvères show a very democratic spirit, as Wace when he makes his rebellious peasants say, 'We are men even as the nobles are, we have the same limbs, and as great hearts, and can suffer as much.' But the more the knight became separated from the poor man by increasing refinement and splendour of living; and the more knighthood developed into an exclusive order, the more did the pride of birth and the spirit of caste find room to grow. The knight forgot his vocation of defender of the poor, and thought only of renown in tournaments and battles. And thus chivalry left to later ages the bitter inheritance of class prejudice, the contemptuous dislike of the well-born man for the churl and the trader.

DATES.

The first crusade, and taking of Jerusalem	1099
Second crusade, preached by St. Bernard	1147
Jerusalem retaken by the Turks	1187
Third crusade (Richard I. and Philip of France)	1189

CHAPTER XV.

HENRY II., king of England, overlord of Wales and Ireland, and of half France, died broken-hearted and defeated in 1189, at the close of an ignominious war with his rebellious son Richard, and Richard's crafty ally, Philip Augustus, king of France. The reign of Richard I. fills up the next ten years, and closes the twelfth century. We need not dwell upon its details. The history of the third crusade, on which Richard set forth as soon as he could gather the needful funds, is no part of the history of England; the wars between Richard and Philip, who became his rival and his bitter foe, though they mark the beginning of the separation of the French provinces from the English kingdom, affected England chiefly through the drain of money which they necessitated. During the whole of his reign, Richard scarcely spent six months in England. But though our country was without a king, she had a Government. The administrative machinery organised by Henry II. worked on in the hands of Richard's ministers, and was even developed farther in the direction of self-government. Thus the grand jury was made elective in every county; and the coroners, whose office was instituted in Richard's reign, were chosen by the whole body of freeholders; and in 1198, when Richard imposed a new land-tax, the principle that the county should declare its own liability through its representatives in the county court, was carried out even more fully than it had been in his father's time. The baronage

Reign of Richard I.

remained quiet during Richard's reign ; the king's brother John vainly tried to wrest the sovereignty into his own hands during his brother's captivity ; and in spite of the oppressive taxation which was called for by the king's ransom and his constant wars, trade and wealth increased under the influence of peace and order.

The reign of Richard I. may be regarded as a pendant to that of Henry II.; in the thirteenth century a new period begins, which has the Great Charter for its starting-point. The history of the twelfth century has shown us how England was saved from the anarchy of feudalism and made a solid State with a central government, while the local self-governing institutions which she had possessed from the earliest times were preserved and developed. Before we take leave of the period we must sketch some of the other influences which make it a decisive epoch both in English and European history, and glance at the social condition of the people at large. The twelfth century was the time in which the great forces which were to mould the later history were slowly beginning their work.

We may roughly describe the most striking feature of the twelfth century by saying that then people began to think. A new morning of thought had dawned at the end of the eleventh century. Not that the human mind had been entirely dormant for six centuries ; from time to time thinkers had arisen, but their voices found little echo in those unquiet ages. Still, these thinkers busied themselves with the materials which had been handed down to them from the wreck of the old world of thought. Their mental sphere was ruled by the two great master spirits of antiquity ; Plato, the great idealist, and Aristotle, the great apostle of common sense. The works of Plato and Aristotle were not known at first hand ; the very partial knowledge which the middle ages possessed of them was chiefly got through the translations and commentaries of Boethius, the same Roman philosopher whose 'Consolations of Philosophy' it had been the pleasure of our king Alfred to translate for his people, and whose writings were of supreme influence in the early part of the middle ages. The food provided for the human mind from this and some few other sources was scanty indeed. A part of Aristotle's Logic, and some fragments of

The dawn of thought.

Plato, were all that the middle ages possessed of these great authors before the thirteenth century. Nevertheless, from these scanty materials the energy of young thought developed the great controversy between Nominalism and Realism, which filled the whole mediæval period. This controversy existed in germ from the ninth century onward, but it only burst forth at the end of the eleventh century, when Roscellin, the Nominalist, boldly applied the principles of his philosophy to theology, and thus kindled a strife which could not henceforth be suppressed. When Roscellin had spoken, the systems of Realism and Nominalism suddenly appeared full-grown. The teaching of Plato, worked out under the influence of Christian beliefs, had produced the philosophy known as Realism, which seems to have tacitly prevailed until attacked by Roscellin. The Realists maintained that abstractions such as humanity, colour, virtue, &c., were not mere words, but realities existing apart from the objects in which they are found. The senses, they said, are no trustworthy guides to knowledge; what we see and handle has no real existence; God is the only real existence, and from partaking of His essence all created things derive what they have of reality, and universals (that is, abstractions or general ideas) are realities because they are His thoughts. But against this philosophy arose a protest on the part of the disciples of common sense, which was the origin of Nominalism. Roscellin (canon of Compiègne about the year 1092) was the first great speaker on the side of the Nominalists. 'These universals, genus and species, qualities and parts,' he said, 'are mere words. If they exist, show me them; let me hear and touch them. The virtuous man is a reality, but virtue is only a name. Individuals alone have real existence; abstractions are only logical constructions. The evidence of the senses alone is trustworthy; all else is the mere creation of the intellect.'

With Roscellin begins an unbroken chain of thinkers who carried on the controversy between Realism and Nominalism until the end of the middle ages, and developed in all its elaboration the Scholastic philosophy. This controversy has provoked much laughter in modern times; the schoolmen and the scholastic philosophy have been favourite objects of derision, and modern philosophers have despised them for wasting their time and their zeal on mere verbal hair-splitting. Yet we shall never understand history unless we are willing to believe that the men of past ages had good reasons for most things that they did and thought. At the bottom of the Realist and Nominalist controversy lay the great problem of Ontology, the question of the nature of Being. What is real existence? Is it matter—that which we see and touch? Or is it Spirit; something beyond what we see and touch?

This question indeed did not distinctly appear on the surface, because the distinction between Matter and Spirit was not formulated so precisely as it has been since. That there is but one substance, under many forms, had been the thought of the whole ancient world; and both Nominalists and Realists believed in the unity of substance, though the Nominalists took it in a material sense, the Realists in a spiritual. Thus logically, Nominalism tended towards Materialism; and Realism towards Pantheism; and this question of substance lying at the basis of the controversy made it more than a mere verbal dispute. So far from this question being one which we have dismissed and done with at the present day, speculation is constantly returning upon it; and perhaps the only advantage which the nineteenth century has over the twelfth is that it comes better prepared for the discussion. The mediæval controversy about words and things was most necessary as a prelude to juster ideas of what reasoning can do and what it cannot do, and what the limits of our knowledge must be. And it was perfectly natural that in the dawn of thought men should attack the hardest problems first, and attack them in that form in which they were presented by the common usage of language.

Materialism and Pantheism.

With this controversy began the intellectual education of Europe. It broke forth at a time when many influences were combining to open the world of thought to the rude nations of the West. The Crusades gave a great stimulus to the human mind by the new scenes and new questions which they introduced. The Christian nations were not long in finding out that they had much to learn from their Mohammedan enemies. The Mohammedans had been the first inheritors of the ancient wisdom of the Greeks.; and at a time when Europe was still sunk in barbarism they had brilliant schools in all the various parts of their empire, which extended from Persia to Spain. Their translations of and commentaries on Aristotle and Plato were eagerly studied by the scholars of the West, who flocked to the Arabian schools at Cordova, Salamanca, or Salerno, for the study of philosophy, as well as for that of medicine and alchemy. Many Englishmen distinguished themselves not only by pilgrimages to these Arabian schools in search of learning, but by translating numerous classical works from Arabic versions. The thirteenth century was the great epoch of translations from the Arabic; but in the twelfth century Athelard of Bath, an English scholar, translated the elements of Euclid from the Arabic for the instruction of the West, besides other works, arithmetical or astronomical. Jewish Rabbins were sought out for instruction in Hebrew as well as in medicine, for which their schools were as famous as those of the Mohammedans. A new eagerness for knowledge sought for food on all sides. There was a revival of classical literature along with the eager study of Roman law. Never indeed was there a time of greater intellectual activity than the twelfth century.

The Arabian schools.

The universities which were rising in Europe during the first half of the century were at once a sign and a stimulus of the new craving for knowledge. They became the organs through which a common pulse of intellectual life beat throughout Europe. Intellectual growth becomes easy when the intellect thus finds a focus and a common life. The University of Paris was the intellectual centre of Europe in the beginning of the twelfth century, and was drawing to itself the scholarly youth of all European nations. The English among other nations had their own college there. The concourse of scholars was so immense that king Philip II. had to enlarge the bounds of the city. The lectures of the famous teachers of the day on the driest subjects were flocked to by admiring crowds; and the controversy concerning Universals was a subject of dinner-table conversation. The students appear to have led very hard lives in poverty and severe study. A satirist of the twelfth century 'pictures them, after having spent a great part of the night in study, roused from their sleep before daylight

The Universities.

to attend the lectures of the masters, treated there with continual rudeness, and finally, after having surmounted all the difficulties of their path, obliged to see the rewards and honours distributed with unjust partiality.'

The participation of England in the intellectual development of the time is shown by the rise of the University of Oxford. We first hear of it in the reign of Stephen, through the lectures given there on Roman law by the Lombard Vacarius. By the end of the twelfth century it had risen to a high rank among European universities, and some of the most distinguished minds of the next age—Duns Scotus, Roger Bacon, and Occam—were trained in its schools. The University of Paris was the model of Oxford, as afterwards of Cambridge. The course of study pursued at Oxford and most other universities was that of the Seven Arts, divided into the Trivium and Quadrivium. The Trivium comprised grammar (that is the Latin language), the Logic of Aristotle, and Rhetoric as taught by Cicero and Quintilian. The Quadrivium consisted of Geometry, Astronomy, Arithmetic, and Music. When the student had graduated in these *Arts*, he might advance to the *Sciences* of Theology, Medicine, and Law. At first sight this scheme, whatever its faults of classification and method, appears to open up a considerable field for the student. But when we inquire into the sources of knowledge possessed by the twelfth century, and find that they consisted of a few meagre manuals handed down from the later period of the Roman empire, a few scraps and fragments of the greater ancient authors, generally transmitted at second-hand, we shall wonder not that the students wasted a good deal of time on logical quibbles, or that the study of Roman law led to the neglect of the poets and philosophers (as a writer of the time complains), but that any mental growth was possible on such scanty food. Considered in this light, the intellectual eagerness of the twelfth century is a very wonderful thing. The human mind appeared to have awakened from a long sleep, and to be girding itself to start on a new pilgrimage, to scale all heights and sound all depths. All this mental development, even the universities themselves, had grown up under the countenance or even the direct influence of the Church. It remained to be seen whether the Church would consent that the intellect should play the great part which it now for the first time aspired to. The supreme importance of the twelfth century lies in the fact that the course was then chosen which was to alter the whole future relations of the Church and mankind.

To understand the mutual attitude of the Church and the new intellectual awakening, we must imagine how a *The Church and intellectual development.* child who has been brought up from its earliest years under a wise and loving teacher, who has derived from her all its moral and intellectual training, grows up in profound respect for that teacher, and believes her every word to be indubitable truth. But the child has a quick and lively mind; the very lessons its teacher has given it teach it to think, and soon it awakes to a knowledge of its own powers. Still it has a reverent disposition, and does not reject all its old lore as soon as it has got new light. On the contrary, it is convinced that the old lore was so good that the new light cannot possibly contradict it, and its first step is to try to harmonise the discoveries of its reason with what it has learned from its teacher. So long as it does this, the teacher smiles approval. But by-and-by difficulties arise. The child begins to see that the teacher is not infallible, and that great as is its veneration for that teacher, truth has even higher claims. But alas! the teacher is unwilling to confess that she also is mortal. She wishes still to hold her pupil in leading-strings, and she tries to clip the wings of his intellect. Thus arises a gradual estrangement between teacher and pupil, which ends in a complete quarrel; until the child, now grown into a sturdy youth, is strong enough to break forcibly all the restraints his teacher has put upon him, and by this act enters upon the career of his manhood.

This is a true image of the relations of the Church and mankind in their gradual development from the eleventh century to the sixteenth. When first the new power of thought began to be felt, when the questionings of Roscellin about universals had grazed some of the most sacred mysteries of the Church's creed, the gratitude of mankind towards the Church from whom they had learned everything was too great for her influence to be at once shaken off. Her faithful children, while ardently thrilled with the new intellectual impulse of the time, were as deeply convinced that reason could never be the enemy of faith. Of these faithful children the greatest was St. Anselm (of whose life something has already been related), who at the end of the eleventh and beginning of the twelfth century set himself to prove that the whole fabric of Christian doctrine could be built up by reason alone without the aid of authority. The aim was noble, and Anselm brought to the task the powers of a profound and original as well as of an earnest mind; yet the fabric of argument which he built up is very like a house of cards. In truth Anselm, like most of the thinkers of the day, greatly overvalued the capacity of human reason, that is, of reasoning; they thought it capable of solving problems before which it is powerless. They had studied the categories of Aristotle until they had come to believe that all truth must be capable of formal logical proof. And they had not measured the depths of human ignorance, its ignorance of even the nature of thought. Anselm indeed was aware that human words could not measure the infinite and ineffable; yet he continually used them as though they did. He thought that he found a demonstration of the existence of God in the fact of the mind's conception of God, so that he could prove conclusively that only the fool had said in his heart, 'There is no God.' The argument did not convince everybody even then; a monk named Gannilon wrote a book in defence of 'the fool.' St. Anselm, however, did not regard reason as the right instrument for arriving at truth in spiritual things; it could only follow where faith led the way. What he believed he sought to demonstrate by reason, but his motto was : ' He that hath not believed will not understand; for he that hath not believed hath not experienced; and he that hath not experienced cannot understand.'

 But meanwhile workers in other fields than theology were uttering bold words on behalf of the supremacy of reason. Early in the twelfth century Athelard of Bath, who was an original writer as well as a student and translator, speaks thus in a work on natural philosophy: 'What is authority but a halter by which credulous men are led bound into error like brutes? For they do not understand that reason is given to each and all that they

may discern by her sole judgment between true and false.'
Not long afterwards the same maxim was applied in the
sphere of theology and philosophy by a more famous teacher
than Athelard, the Breton Abelard. Instead of
saying with St. Anselm, 'We must believe in
order to understand,' Abelard said, 'We must understand in
order to believe. Inquiry is the prime key of wisdom. To
doubt about particulars is not without use. For by doubting
we come to inquiry, and by inquiry we perceive the truth;
as the Truth himself said, "Seek and ye shall find."'
Abelard attempted to cut the knot of the Realist and Nominalist controversy. He was a Nominalist in so far as he
asserted that a Universal is only a collection of individuals,
and not a real substance apart from them. But his further
assertion that this collection is a substantial reality, and that
in all individuals there is a certain portion of pure universal
essence, was entirely in the direction of Realism.

<small>Abelard.</small>

It was impossible to philosophise without touching theology; and it was impossible to philosophise freely without
coming into collision with some of the dogmas of
the Church. All discussions about Being necessarily had an application to the nature of God, and
consequently to the doctrine of the Trinity. Abelard was no
rebel against Christianity, he always believed himself to be
orthodox in his faith; but he handled theological questions
in a free and broad spirit. He was accused of heresy, and
condemned by two councils. The man who stood forth as his
accuser at the Council of Soissons in 1140 was none other
than St. Bernard, the great saint of the twelfth century, the
perfect model of monkhood. It would have been better for
St. Bernard's fame if he could have let Abelard alone; but
great as St. Bernard was, his greatness was one-sided; the
ascetic ideal, which he represented, is a necessarily imperfect
ideal, one that crucifies some of the best powers of human
nature, and does not allow the whole man to grow to perfection. Feeling, devotion, obedience, were everything in the
monastic ideal; when the intellect stood up to demand free
development for the whole of man's nature, the ascetic revolted in horror and wrath. Abelard seems to have been as
far from asceticism as he was from mysticism; he did not believe the body to be under a curse, he wrote in defence of

<small>Abelard con-
demned by
the Church.</small>

marriage, he had even dropped hints against sacerdotalism. But if Becket was too strong for Henry II. in 1163, much more was Bernard too strong for Abelard in 1140. The age with all its intellectual vivacity had as yet no thought of renouncing its teacher; the hold which asceticism, religious exaltation, ardent imagination had on its mind, was far too strong. St. Bernard and authority triumphed.

Yet the apparent victory of St. Bernard and defeat of Abelard had the same kind of result as the apparent victory of the martyr Becket over the constitutional king. Although the majority sided with the Church, and for the rest of that century and the next the greatest thinkers continued to follow St. Anselm in trying to work from authority to reason, yet a powerful minority remained to hand on the torch of free thought, and prepare the slow current of reaction which led at last to the overthrow of Church authority altogether. Even at the table of Becket there were to be found men who defended Abelard, and spoke slightingly of St. Bernard. And from this time, as thought went on playing on religious questions, heresies sprang up in various parts of Europe. The first persecution for heresy in England took place in 1160. Vainly did the Church try to stamp out these movements with a strong and cruel hand; vainly in the next century did she seek to rivet her authority more firmly on the necks of every individual by establishing the confessional; from henceforth she was fighting a losing battle; the activity of the human mind, once awakened, could never more be crushed. The great schoolmen of the next century, who made it their task to reconcile Christianity with reason and the wisdom of antiquity, though they always assumed the absolute truth of the Church's dogmas, yet by calling in reason to the aid of faith furthered the development of reason. In philosophy Abelard's solution of the Nominalist and Realist dispute was tacitly accepted, while his opinions (which seem to have been scarcely understood by his age) were openly condemned. A distinguished school of Realists existed until the end of the twelfth century, throwing themselves more and more into a mysticism which tended, as Abelard had foreseen, towards Pantheism; but Conceptualism, as the doctrine of Abelard has since been called, was virtually in possession of the schools, and was adopted by Albertus

Magnus and St. Thomas Aquinas, the great teachers of the thirteenth century.

But although the attitude which the Church took towards free thought in the twelfth century was fatal to her future influence, it is far from likely that the triumph of free thought and of Abelard's principle—'We must understand in order to believe,' would have been an unmixed good. With minds wholly untrained to observation and experiment, with a stock of knowledge so meagre, the age was not yet ripe enough to plunge into such an ocean; the instinct which made it cling to authority, to the authority of the Church in matters of dogma, of Aristotle in philosophy (when in the next century he became more fully known through translations from the Arabic) was in the main sound. Listen to the words of a Realist of the twelfth century, and we shall see that it was in no ignoble spirit that that age accepted the guidance of faith. Hugh of St. Victor says : 'Faith can aid herself with reason in the things which are according to reason, and can bid reason be silent and respect her authority in those things which are above her, and for this submission reason will find motives in her own nature; but it is impossible that faith should present to her objects which are evidently contradictory to her knowledge, God being equally the author of the light of reason and of that of faith.' In truth, the provinces of knowledge and faith had yet to be separated ; and even to-day the last word has not been said in this controversy.

If we say that the end of the twelfth century marks the time when the influence of the Church, having reached its zenith, began to wane, we must guard ourselves against fixing too hard and fast a date for a change so very slow and gradual, and with so many counter currents. *Decline of the Church's influence.* The Church had still much good work to do, such as the sending forth of the Franciscan order in the next century. But what we distinctly observe is a decline in that respect for the monastic ideal, which had hitherto been dominant in the popular mind. Not only do we find the most eminent churchmen of the day inveighing against the corruption of the monastic orders (especially of the great order to which St. Bernard had belonged, the Cistercians), but we find them seriously maintaining that though the contemplative life may be safer than the active, the latter is more useful and glorious, because it is to the profit of many, not of one only. Giraldus Cambrensis, speaking of the austerities of the order of Grammont, who were obliged to beg for necessaries, says that as long as men can support themselves by their own industry, they have no right to tempt God. Mapes, in a poem attributed to him on the Body and the Soul, instead of treating the body as the source of all evil, makes it rebuke the soul for having allowed it to become master where it ought to have been servant, and say that the soul is the greater sinner. Giraldus says that whereas monasticism was formerly a way of dying to the world and living to God, it is now become a way of dying to God and living to the world. In all accusations brought by churchmen against monks, something must be allowed for the rivalry and hatred which always existed between the secular and the regular clergy, though the writers above quoted are quite as severe against their own order as against the monks. But we have more certain evidence still of the decline of monasticism in public favour. During the twelfth century, when monasticism was at the height of its glory and influence, 418 monasteries were founded in England. In the next century only about a third of that number were founded, and in the fourteenth century only twenty-three. After this, for 150 years before the Reformation, people gave up founding monasteries, and built hospitals and colleges instead. Monasticism was dead long before the Reformation came to bury it.

The fact that after the twelfth century the monastic life began to cease to be the ideal of Christian people was a sign that the Church herself was losing her hold on the popular mind. For the mediæval Church was committed to the ascetic ideal of which monasticism was only the formal embodiment. She was committed to it by her whole system, and especially by the celibacy of the clergy. But the twelfth century opened the door to a larger life, before which the narrow ascetic ideal waned and lost its charm. The new intellectual impulse; the development of another ideal of Christian manhood through chivalry; the elevation of women's position through the same influence; the development of trade, offering a career to the non-noble ; the growth of a class of educated laymen, poets, lawyers, merchants' clerks ; all these were so many new openings for all ranks of society, rendering the old attraction of the Church less powerful. The evil practical effects of celibacy, the ignorance, rapacity, and irreligion of all ranks of the clergy, have been fully exposed to us by Giraldus and other writers of the twelfth century. 'The house of the Lord has become a den of thieves,' is their text. For a long while the popular mind clung to the system, while it condemned the individuals. But as thought began to play more and more on ecclesiastical subjects, as controversies between kings and prelates gave rise to the discussion of questions before unraised, above all as papal aggressions roused the resentment of the English nation, now waking to consciousness of itself, the faults of the clergy were traced to the faults of the system, and mockery and hatred gradually took the place of trust and love.

While thus in the twelfth century the mines were being silently laid which were to overthrow the great power which had hitherto ruled supreme in the moral and intellectual sphere, another revolution was being quietly prepared, in the rise of a third estate between the noble and the peasant, through whose agency the old feudal constitution of society was one day to be dissolved. We have seen how Feudalism in England had been curbed and compressed from above by the organisation of a central government. The independent lordship of the noble was henceforth to be held in check by the king's justices; the power of the nobles as a military class was weakened by the establishment of scutage. But the rise of the industrial communities of the towns was destined to put an end to the economic system of feudalism, in which the labour of production had been carried on by the many for the profit of the one. During the twelfth century the English towns begin to push themselves into light. They had grown up in old times out of those village communities which had either received an independent share in the first distribution of land, or had gathered round some great monastery or the abode of some powerful noble. In sites favourable for trade these villages grew into towns. As these towns had been villages to begin with, their early institutions were those of the village. They had their free meetings, made their own by-laws, and chose their own officers. Their various trades formed themselves into guilds, not very unlike our trades-unions, while the general body of

Rise of the towns.

the citizens formed the merchant guild, which afterwards became the governing body of the town. Though with the growth of feudalism they probably fell more and more under the dominion of their king or earl or monastery, they nevertheless had risen before the Norman conquest to a position of such importance that many towns had been able to make a bargain with the king or earl to pay a fixed sum of money instead of the various dues to which they had been liable.

The Norman conquest, though at first it brought ruin and desolation to many towns, gave a fresh spur to their trade, through the number of foreign craftsmen and traders who came to settle in English towns, and the increased intercourse with the Continent. The wool trade, for example, was brought to England by the conquest. *The towns after the Conquest.* Many Flemish weavers came over with the Conqueror, whose wife was from Flanders, and under the two following reigns the manufacture throve and increased. Henry II. had the wisdom to protect and encourage the foreign merchants settled in London, by whom the trade of that city was chiefly carried on. Thus the foundations of the manufacturing and commercial greatness of England were laid in the first instance by foreigners. England was then an agricultural rather than a trading country, and the country which cannot now grow corn enough for her own food exported corn to Norway. Under the rule of order which most of the Norman kings kept up, the towns increased in wealth, and in the twelfth century they began to struggle for the ancient freedom which the Anglo-Saxon township had possessed.[1] The privileges which they sought to wrest from the king, the noble, or the monastery in whose demesne they lay, and to whom they were considered to belong, were the confirmation of their merchant guilds, the right to manage their own affairs, to have their own courts of justice according to their own local customs, with exemption from the jurisdiction of the courts of the shire and hundred, to elect their own magistrates, and to

---

[1] 'In the silent growth and elevation of the English people the boroughs led the way ; unnoticed and despised by prelate and noble, they had alone preserved the full traditions of Teutonic liberty. The rights of self-government, of free speech in free meeting, of equal justice by one's equals, were brought safely across the ages of Norman tyranny by the traders and shopkeepers of the towns.'—Green, *Short History of the English People*, p. 89

compound for the taxes by a fixed sum, free from the exactions of the sheriff. Need of money made Henry II. and his sons Richard I. and John willing to sell charters to the towns, by which these privileges were secured to them. The nobles were influenced by the same reasons; and 1,500 royal and 49 baronial charters which are still extant give us an idea of the extent of this revolution, which however was not always accomplished without a struggle, sometimes, as in the case of St. Albans, a bloody and in the end disastrous struggle.

Political power was not one of the objects sought by the towns in the twelfth century; they did not yet aspire to a voice in the government of the country. The city of London alone possessed such a voice. She took an important part in the election of Stephen to the crown. In his reign her power and wealth were so great that the barons called her 'the head of all the realm.' The Bishop of Winchester, Stephen's brother, when holding a council at Winchester to declare Matilda queen, said: 'We have despatched messengers for the Londoners, who, from the importance of their city in England, are almost as it were nobles, to meet us on this business, and have sent them a safe-conduct; wherefore let us wait for them.' It is said that London furnished 20,000 horse and 60,000 infantry in Stephen's time. Yet London did not obtain its recognition as a self-governing corporation till 1191; the right to elect its mayors annually was granted by John in 1215. But though in the next century the towns were called upon to send representatives to the great council of the nation, the fact of primary importance in their history is not that through them the middle classes rose to political power, but that the rise of the industrial system put an end to the social economy of Feudalism. We have seen how the village community, growing its own food, and supplying all its own wants, was succeeded by the feudal community, the lord surrounded by his dependents, who were bound to cultivate his fields, and to supply him with such articles as his womenkind did not manufacture in his own household. But as the village becomes a town, and the traders and manufacturers of the town, increasing in wealth and importance, are able to throw off the yoke of the lord, and to compound for their services in kind by fixed payments

Industry and Feudalism.

in money, we can see that a death-blow has been struck at feudalism as a social system. The new power of Industry will be fatal to an order of things which encourages fighting and idleness and despises work. We may be sure that the class which has thus secured its position will soon rise to political power. And we already see the self-sufficing community of early times changed for a broader system of division of labour, whereby the towns and hamlets of England are linked through trade and commerce with the larger life of the world.

While we look with pleasure on the emancipation of the towns as the sign both of the rise of a middle class and of the strong spirit of English independence, we must not forget that the word freedom in the twelfth century had not that large sense which it has now. Freedom, indeed, as we conceive it, did not exist then; it means now the possibility of development shared equally by all, and limited only by its universality; it meant then privilege, the private franchise, not the common right. Only certain classes enjoyed the franchise of the city, and there was an eternal feud between them and the unprivileged. It was a glorious thing that the serf who fled from his tyrannous lord could be received into the guild of the city, and if he remained there a year and a day, could not be recovered by his lord any more. But the same merchant guild was often tyrannous in relation to other interests, as, for example, to the craft guilds. The merchant guild at first included all the traders and manufacturers of a town; and as long as all handicraftsmen were also merchants, the tailors, for example, importing their own cloth, there was no separation of interests in the town. But with increasing wealth came division of labour, and then only the wealthier citizens became merchants, and the different guilds of weavers, fullers, tailors, and others, were confined to craftsmen only. The struggle of the craft guilds with the merchant guild for civil power belongs to the thirteenth and fourteenth centuries, and therefore does not come within the scope of the present work. But the unequal distribution of public burthens between the richer and poorer citizens was the cause of the first popular insurrection in England, the conspiracy of William Fitzosbert in the city of London in 1196.

Narrowness of Merchant Guilds.

The craft guilds themselves, though their professed aim

was 'the better maintenance and profit of the poorer sort,' only sought to secure this aim by obtaining monopolies. We must stay for a moment to glance at these guilds, which were such a marked feature of our ancient towns. and which date from Anglo-Saxon times. At first they appear to have been almost like clubs, meeting for good-fellowship and for religious services, and providing wax-lights, masses, and burial services for departed members. Others were formed as mutual assurance societies; others for works of charity. The craft guilds in many respects resembled our modern trades-unions; like them they had their praiseworthy side in so far as they aimed at the protection of the weak against the strong, and their bad side in so far as they meant the tyranny of the weak or the lazy over the strong. They insisted that none should carry on their trade who did not belong to their guild, and that all other craftsmen should strictly confine themselves to their own craft. They kept the management of their craft entirely in their own hands, and the minuteness with which they regulated all its conditions and processes must have been very vexatious, and a great hindrance to improvements. They obtained in time the right to be sole judges of their members in accusations relating to their craft. Rattening (taking away tools) was made use of to enforce the payment of fees and fines from guild-brothers. They limited the hours of work, and enforced certain holidays, to prevent competition. Every guild-brother was surrounded by restrictions on the free development of his industry. On the other hand, those who met with losses had a claim for help from the funds of the guild. Of course the guilds attempted to fix prices; it was the universal belief of the middle ages that this was a matter which could be and ought to be regulated by authority. The guilds bought from the kings the right of enforcing their privileges; and from them are descended the chartered *Livery Companies* of London, so called from the distinctive dress, which was the badge of every guild.

In one important respect there was no parallel between the guilds and modern trades-unions. They were not associations to protect the interests of Labour against those of Capital. Until the middle of the fourteenth century there was no working class distinct from the employers of labour.

The master craftsmen all worked with their own hands, employing for the most part only apprentices, who after their seven years' term of service themselves became masters. Disputes between labour and capital were as yet unheard of. It was not until the abolition of serfdom that difficulties of that kind came to the front.

The treatment of the Jews is a sad page in the civic history of the middle ages. The Jews had settled in England after the Norman Conquest, and were protected by the Norman kings; not for any respect they had for this ancient and most industrious nation, but because their love of money was stronger than their religious prejudices. The Jews were the only money-holders in Europe, and the Norman kings protected them from the bigoted hatred of their Christian subjects only in order that they might wring money from them themselves. In all the larger towns the Jews had their separate quarter called the Jewry, and were regarded with bitter jealousy by their fellow-citizens. When King Richard I. came to the throne the third crusade was already proclaimed, and the outburst of crusading spirit was one cause of the frightful massacres of the Jews, which began in London on the very day of the king's coronation, and spread to Lynn, Stamford, Lincoln, and York. The following account of the fearful tragedy of York is taken from William of Newburgh, a contemporary chronicler.

The Jews.

Benedict and Jocens, the chief Jews of York, had built themselves houses which were like kings' palaces, stone houses being then very rare in towns. It was very grievous to the Christians to see the prosperity of the Jews, especially when they were conscious that they owed them money. Benedict was killed in the massacre of the Jews at London, but Jocens escaped. When King Richard I. left England a great conspiracy was formed against the Jews of York, chiefly by some nobles who were greatly in debt, and youths who had taken the cross and wanted money; the graver citizens held aloof, knowing the Jews to be under the royal protection. On a stormy night the conspirators set fire to the city, that under cover of the fire they might plunder more easily. They broke into the house of Benedict, slew all whom they found, and made off with the booty, after having set fire to the house. Jocens and other Jews, terrified by this, took refuge in the castle of York, with their wives and children and their treasures. The mob then plundered and burnt the Jews' quarter, and slew all the Jews they could find who refused baptism. Unfortunately, the commander of the castle having gone out on business, the Jews in the castle were in a state of such terror and distrust that on his return they would not let him in. He forthwith went to the sheriff, who happened to be in the city with some of the forces of the shire, and the sheriff indignantly ordered siege to be laid to the castle. The mob rushed to the work with such fury that the sheriff repented of his command, and tried to hold back the besiegers, but it was too late. The handicraftsmen, the youth of the city, crowds of country folk, and not a few soldiers, formed the body of the besiegers; the clergy also were represented; a certain hermit distinguished himself by his savage eagerness in leading on the besiegers, and he was the only one of them killed, by a stone from the walls. As the Jews had neither sufficient food nor means of defence, it was soon plain that they could not hold out long. They held a council of despair. Then arose an ancient Rabbi, much revered by them all, and said: "God, to whom no one can say, Why dost thou do this? commands us now to die for our law. And behold, our death is in the gates, as ye see; unless ye choose what is worse than death, to die apostates. Therefore with our own hands let us willingly give to the Creator the life which He demands, without waiting for the cruelty of our enemies." The greater part of the Jews followed his advice; having destroyed or spoilt their treasures as far as they could, they set fire to the roof of the castle, and then cut the throats of their wives and children, and their own. In the morning the survivors showed the horrible sight to the Christians, and begged for mercy, offering to receive baptism. Most people were moved with horror and pity, but one Richard Mala Bestia (or the Evil Beast) and the chief conspirators enticed them out of the castle, and murdered them all. The conspirators then went to the cathedral, and destroyed the schedules of their debts, which were kept there.

Though we are expressly told that the graver citizens held aloof from this deed of blood, and though no doubt the worst share of the blame belongs to the low rough population which is even now to be found in our towns, yet it is plain that the better citizens winked at these outrages, and tried to screen the criminals, and that a spirit of cruel hatred to the Jews was almost universal. The chronicler who relates to us this tragedy, while perfectly aware of the wickedness and cruelty of those who did the deed, nevertheless rejoices in it as God's judgment on a 'perfidious nation'!

A writer of the twelfth century has left us an interesting description of London, from which we may form an idea of city life in the time of Henry II. London, which covered but a very small area then compared with its enormous extent at the present day, was surrounded by walls, the course of which is indicated by the names, still preserved, of their ancient gates; Ludgate, Newgate, Aldersgate, Cripplegate, Moorgate, Bishopsgate, Aldgate. On the east side it was defended by the massive Tower which William the Conqueror had built to hold it in awe. The manners and customs and government of the city, says this writer, were admirable, everything being carefully regulated; drunkenness and fires were the two great plagues. We however should find in the minuteness with which everything was regulated the note of a society just emerging from barbarism. The prices of bread, beer, wine and clothing were fixed by law; every act of the citizen was watched over by the law; his food, his dress, and even the cutting of his hair and nails were prescribed to him; the baker at his oven, the tradesman at his counter, were never safe from the intermeddling of the law. This over-legislation however was a vice of the age. It had rough men to deal with, and could only use rough methods. For example, the baker of bad bread was to be dragged on a hurdle from Guildhall to his own house, through the dirtiest and most public streets, with the bad loaf hanging to his neck. But on the whole there was much good sense in the laws by which the city was governed; and more attention was paid to sanitary matters, and to the general welfare of the community, than the middle ages often get credit for. Even in the twelfth century the public fountains of London were supplied with water by a system of leaden pipes. As the streets were not lighted by night, the watch when they made their rounds carried kettles of burning pitch upon high poles. All taverns

London in the twelfth century.

had to be closed at curfew bell, and no one was allowed to wander about the streets with arms at night, unless it were some great lord, or some of his following. Yet in the days of Henry II. there were great disturbances; at one time, the sons of some of the richest of London citizens used to maraud by night in the streets, killing everyone they met, and breaking into houses. One of the wealthiest of the citizens was hanged for his share in these disorders.

Clerkenwell, Holywell, and St. Clement's well were then clear streams, flowing over gravelly beds, whose banks on summer evenings were the favourite walks of the scholars [1] and youths of the city. In a field outside the gates (Smithfield) a great horse and cattle fair was held every Saturday. A vast forest lay round the city, abounding in all kinds of game, including wild cattle, boars, and stags. The burghers of London had the right of hunting through Middlesex and Hertford, in the Chiltern Forest, and in part of Kent. To the north of the walls lay the swamps of Moorfields, which when frozen over in winter were covered with crowds of skaters. They used a kind of skate made of the thigh-bones of oxen, and used to play most warlike and dangerous games on the ice; the martial spirit was so strong that such sports were eagerly entered into. Games and amusements of all sorts took up a good deal of the citizens' time in those days, when life did not rush along as fast as it does now. In carnival time, the great game of the London schoolboys was cockfighting, carried on in the presence of their masters; the forenoon was devoted to this. Afterwards, they all went to play ball in a large field near the city; the different studies had each their ball, and so had the different office-bearers of the city. The parents and rich men of the city came on horseback to watch the games. Every Sunday in Lent, there were sham fights in the fields; the youths of royal, episcopal, and baronial houses mingled with the citizens' sons. In the Easter holidays there were games on the river, a sort of tilting in boats (water-quintain), not without danger; London bridge and the balconies of the houses were then covered with spectators. In summer there were all kinds of

Amusements of the citizens.

---

[1] There were three great schools in London, connected with the abbeys of Westminster and Bermondsey and the church of St. Paul's.

games, archery, races, leaping, wrestling, stone-throwing, slinging; then dancing with the girls by moonlight. In winter, the forenoon of holidays was given to bull or bear-baiting, especially in the fields between Southwark and Lambeth. Besides these amusements, the great conventual establishments, which were numerous in London, gave miracle plays, theatrical representations of sacred history or the lives of the saints.

Some allusion has already been made to the changes in social and domestic life introduced into England by the Norman Conquest. The rude hall of the English noble was changed for the stately castle of the Norman, in which a more refined life was possible; we are told that the Normans gladly spent on noble dwellings wealth which the English were willing to squander in meat and drink. Furniture, however, was still scanty, chairs were rare, and even in such a palace as Becket's, some knights had to sit on the floor. Chimneys were introduced by the Normans, though it was long before they became common in ordinary houses. Such houses, even in cities, were built of wood; and the principal change that took place in them was that the *chamber*, or women's apartment, was added on to the hall which had formerly been the only room, and opened out of it. It was the sleeping-room of the master of the house, while the hall still served the purpose of kitchen, parlour, and dining-room, besides being the common bedroom of the rest of the household. Sometimes the chamber was above the hall, and was then called the solar or garret. Judging from illuminations, these houses with their high-pitched roofs, carved eaves, timbered gables, and doors inlaid with metal work, must have been very picturesque objects. But being built of wood, they were very liable to fires, which were the great pests of towns in those days. Stone houses were brought in by the Jews, who found it needful to live in strongly-protected homes. After the great fire in London in Stephen's reign, houses of stone or tile became more common. The poorer classes lived in mere wooden huts, which could be taken down and carried away to be set up elsewhere. Glass windows were beginning to be used, but did not become common till the middle of the thirteenth century. Tapestry hangings on the walls became fashionable after the first crusade.

Domestic life in the twelfth century.

All the arts received a great impulse in the twelfth century, but especially architecture. Architecture was indeed the great art of the middle ages, the great language of living stone which it spoke as it has never been spoken before or since. Nearly all our noblest cathedrals can show portions of twelfth century work, in the style which we are wont to call Norman. The Normans were great builders, and have covered their native province with magnificent monuments of their genius. Painting was used chiefly to illustrate sacred subjects on the walls of churches, or to adorn the manuscripts which were copied in the monasteries. All the year round, in the cold winter as well as the cheerful summer, the monk sat in the open cloister, laboriously illustrating his parchment manuscript of Psalter or Missal with gay pictures in which the personages of sacred story were dressed as knights and ladies of his own day, and lavishing his pains on elaborate borders, rich with birds and flowers. Music had made some advances; organs of a clumsy kind were used in churches; and the modern violin, noblest of instruments, was being slowly developed out of the awkward-looking crowth or rote, which appears to be of Celtic origin. Church song was always in unison, but in Wales and Yorkshire the country people sang songs in parts. Even in the twelfth century there were discriminating critics who were susceptible to the higher influences of music, but condemned what they called the enervating character of the fashionable music of the day, as well as the songs sung at banquets. Dramatic art was taking its first beginnings in the representations of sacred history and legends of the saints which were carried on in the monastic schools. The first recorded performance of these miracle plays or mysteries, as they were called, took place at the monastic school at Dunstable, where Henry I. was holding his court; but there can be no doubt that such performances were common in the twelfth century. The stage, like the university, grew up under the wing of the Church. The professional actor was a character held in the lowest esteem at that time, and no wonder, for under the name of actor appears to have been meant only the buffoon or juggler who amused the company at feasts; and John of Salisbury expresses his wonder that illustrious houses could tolerate the indecency of these people. Indecency, indeed, was a prevailing feature of these amusements as well as of the ordinary conversation of the middle ages. But though no secular drama yet existed, it was some compensation that the whole of life was dramatic. The mass itself was a drama; the symbolic forms which were used to impress all important transactions on the mind, the gorgeous pageantry which was a necessary feature of all solemn occasions, must have furnished the very poorest with constant spectacles which relieved the monotony of their burdened life.

It has already been said that the position of women of the higher classes was improved by feudalism and chivalry. There was some drawback to this in the fact that the feudal lord assumed the paternal right of giving away wards and widows in marriage, and we are told that wards were bought and sold as commonly as beasts. The women of the middle and lower classes seem to have borne a bad character in the middle ages; the literature of the time delights in depicting their low morals and bad temper. There may be some slander in this; but when the home-life, under the influence of ascetic ideas, was regarded with' contempt, women's position in it was not likely to be respected, and women who were not respected were not likely to respect themselves. The refinements of romantic homage were reserved for the ladies of the castle. *Position of women.*

There is much difficulty in tracing the history of the peasantry during the three centuries immediately following the Norman Conquest. We know that among the Old-English there were many classes of peasant labourers, bound to the soil, and under the authority of a lord, while there were also personal slaves (theows) who had no relation to the land at all. In Norman times the personal slaves seem to disappear, and the different classes of cottars, borderers, &c., are all merged in the villein, whose position, as far as it can be traced, got worse as time went on. The more rigid feudalism introduced by the Conquest was unfavourable to the privileges which the peasants had possessed before. They could no longer purchase their own freedom, for all their earnings belonged to their lord; their goods might be seized to pay their lord's debts if his own goods did not suffice. They had no power of escape, for if they left their land, they were liable to be pursued as strays. They had *The peasantry.*

R

no legal rights against their masters; they could be sold or transferred with the land on which they dwelt; and they were probably treated with greater contempt and oppression by their Norman than their English masters.

The villein, who had once been the free ceorl of the village community, was now a labourer, whose services were paid for in land. The services rendered by the Bishop of Durham's villeins in the twelfth century may give us some idea of those generally rendered by villeins throughout the country, though local custom differed in different shires. The villeins of Boldon had to work 144 days in the year for their lord, besides some extra work in ploughing, harrowing, and reaping time; they had also to pay 3s. 10d. in money (equal to 11s. 6d. of our money, five cartloads of wood, half a chaldron of oats, two hens, and twenty eggs. For these services they held about thirty acres of land, with a house attached. Considering that they had also rights of pasture on the then very extensive commons, and rights of cutting firewood or turf in the forests and moors, it would seem that though their work was hard, a fair amount of comfort might go along with it, as long as the lord was considerate. But if he were greedy, there were many exactions he could make. He could compel them to bring all their corn to his mill to be ground, and their flour to his oven to be baked. The villein could not marry his daughter without paying a certain sum for his lord's permission; and we are told how the earl's bailiff in a certain county did not scruple to seize the last cow of a poor household in payment for this tax. We have evidence that the lord sometimes resorted to still more vexatious exactions, since there were none to hinder him if he dared to set custom and public opinion at defiance.

But custom was a great protector in those days of unwritten law. Although the villein had no legal rights, he could urge against new exactions that they were contrary to ancient custom, and only a very hardened tyrant would dare to set at naught such a plea. In Anglo-Saxon times the services of the peasant had been fixed, and he could still plead this fixity against all but the very worst of Norman lords. Although the land which had once belonged to the village community had now become the lord's land, of which the villein was only the tenant, he still retained some of the ancient communal rights; he had a voice in the affairs of the parish; and he was represented at the shire-moot. Custom gave him a sort of title to the land which was allotted to him as the wages of his labour, and ultimately this title was acknowledged by law, and the villein became the copy-holder of later times.[1] Though he could not buy his own freedom, he could that of his children; and a writer of the twelfth century tells us that the villeins sought for education for their children more eagerly than the nobles, that they might be able to rise in life. If they could escape and obtain admission into the guild of a town, and could remain there unclaimed for a year and a day, they became legally free, and their lord had no further claim upon them. In general, their position was protected by the Church, and by the opinion of the better minds of the age, who, like John of Salisbury, taught that government should exist for the welfare of the greatest number, namely, the poor. Already in the intellectual ferment of the twelfth century the inequalities of rank and property were discussed in a free and republican spirit, and very distinguished churchmen had no scruple in advocating opinions which the present age would call rank communism.

The poor must often have suffered greatly from the great changes in price to which food was liable in the middle ages. There was no systematic storing of corn, except in the granges of great monasteries. The crops were disposed of very soon after harvest; people lived from hand to mouth, and often one harvest was consumed before the next came in. We can understand, therefore, what dreadful meaning lies in the *famines* so often recorded in those days. There were no poor-laws then, but the state of feudal dependence in which all the poorer classes of the country lived provided them with a resource in the charity of their lord. But in times of famine the great lords themselves cannot always have been provided with resources to feed the immense swarms of their dependents, and it follows that great numbers of the poor must have simply died.

[1] His name being entered on the roll of the lord's court as a customary tenant, the common law gave him a title by *copy* of the court roll, on performing the customary services, or paying a commutation in money.

Conclusion. I have tried in this little book to set before the reader a faithful picture of the early and middle ages of English history, chiefly with regard to those forces, whether inward or outward, which were the moulding powers of our history, and have neglected, for the sake of brevity, those outward events which were but straws on the current. I pause at the end of the 12th century, because I believe that after that period the student will meet with no new forces which require explanation before they can be understood in their true character by a modern. If I have at all helped the inexperienced reader to grasp the development of feudalism out of clanhood, to recognise how far our Old-English institutions survived the Norman Conquest, and out of what elements a system of government arose under Henry II.; if he has observed the relations of the English kingdom to the surrounding Keltic populations; if he has formed an idea of the position and influence of the mediæval Church, its work in the education of Europe, and its attitude towards the new learning of the twelfth century, he will be better able to follow out in larger histories the evolution of modern government, society, and thought from elements which he has seen preparing in the twelfth century, and my aim will be fully accomplished.

AUTHORITIES USED IN THE FOREGOING CHAPTERS.

CHAPTERS I. and II.—Cæsar, De Bello Gallico; Tacitus, Germania; Sir Henry Maine's Village Communities, Ancient Law, and Early History of Institutions; Kemble's Saxons in England; Freeman's Norman Conquest, vol. i.; Palgrave's Rise of the English Commonwealth; Lappenberg's Geschichte von England, Band i.; Gneist's Geschichte der Self-Government; Stubbs' Constitutional History of England, vol. i.; Schmid's Gesetze der Angelsachsen; Stubbs' Select Charters; Wright's The Kelt, the Roman, and the Saxon; Guest On the Early English Settlements in Britain; Kemble's Beowulf; Garnett's Philological Essays; Robertson's Scotland under her Early Kings; Pearson's History of England, vol. i.

CHAPTER III.—Bede's Ecclesiastical History; Anglo-Saxon Chronicle; Thorpe's Northern Mythology; Milman's Latin Christianity; Michelet, Histoire de France, vol. i. 2. i.; Guizot, Histoire de la Civilisation en France, ch. xiv.; Thorpe's Cædmon; Stevenson's Preface to Abingdon Chronicle; Brewer's Preface to Giraldus Cambrensis, Spec. Ecc.; Haddan and Stubbs' Councils and Ecclesiastical Documents; Hook's Lives of the Archbishops of Canterbury; Wright's Biographia Britannica Literaria, A. S. period.

CHAPTER IV.—Kemble, Maine, Palgrave, Stubbs, Freeman, as above; Nasse's Land Community; Anglo-Saxon Chronicle; Lappenberg.

CHAPTER V.—Asser's Life of Alfred; Anglo-Saxon Chronicle; Pauli's Life of Alfred; Schmid's Gesetze der Angelsachsen; Sharon Turner's History of the Anglo-Saxons; Taylor's Words and Places; Earle's Philology of the English Tongue.

CHAPTER VI.—Worsaae's Danes in England; Mallet's Northern Antiquities; Dasent's Burnt Njal Saga; Robertson's Scotland under her Early Kings; Taylor's Words and Places; Anglo-Saxon Chronicle; Florence of Worcester; Simeon of Durham; Burton's History of Scotland, i.; Dunstan's Life in Anglia Sacra; Robertson's Historical Essays; Thorpe's Codex Exoniensis; Kemble's Codex Vercellensis; Wright's Biographia Britannica Literaria.

CHAPTER VII.—Anglo-Saxon Chronicle; Palgrave's England and Normandy; Stubbs' Constitutional History, and Select Charters; Guizot's Civilisation en France, i.; Kemble, Maine, Gneist, Schmid, Nasse, Freeman, as above; Boldon Buke, with Greenwell's Glossary; Dasent's Burnt Nial Saga, Wright's History of Domestic Manners, Pearson's History of England, i.

CHAPTER VIII.—Anglo-Saxon Chronicle; Life of Edward the Confessor, in Rolls Series; Freeman's Norman Conquest, vols. ii. and iii.

CHAPTER IX.—Anglo-Saxon Chronicle; Florence of Worcester; Simeon of Durham; William of Malmesbury; Ordericus Vitalis; Freeman's Norman Conquest, vol. iv.; Stubbs' Select Charters, and Prefaces to Benedict of Peterborough, vol. ii., and Roger of Hoveden, vol. ii.; Gneist's Geschichte der Self-Government in England; Morga's England under the Normans; Ellis's Introduction to Domesday Book; Palgrave's England and Normandy.

CHAPTER X.—Eadmer, Vita Anselmi, and Historia Novorum; Milman's Latin Christianity; Church's St. Anselm; Michelet's Histoire de France, book iv. ch. ii.; Lanfranci Epistolæ.

CHAPTER XI.—Anglo-Saxon Chronicle; Ordericus; William of Malmesbury; Eadmer, Historia Novorum; Gesta Stephani; William of Newburgh; Stubbs' Select Charters and Prefaces, as above; Palgrave's England and Normandy; Pearson's History of England; Maine's Ancient Law, and Essay in Cambridge Essays for 1856; Hallam's Middle Ages; S. Bernardi Vita Prima; S. Thomas Cantuar., Lives and Letters, Giles' edition; Robertson's Becket; Milman, vols. iv. and v.

CHAPTER XII.—S. Thomas Cantuar., Robertson, Milman, Hallam, as above; John of Salisbury, Epistolæ; Stanley's Memorials of Canterbury; Freeman's Lectures on the Growth of the English Constitution.

CHAPTER XIII.—Roger of Hoveden; Benedict of Peterborough; William of Newburgh; Giraldus Cambrensis, De Instruc. Prin., Jordan Fantosme; Stubbs' Select Charters, Constitutional History, and Prefaces, as above; Gneist; Pauli's Geschichte von England; Allen's Royal Prerogative; Earle's Philology of the English Tongue; Guest's History of English Rhythms, vol. ii.; Morris' Outlines of English Accidence; Madden's Layamon; White's Ormulum; Wright's Biographia Brit. Literaria (Anglo-Norman period); [Wales] Ordericus Vitalis; Giraldus Camb.; Warrington's History of Wales; Lyttleton's History of Henry II.; [Scotland], Palgrave's England and Normandy; Burton's History of Scotland; Simeon of Durham; [Ireland], Giraldus De Invectionibus, and de Expug. Hib.; Maine's Early History of Institutions; Bernard's Vita S. Malachiæ.

CHAPTER XIV.—Michaud's Histoire des Croisades; Guizot, Civilisation en Europe, ch. viii.; Civilisation en France, ch. v. vi.; St. Palaye, Mémoires sur la Chevalerie; Pearson, History of England, i.; Villemarqué's Romans de la Table Ronde; Holland's Chrestien von Troyes.

CHAPTER XV. — Stubbs' Constitutional History and Select Charters; Anselm's Monologium; Cousin, Introduction aux Œuvres Inédits d'Abelard; Rousselot, Philosophie au Moyen Age; Maurice's History of Mediæval Philosophy; Wright's Biographia Brit. Lit, A. N. period; Green's Papers on Oxford in 'Macmillan's Magazine'; Mullinger's History of Cambridge; Hallam's Literature of Europe, i.; Poems of Walter Mapes (Camden Soc.); Giraldus Camb. Gemma Ecclesiastica; Pearson's Historical Maps; [Towns] Stubbs; Thompson's Municipal History: Brentano's Geschichte der Englischen Gewerkvereine; Gneist's Self-government: Green's Short History of the English People; FitzStephen, Vita Becket; Liber Albus; Pauli's Bilder aus Alt-England; Wright's History of Domestic Manners; Lacroix's Arts in the Middle Ages; [Villenage] Dialogus Scaccarii; Glanvill, De Legibus Angliæ; Greenwell, Boldon Buke; Stubbs; Eden's History of the Poor, i.

NOTE TO FIFTH EDITION

I have said in the text 'it would seem more likely that they (the men of the mark) were always more or less under the sway of some lord (the lord of the manor of later times).' Since this was written this view has been more than confirmed by the publication of Mr. Seebohm's 'English Village Community,' a work which should be studied by all who wish to understand the early history of English institutions. I scarcely think that he has produced evidence to rebut the belief in the destructive nature of the English conquest, which is so much confirmed by archæology; but he seems to me to have established a very strong presumption that there never were any *free* village communities in England, but that the cultivation of the land was carried on from the earliest times by men who were almost in the same position as the serfs of later times. On the other hand, M. Paul Vinogradoff, in his recent work on Villeinage in England, argues that the communal organisation of the peasantry can never have arisen out of a manorial community of unfree serfs, but that the manorial organisation has been superimposed on a community originally free.

INDEX.

ABE

ABELARD, 226
Agricola, 5
Aidan, 22
Alaric the Goth, 7
Alcuin, 33
Aldhelm, 70
Alfred, King, 45-60
Allodial tenure, 36, 79
Alnwick, battle of, 185
Amusements in twelfth century, 238
Angles, 8, 9, 11; personal appearance, 17
Anglesea, Isle of, 120, 125
Anglo-Saxon Chronicle, 65, 95, 124, 207
Anselm, St., 135-143; his philosophy, 225
Arabian schools, 222
Architecture, 241
Aristocracy among the Teutons, 13
Aristotle, 219, 222, 225
Art, 69, 241
Aryan race, 3
Asceticism, 26, 28
Ashdown, battle of, 46
Assembly, national, of Teutons, 13
Asser, 56
Assize, Grand, 182; of Arms, 182
Athelard of Bath, 222, 225
Athelney, 50
Athelstan, 65
Augustine, St., 20
Authority, reason and, 225

BARONAGE, revolt of, 183
Battle Abbey, 108
Becket, Thomas, 161-179
Bede, the Venerable, 8, 20, 23, 24, 54
Benedict Biscop, 69
Benedict, St., 24
Bernard, St., 157, 226
Bernicia, 62
Bertha, Queen, 20
Bible, 53; Vulgate, 54

COL

Blood-revenge, 14
Boethius, 31 (note), 55, 219
Boniface, St., 33
Bookland, 37
Border earldoms, 120
Brehon Law, 197
Bretwalda, 41
Britain, 3, 5-7
Brunanburh, battle of, 65

CÆDMON, 25, 70
Cæsar, Julius, 5
Caledonians, 7-17
Castles, 79, 122, 150, 186, 212
Ceorls, 13, 36, 79, 83, 242
Cerdic, 17
Chancellor, 148, 162
Charlemagne, 33, 42, 202
Chester, 59, 136
Chieftain and followers, 15, 38, 210
Chivalry, 210-216
Christianity, 10, 19, 29, 211
Church, Roman, 19; British and Welsh, 10, 19, 194; Scottish, 22; Irish, 32, 197; Mediæval, 126-158, 160, 164; influence on art and learning, 70; on intellectual development, 224; threatened with feudalisation, 128; zenith of influence, 228; Church and State, 32, 88, 130, 164
Cistercians, 156
Civilisation, 2; of Teutons, 16
Clanhood, 3, 12, 174; in Ireland, 197
Clarendon, Constitutions of, 168, 180, 181
Class prejudices, 217
Clergy, 32, 53, 55, 68, 126, 159; marriage of, 69, 129-131, 142; benefit of, 158
Clyde river, 5, 11, 48, 67
Cnut, 76
Coinage made uniform, 153
Columba, St., 22

Columban, St., 24
Commendation, 37, 79
Compurgation, 87
Conquest, Roman, 5; English, 8-10; Danish, 73; Norman, 111-114, 116; of Anglesea, 120, 125; of Monmouthshire, 98; of Cumberland, 194; of South Wales, 193, 194; of Ireland, 198
Constantinople, English soldiers there, 123
Conversion of Kent, 20; of Northumbria, 21; of Germany, 33; of Scandinavia, 64, 76
Cornwall, 10, 11, 42, 43
Coronation oath, 145
Council, Great, 121, 148
Courts, popular, 13, 40, 80, 132, 148; clerical, 132, 158, 169; King's Court, 147; of Exchequer, 148
Craft-guilds, 233, 234
Crusades, 205; influence of, 207; darker side of, 209; against Albigenses, 209
Cumberland, 10, 62, 66, 120, 152, 194
Cumbria, or Strathclyde, ancient kingdom of, 11; conquered by Eadbert, 41; independent of Egbert, 42; conquered by Danes, 48. (See Strathclyde)
Curia Regis, 147

DANEGELD, 72
Danes, 43-51, 57; settlements in England, 61; conquered by Edgar, 66; conquer England under Sweyn and Cnut, 72-74; results of conquest, 76; kept off by William I., 112, 120
Democratic feeling, 161, 217, 243
Denalagu, 62, 66, 74, 189
Denmark, 76
Devon, 10, 11
Domesday Survey, 122
Domestic life, Old English, 85; in the twelfth century, 239
Dorset, 11, 49
Druids, 4, 5
Dunstan, St., 68-70, 145

EADBERT OF NORTHUMBRIA, 41
Ealdormen, 35
Earldoms, four great, 77, 89, 119
East Anglia, 11, 17, 44, 51, 62, 64, 72, 89, 95, 96
Edgar, 66, 68
Edgar Atheling, 100, 110
Edinburgh, 67
Edington, battle of, 50
Edmund of East Anglia, 44
Edmund I., 66; Edmund II. (Ironsides), 73, 110, 145

Edred, 66
Education, 32, 53, 212, 223
Edward the Confessor, 88-100
Edward the Elder, 64
Edwig, 69
Edwin of Northumbria, 21, 22
Edwin and Morkar, 98, 103, 106 111, 115
Egbert of Wessex, 42
Eleanor of Aquitaine, 152, 187
Elfgar, Earl, 96, 97
Emma of Normandy, 75, 93, 101
End of world expected, 74, 203
England, name of, 99 (note)
English settlements in Britain 8; nationality founded, 64; permanence of, 75; fusion with Normans, 189; empire, 119, 192; language, 189; literature, 54, 191; poetry 16, 65, 70, 190, 191
Ethelbald of Mercia, 41
Ethelbert of Kent, 20
Ethelfleda, Lady of Mercia, 59, 64
Ethelred I., 44, 47, 48; Ethelred II., 72, 73, 75
Ethelwulf, 44, 45
Eustace, Count, 91
Excommunication, 135, 175
Exeter, 49, 58, 111

FAMILY, the, 3, 14, 86
Famines, 243
Farnham, battle of, 58
Feorm, 91 (note), 146
Feud, 14, 30, 86
Feudalism, origin of, 38, in France, 77; in England, 76, 78, 152; a necessary stage, 81; after the Conquest, 117; in Scotland, 196; its end, 181, 232
Feudal jurisdictions, 77, 80; tenures, 79, 117; virtues, 82, 210
Five Danish cities, 62, 64
Flemings in Pembroke, 194
Flemish weavers, 231
Folkland, 37, 77, 91 (note)
Forest, New, 123, 139; forest laws, 123, 187
Frankpledge, 81
Freedom, 83, 84, 233
Frith-guilds, 80
Frontier, English, finally settled, 195
Fusion of English and Normans, 189; of barbarian and Christian ideas, 25, 211
Fyrd, 52, 185

GAELIC KELTS, 4, 28
Gauls, 4, 5
Germany, 8, 33
Gildas, 8

GIR

Giraldus Cambrensis, 128 (note), 198, 199, 200, 229, 230
Godfrey de Bouillon, 207
Godwin, Earl, 89-95
Grand Assize, 182
Gregory I., pope, 19; Gregory VII., 128
Griffith of Wales, 96-97
Guilds, 81, 233

HARALD HARDRADA, 103
Harold Godwinson, 90, 95, 97, 100-108
Hasting, the Dane, 58
Hastings, battle of, 107
Heathenism, 18, 25
Hengist and Horsa, 8
Henry I., 139; his charter, 145
Henry II., 152; his reforms, 153, 182; quarrel with Becket, 166-179; character, 187
Heptarchy, 11
Hereward, 115
Hildebrand (Gregory VII.), 105, 128, 137
Holy Land, 201
Homage, oath of, 38
Home life, 213, 239
Hospitallers, 212
House-carls, 76, 106
Hundreds, 13, 80; Hundred moots, 13, 40
Husbandman, 30, 31, 160, 217
Hypocrisy of middle ages, 215

INDIA and Alfred, 56
Industry and feudalism, 232
Infanticide, 29
Innocent III., pope, 209
Institutions, Roman, 6; Keltic, 4; Teutonic, 12; Old English, 34; Danish, 63; feudal, 77; Irish, 196
Investitures, 129, 140, 142
Iona, 22
Ireland, 22, 133, 196, 199, 201

JERUSALEM, 56, 203, 206
Jews, 235
Judicial reforms of Henry II., 182
Jurisdictions, feudal, 77, 80
Jury, trial by, 87, 183; inquiry by, 183, 186
Justices in Eyre, 182
Justiciar, 147
Jutes, 9-11

KELTS, 4, 5, 9, 42, 192-197
Kent, 9, 11, 21

NEW

King, among Old Saxons, 13, 34; elective, 40, 100, 110, 111; his power growing, 35, 52, 76, 154; the Norman or Angevin king, 160; supremacy established, 181
Kingdoms, early, 11
Knighthood, 211; ideal, 215
Knights Templars and Hospitallers, 212

LABOUR, 29, 30, 234
Lancashire, 62, 115
Land, 12, 36, 79, 116-118
Language, English, 189
Law, Alfred's code of, 53; Cnut's law, 99; English laws preserved, 115; forest laws, 123, 187; Roman, 154, 223
Leofric, Earl of Mercia, 89
Lindisfarne, 23, 24
Literature, English, 54, 61, 70, 191; chivalric, 214
London, 48, 52, 58, 59, 73, 94, 99, 110, 111, 115, 232, 237
Lords and vassals, 15, 35, 37, 77, 79, 117, 121
Lothian, cession of, 67, 76, 195
Louis VII. of France, 184
Lowlands of Scotland, 196

MALCOLM CANMORE, 195
Maldon, battle of, 72
Man-bote, 14 (note)
Man, Isle of, 120
Manorial system, 36, 80, 82, 121
Margaret of Scotland, 195
Mark, 12, 37, 79
Materialism, 221
Matilda, Empress, 149, 152
Matilda of Scotland, 141, 145
Mediæval Church, 126, 128, 143, 158, 164-180
Merchant-guilds, 233, 234
Mercia, 11, 41, 49, 51, 62, 64, 67, 77, 89, 96, 98
Miracle plays, 240
Mission of Augustine, 20; of Scottish Church, 22; of England to Germany, 33; to Scandinavia, 64, 76
Mohammedanism, 202, 221
Monasticism, 30, 32, 68, 156, 229
Monmouthshire, conquest of, 98
Murder of Becket, 179
Music, 240

NATIONAL feeling, wanting, 74, 111; developing, 95, 102, 109
Nationality, English, founded, 64
New Forest, 123, 139

Nobles, among Old Saxons, 13; in England, 35; in France, 77; in Cnut's time, 79; their domestic life, 85; after the Norman Conquest, 121; under Henry I., 147; under Stephen, 150; under Henry II., 182–187; life in castles, 212; pride of birth, 217
Nominalism, 220
Normandy, 73, 75, 89, 93
Northampton, council of, 171
Northern counties, 119, 120, 153, 195
Northumberland, modern county, 66; first distinguished from Yorkshire, 111; conquered by William I., 119; held by Scotch king, 152; restored to Henry II., 153
Northumbria, kingdom of, 11; conversion, 21; Bretwalda, 41; colonised by Danes, 49; submits to Edward, 64; to Athelstan, 65; to Edred, 66; divided by Edgar, 67; one of the four great earldoms, 77; earldom of Siward, 89; of Tostig, 95, 98; divided again, 111; its learning, 53; emigration to Scotland from, 195
Norwegians, 62, 66, 103, 120, 195

ODO OF BAYEUX, 120, 124
Offa of Mercia, 41; Offa's dyke, 41, 97
Old English, the, origin, 9; appearance, 17; poetry, 16, 45; religion, 18; institutions, 34
Ordeal, 87
Orderic, 144, 192, 194
Organisation, 2; of the Church, 27
Oswald of Northumbria, 22
Oxford University, 61, 223

PAINTING, 70
Pale, English, 199
Pall, the archbishop's, 137
Pantheism, 221
Papacy, 19, 126, 132, 157, 181
Peasantry, 241
Penda of Mercia, 22
Penitential system, the, 32, 88
People, the English, 36, 138, 143, 186, 189
Peter the Hermit, 203
Peter's Pence, 76, 198
Picts, 7, 8, 17, 67
Pilgrimages, 201
Plato, 219, 222
Poetry and the Church, 70
Priest, ideal of the true, 159
Public opinion, 93

QUADRIVIUM, 223

REALISM, 220
Reason and authority, 225
Reforms of Alfred, 52; of Gregory VII., 128; of William I. and Lanfranc, 130; of Henry II., 153, 181
Religion, of Teutons, 18; Christian, 26; influence of, 29; religion and art, 69; and reason, 225
Religious magic, 26
Representation, origin of, 40, 183
Revival, intellectual, 219; monastic, 68
Richard I., 185, 218
Robert, Duke of Normandy, 141, 145, 207
Robert Mowbray, 144
Robert of Belesme, 147
Rolf of Normandy, 74
Roman Church, 19; mission to England, 19; contest with Scottish Church, 23; appeals to Rome unknown in Old England, 130; Lanfranc and Rome, 133; loss of credit, 181
Roman conquest of Britain, 5, 6; roads, 6; wall, 7
Roman law, 154, 223
Roscellin, 220
Royal power, 13, 34, 76, 119, 154, 160, 181
Rufus, William, 134–143
Runes, 17

SAXONS, 7, 8, 9
Schleswig, 9, 14
Scholastic philosophy, 220
Schools, 32, 54, 223; in London, 238 (note); Arabian, 222
Scotland, anglicised under Malcolm and Margaret, 196
Scots come from Ireland, 17; submit to Edward the Elder, 64; defeated at Brunanburh, 65; allies of Edmund, 66; advance into Lothian, 67; submit to Cnut, 76; to William, 119, 125; to Henry II., 153; defeated at Alnwick, 185
Scottish Church, 22, 23, 196
Scutage, 186
Senlac, battle of, 107
Serfs, 36, 63, 77, 83, 84, 121, 170, 208, 241
Settlements, English, 8; Danish, 46–61; Scots in North Britain, 17; Flemings in Pembrokeshire, 191; English and Normans in Scotland, 195; South English in Cumberland, 195; Norwegians in Cumberland, 62
Shiremoots, 13, 40, 80, 132, 148
Shires, 13, 35, 61
Simony, 127, 129
Slavery, 3, 6, 16, 30, 84

SOC

Society, feudal, 83
Stamford Bridge, battle of, 104
State, Church and, 32, 164
Stephen, 149
Strathclyde, ancient kingdom of, 11; overrun by Danes, 48, 62; submits to Edward the Elder, 64; to Edgar, 66; to Cnut, 76; part of Scotch kingdom, 195. (See Cumbria)
Strongbow, Earl of Pembroke, 199
Sussex, 11, 42
Swegen or Sweyn Godwinson, 90
Sweyn, King of Denmark, 73
Synod of Whitby, 24

TACITUS, 14, 16
Taxation, 125, 134, 146, 166, 183, 218
Templars, Knights, 212
Tenure of land, 35, 36, 79, 84, 121, 242
Teutons, 3, 4, 7, 8, 12, 18
Theodore, Archbishop. 25
Thingwall or Tynwald, 63
Thomas Aquinas, 228
Thomas Becket, 161
Tostig, 98, 102, 104
Tournaments, 217
Tower of London, 122, 144
Towns, 77, 123, 149, 230, 231
Townships, 37
Trivium, 223
Trouvères, 216
Turks, 203
Twelfth century, important period, 154, 222

UNIVERSITIES, 222
Urban II., 204

VALHALLA, 18
Vassalage, 38, 77, 79, 117, 121

YOR

Village life, 85
Villeins, 84
Vitality of popular institutions, 81

WACE, ROBERT, 190
Wales, see Welsh
Wallingford, peace of, 152
Waltheof, Earl, 113, 115
Watling Street, 51, 61, 64
Wedmore, treaty of, 51
Welsh, 4; relations with English, 10, 22, 42; independent kingdom, 11; Christian, 19; submit to Alfred, 57; to Edgar, 66; wars with Harold, 96–98; join Edwin and Morkar, 112; submit to William I., 120, 125; to Henry II., 153; English ascendency maintained by Norman kings, 192–194; character and customs, 193
Wergilds, 14, 62
Wessex, 11, 42, 46, 49, 57, 61, 76
Westminster Abbey. 99; Hall, 144
Westminster, council of, 166
Westmoreland, 120, 152
West Wales (Cornwall and Devon), 11
Whitby, synod of, 24
William I., 93-124
William II., Rufus, 134, 143
William the Lion, 196
Winchester, old capital of England, 100
Witenagemot, or Wise Men's Meeting, 21, 35, 39, 73, 74, 99, 121, 148
Woden, or Odin, 13, 18, 34
Women, position of, 16, 26, 29, 213, 216, 241
Wulfstan, St., and the slave trade, 84

York, 22, 34, 64, 66, 112, 113, 235
Yorkshire, 61, 62, 111 (note), 112, 114

www.ingramcontent.com/pod-product-compliance
Lightning Source LLC
Chambersburg PA
CBHW032204230426
43672CB00011B/2509